First Language Use in Second and Foreign Language Learning

SECOND LANGUAGE ACQUISITION
Series Editor: Professor David Singleton, *Trinity College, Dublin, Ireland*

This series brings together titles dealing with a variety of aspects of language acquisition and processing in situations where a language or languages other than the native language is involved. Second language is thus interpreted in its broadest possible sense. The volumes included in the series all offer in their different ways, on the one hand, exposition and discussion of empirical findings and, on the other, some degree of theoretical reflection. In this latter connection, no particular theoretical stance is privileged in the series; nor is any relevant perspective – sociolinguistic, psycholinguistic, neurolinguistic, and so on – deemed out of place. The intended readership of the series includes final-year undergraduates working on second language acquisition projects, postgraduate students involved in second language acquisition research, and researchers and teachers in general whose interests include a second language acquisition component.

Full details of all the books in this series and of all our other publications can be found on http://www.multilingual-matters.com, or by writing to Multilingual Matters, St Nicholas House, 31–34 High Street, Bristol BS1 2AW, UK.

SECOND LANGUAGE ACQUISITION
Series Editor: David Singleton

First Language Use in Second and Foreign Language Learning

Edited by
Miles Turnbull and
Jennifer Dailey-O'Cain

MULTILINGUAL MATTERS
Bristol • Buffalo • Toronto

Library of Congress Cataloging in Publication Data
A catalog record for this book is available from the Library of Congress.
First Language Use in Second and Foreign Language Learning/
Edited by Miles Turnbull and Jennifer Dailey-O'Cain.
Second Language Acquisition: 44.
Includes bibliographical references and index.
1. Language and languages--Study and teaching. 2. Second language acquisition--
Study and teaching. 3. Second language acquisition research. 4. Discourse analysis.
I. Turnbull, Miles. II. Dailey-O'Cain, Jennifer.
P53.F53 2009
418.0071–dc22 2009026141

British Library Cataloguing in Publication Data
A catalogue entry for this book is available from the British Library.

ISBN-13: 978-1-84769-196-5 (hbk)
ISBN-13: 978-1-84769-195-8 (pbk)

Multilingual Matters
UK: St Nicholas House, 31–34 High Street, Bristol BS1 2AW, UK.
USA: UTP, 2250 Military Road, Tonawanda, NY 14150, USA.
Canada: UTP, 5201 Dufferin Street, North York, Ontario M3H 5T8, Canada.

Copyright © 2009 Miles Turnbull, Jennifer Dailey-O'Cain and the authors
of individual chapters.

The policy of Multilingual Matters/Channel View Publications is to use papers
that are natural, renewable and recyclable products, made from wood grown in
sustainable forests. In the manufacturing process of our books, and to further
support our policy, preference is given to printers that have FSC and PEFC Chain
of Custody certification. The FSC and/or PEFC logos will appear on those books
where full certification has been granted to the printer concerned.

Typeset by Techset Composition Ltd., Salisbury, UK.
Printed and bound in Great Britain by MPG Books Group.

Contents

Acknowledgements

The editors would like to thank Glenn Levine for giving many of the authors in this book the opportunity to gather and explore this topic at a fruitful workshop in February 2007 in Irvine, California. We would also like to thank Barbara Rohde for the book's cover art, and Rebecca Hatch, Aaron King, Frank Orlando, Brittany Perry and David Rohde for assistance in staging it.

Contributors

Carl Blyth is the Director of the Texas Language Technology Center and Associate Professor of French Linguistics in the Department of French and Italian at the University of Texas at Austin. His most recent publications include *Teaching French Grammar in Context* (Yale University Press, 2007, co-author) and *Pause-café: French in Review* (McGraw-Hill, 2009, co-author). He also serves as the Series Editor of the annual volume *Issues in Language Program Direction* (Heinle).

Jennifer Dailey-O'Cain is an Associate Professor of German applied linguistics at the University of Alberta in Edmonton, Canada. Alongside her work on codeswitching in the classroom, her research also includes work in language, migration and identity in both Germany and German-speaking Canada, and language attitudes in post-unification Germany. Major recent publications include articles in the *Modern Language Journal*, the *International Journal of Bilingualism*, the *Canadian Modern Language Review* and the *Zeitschrift für angewandte Linguistik*.

Michael Evans is Deputy Head of the Faculty of Education at the University of Cambridge. He is co-director of a DCSF-funded study, 'Language Learning at KS3: the impact of the KS3 Modern Foreign Languages Framework and changes to the curriculum on provision and practice' (2006–2008). Recent books include (as editor) *Foreign Language Learning with Digital Technology* (Continuum, 2009) and (as co-author) *Foreign Languages: Teaching School Subjects 11–19* (RoutledgeFalmer, 2007).

Janet M. Fuller is an Associate Professor of Anthropology at Southern Illinois University at Carbondale. She has done research on Pennsylvania German, discourse markers, and the courtesy title 'Ms'. Her current research focuses on pre-teen bilinguals in the classroom, based on fieldwork among Spanish-English bilinguals in southern Illinois and English-German bilinguals in Berlin, Germany. Her interests include codeswitching, identity, language ideology and gender.

Glenn S. Levine (PhD University of Texas at Austin) is Associate Professor of German at the University of California, Irvine. His areas of research include second-language acquisition and socialization, and curriculum design and teaching. His publications deal with code choice in second-language learning, constructivist, ecological, and critical approaches to curriculum design and teaching and issues of language program direction.

Grit Liebscher is an Associate Professor of German at the University of Waterloo in Canada, and she is a sociolinguist with a focus on interactional sociolinguistics and conversation analysis. Her research interests include language use among German-Canadians and language and migration in post-unification Germany. Major recent publications include several book chapters as well as articles in the *Modern Language Journal*, the *International Journal of Bilingualism*, the *Canadian Modern Language Review* and the *Zeitschrift für angewandte Linguistik*. She has also co-edited (with a team of scholars from the University of Waterloo) a book on Germans in the North American diaspora.

Ernesto Macaro is Professor of Applied Linguistics at the University of Oxford where he teaches on the Masters in Applied Linguistics and Second Language Acquisition and on the postgraduate language teacher education programme (PGCE). He has carried out research and published widely on the topics of codeswitching in second language classrooms and on language learner strategies. He has published in venues such as *Modern Language Journal, Applied Linguistics and Language Learning*.

Brian McMillan holds a MEd from the University of Prince Edward Island, Canada. He has taught both French and English in a variety of contexts in Canada and in Japan. His research interests include L1 use in L2 teaching and learning, Vygotskian sociocultural theory, teacher training and learner autonomy. Brian is currently teaching English and working on research into student and teacher use of the TL and L1 at Hiroshima Bunkyo Women's University and at Kanda University of International Studies in Chiba, Japan.

Krisztina Nagy was trained as a Primary School Teacher in her native Hungary and taught there for five years. Then, she trained in London to use the Montessori Method and taught for three years in a Montessori school. Subsequently she did a course in Scotland on teaching children with learning difficulties, and worked as a Learning Support Teacher. She completed an MA at Stirling University on Teaching English as a Foreign Language and is about to defend her doctoral dissertation (Stirling) upon which the chapter in this volume is based. Krisztina has presented papers at various conferences on language learning in primary schools. Her creative spirit is expressed in her use of new, interesting materials for carrying out research.

Kim Potowski is Associate Professor of Hispanic linguistics at the University of Illinois at Chicago. Her research focuses on Spanish in the United States, including a book about a dual immersion school and recent studies about discourse markers, Spanish use in *quinceañeras*, and 'MexiRican' ethnolinguistic identity. She directs the Heritage Language Cooperative, which promotes research and teacher development. Her 2009 book *Language Diveristy in the U.S.* (Cambridge University Press) profiles non-English languages spoken in the United States.

Daniel Robertson has taught EFL and applied linguistics in Italy, Germany and the UK. His PhD (University of Edinburgh, 1991) is concerned with the acquisition of English by L1 German learners of English. Since completing his PhD he has held research and teaching positions at the universities of Edinburgh, Leicester and Stirling. His research interests include generative approaches to second language acquisition, classroom discourse and the cultural contexts of ELT.

Miles Turnbull is an Associate Professor in the Faculty of Education at the University of Prince Edward Island. He is Coordinator of Graduate Programs and works in the pre-service program in French second language teaching, as Coordinator of the Bachelor of Education-French Education. Miles' research has been funded by the Social Sciences and Humanities Research Council of Canada, Canadian Heritage, The Education and Quality Assurance Office of Ontario, and the Canadian Association of Second Language Teachers. In 2006, Miles was named research scholar in residence in official languages funded by the Social Sciences and Humanities Research Council of Canada and the Department of Canadian Heritage. Miles is currently Past-President of the Canadian Association of Second Language Teachers.

Introduction

MILES TURNBULL and JENNIFER DAILEY-O'CAIN

In recent years, the debate over target language and first language use in teaching and learning second and foreign languages has resulted in an extensive body of literature. Despite this surge in interest for this topic in the past 10 to 15 years, however, no single book, edited volume, or special issue of a journal has been published within that time period to unify what is known about this topic. Moreover, a majority of studies and articles relating to this topic have examined the issues from either a pedagogical perspective or from a sociolinguistic one; few have combined both perspectives. Consequently, the overall goal of this edited volume is to do just that. Drawing on sociolinguistic, pedagogical and critical theories, this volume offers new and fresh perspectives on an age-old and controversial issue in applied linguistics and language teaching by focusing on the use of the first language in communicative or immersion-type classrooms, situations where first language use is generally expected to be rare or nonexistent. Through this focus, the volume as a whole demands a reconceptualization of codeswitching as something which is natural for bilinguals to do – and not just proficient ones, but also aspiring ones – and classroom codeswitching as being inherently linked with bilingual codeswitching. Although the chapters in this volume explicitly explore these links to greater and lesser degrees, all of them cast the second-language learner in the communicative or the immersion classroom as a developing bilingual (Byram, 1997; Kramsch, 1993) rather than as a poor imitator of the monolingual native speaker, and by doing so, imply that selective and principled codeswitching in the second and foreign language classrooms can be seen as a reflection of what bi- and multilingual speakers do in everyday life.

While all authors fit within this core framework, the volume nonetheless presents contrasting views, both in terms of the amount of first language use that should be allowed and in terms of the communicative and pedagogical reasons for teacher and learner codeswitching. These contrasting views are not surprising, given that the authors come from many different backgrounds and methodological traditions. We also anticipate that at least parts of the volume will be controversial for some readers. We expect, accept and encourage this controversy, since we believe that the resulting debate has the potential to lead to even further stimulating work. We therefore offer this volume up not as a definitive 'one true answer' to put a halt to this discussion once and for all, but as a state-of-the-art overview of where research in the field currently stands, and as a jumping-off point for further conversation and inquiry.

Finally, we would also like to stress very clearly up front that we do not equate the use of the first language in the second or foreign language classroom with passing out a license to overuse of the first language, that is, to become so dependent on the first language that teachers and learners cannot function in a second or foreign language classroom without it. Whatever benefits first language use may bring, it is clear that the ultimate goal of a second or foreign language classroom remains the learning of the target language; practices that undermine this ultimate goal must be avoided.

So Why the Controversy?

It is perhaps unavoidable that many second and foreign-language educators and researchers have developed strong beliefs about the most effective way to master a language – beliefs that are not always grounded in theory or research. In some cases, official policies in certain language learning contexts that officially ban first language use by teachers and students may be the source of some of these strongly held beliefs. In other cases, beliefs that educated speakers, native speakers and advanced bilinguals do not and should not switch back and forth from one language to another may be the source. Many educators also believe that avoiding interference from the learner's first language is necessary in effective language teaching and learning, and these educators may believe that avoiding codeswitching is the only way to ensure that the learner's first language does not interfere with target-language development. For many second and foreign-language educators, any notion of first language use in language teaching and learning connotes the dreaded grammar-translation methods that communicative language proponents loathe – after all, unless it is compensated by further target-language talk, codeswitching reduces exposure to that all-important comprehensible input in the target language (Krashen, 1982). As this argument goes, codeswitching also detracts from opportunities for negotiating meaning while interacting with other learners or native speakers in the target language.

Target-language immersion programs may have also played a significant role in promoting exclusive target language use in second and foreign language teaching (McMillan & Turnbull, this volume). These programs, which originated in Canada, are cited by some as the most successful language programs ever (Krashen, 1984; Obadia, 1996), and a core principle of them is exclusive target language use. Due to the success of immersion programs in producing functionally bilingual graduates, we believe that many educators around the world cite this success as rationale to support exclusive target language use by teachers and students in second and foreign language teaching. Moreover, many curriculum developers and leaders in immersion education are rarely open to entertaining any discussion of codeswitching in these programs.

The Virtual Position and the Maximal Position

As Macaro (2005) points out, there is a continuum of perspectives on target language and first language use. On one extreme, there is the position of exclusive use of the target language, which Macaro refers to as the virtual position. Proponents of the virtual position see no pedagogical or communicative value in the first language at all. These proponents draw on the L1 = L2 learning hypothesis (Ellis, 1986; Krashen, 1981); they argue that since the first language is the only language present during L1 acquisition, the second or target language should be the only language present or available when a second or additional language is acquired. Proponents of a virtual position also draw on Krashen's popular comprehensible input hypothesis (Krashen, 1982) which argues for exposing learners to a flood of comprehensible target-language input to ensure mastery of the target language. Further theoretical rationale for exclusive target language use is drawn from Swain's output hypothesis (Swain, 1985). This hypothesis recognizes the importance of comprehensible input for language learning, but argues that comprehensible input alone will not ensure mastery of the target language. Because Swain argues that learners need to speak and write in the target language in order to master it, proponents of extreme versions of the virtual position on target language use may argue that this speaking and writing must always and only be in the target language.

The virtual position's proponents may also cite studies that have shown that the amount of target language input does affect learners' target-language development (e.g. Larsen-Freeman, 1985; Lightbown, 1991; Liu, 2008; Turnbull, 2001). For example, Carroll (1975) and others (e.g. Burstall *et al.*, 1974; Wolf, 1977) have established a direct and positive correlation between learner achievement and teacher use of the target language.

Moreover, researchers like MacDonald (1993; see also Calvé, 1993; Wong-Fillmore, 1985a) argue that target language use will result in increased motivation, since students can see how knowledge of the target language will be immediately useful to them. This theoretical and empirical support for exclusive target-language use has led governments, language school administrators, teacher educators, publishing houses and teachers to accept the virtual position on target language use as *'best'* practice in second and foreign language learning and teaching. Interestingly, authors like Atkinson (1993) and Phillipson (1992) have even suggested that the virtual position on target language use has reached hegemonic status. Among many communicative foreign language and immersion instructors, there is a blind acceptance of the notion that excusive target language is the *best* practice that refuses to entertain any kind of meaningful dialogue about this hegemony, about the realism or desirability of the position or about the potential usefulness of the first language for learners.

However, challenges to the virtual position's hegemony have emerged from many sectors of the research community. Observational studies (e.g. Castellotti, 1997; Duff & Polio, 1990; Macaro, 1997; Polio & Duff, 1994; Rolin-Ianziti & Brownlie, 2002; Turnbull, 1999, 2005) clearly show that teachers vary in terms of the quantity and quality of target language used, even in contexts that are based on principles of communicative language teaching and exclusive target language use. In his review of studies of teacher beliefs across educational contexts and age of learners, Macaro (2000) found that the majority of second and foreign language teachers believe that while codeswitching is often necessary, they also believe it is unfortunate and regrettable. Most participants in the studies Macaro reviewed agreed that the target language should be the *'predominant* language of interaction in the classroom' (Macaro, 2000: 68). Macaro (2005: 66) has also pointed out that no study has yet demonstrated a causal relationship between exclusion of the first language and improved learning.

Problems with the virtual position emerge in studies that examine more than classroom policies and educator beliefs. Some studies also show that learners use their first language even when asked not to, and even when monitored (Behan *et al.*, 1997). Sociolinguists working in this field have also shown that far from simply using the first language when their target-language knowledge is insufficient, learners in fact develop codeswitching practices that resemble those practices used by advanced bilinguals and native speakers (e.g. Dailey-O'Cain & Liebscher, 2006; Liebscher & Dailey-O'Cain, 2004; Ustunel & Seedhouse, 2005). Meanwhile, on the pedagogical side of the field, other studies have found that the first language can be beneficial as a cognitive tool that aids in second-language learning (e.g. Antón & DiCamilla, 1998; Swain & Lapkin, 2000; Watanabe, 2008). These research results have prompted some scholars to soften the virtual position, arguing instead for *maximized* target language use (Swain & Lapkin, 2000; Turnbull, 2001; Turnbull & Arnett, 2002). Proponents of the maximal position agree that the target language can sometimes be more easily processed by making reference to the first language, but also caution that the *overuse* of first language will unduly reduce learners' exposure to target-language input (e.g. Atkinson, 1995; Calvé, 1993; Ellis, 1984). However, it is to be noted that Ellis (1994; see also Cook, 2001; van Lier, 2000) claims that target-language exposure is necessary, but not sufficient to guarantee target language learning, since target-language input must become intake. The target-language input must be understood by students and internalized, and judicious and theoretically principled first language use can facilitate intake and thereby contribute to learning.[1]

Use of the First Language Aids in the Learning of the Second Language

As indicated above, research findings indicate that the first language may contribute to student target-language comprehension, use and learning. Moreover, and contrary to the popular belief supported by the hegemony of the virtual position, small amounts of first language use may indeed lead to more comprehensible input and target-language production. Macaro (2000: 184) also reminds us that too much focus on teacher target language use, with long periods of input modification, may result in teacher-fronted lessons in which individual learners may only be speaking the second language for limited amounts of time (see also Chambers, 1992; Cook, 2005: 59), which goes against the very nature of communicative classrooms. Macaro and Mutton (2002) find that teachers can achieve many language and pedagogical functions in the first language in a very short time, thus still allowing for significant 'discourse space' in the target language.

Cummins' (1996, 2001) language interdependency model, which posits an underlying language proficiency common to the first language and the second language that learners use to support their second-language development, also supports judicious use of the first language in second and foreign language learning and teaching. In fact, many scholars now agree that 'the language of thought for all but the most advanced L2 learners is inevitably his/her L1' (Macaro, 2005: 68). Skinner (1985, cited in Macaro,

2001) argues that some first language use can facilitate connections between the target language and prior knowledge and ideas already developed in the first language. Kern (1994) found that students in a college French class used their first language to reduce working memory constraints, to avoid losing track of meaning, to consolidate meaning in long term memory, to convert the input into more familiar terms, and to clarify the syntactic role of certain lexical items (see also Behan *et al.*, 1997; Macaro, 1997; Swain & Lapkin, 2000; Thoms *et al.*, 2005). The cognitive benefits of the first language may be especially relevant in learning contexts where the cognitive load of many tasks is heavy and students' target-language skills limited. Finally, first language use may help students who are challenged in some way to learn a language. In one study, which examined the use of the first language by a Grade 9 French second language teacher, Arnett (2001) argues that the first language helps students, especially those with learning disabilities, to understand and process the target language.

Several recent studies have used sociocultural theory and a Vygotskian analysis of verbal interaction (which reveals the interrelatedness of speaking and thinking) to examine learners' use of the first language as a cognitive tool in carrying out collaborative tasks. This first language is especially important for learners with a low level of target-language proficiency dealing with challenging tasks and content. Brooks and Donato (1994) found that the learners, especially beginners, often benefit from using the first language when negotiating meaning. They suggest that some use of the first language during second-language interactions 'is a normal psycholinguistic process that facilitates second-language production and allows the learners both to initiate and sustain verbal interaction with one another' (Brooks & Donato, 1994: 268). Antón and DiCamilla (1998) studied adult beginner-level learners of Spanish who used the first language as a cognitive tool for providing each other with scaffolded help, for maintaining cooperation, and for externalizing their internal speech. Behan *et al.* (1997: 41) tape-recorded Grade 7 late French immersion students working in groups to complete a cognitively challenging jigsaw task; they concluded that 'L1 use can both support and enhance L2 development, functioning simultaneously as an effective tool for dealing with cognitively demanding content'. Swain and Lapkin (2000) report that Grade 8 early French immersion students were able to complete a collaborative task more successfully by using some L1. While these students used some L1 in roughly 25% of the turns taken, only 12% of these were off-task; by far, most of students' first language use served important cognitive and social functions. Swain and Lapkin conclude that judicious first language use supports second-language learning and production in the second language. They argue that 'to insist that no use be made of the L1 in carrying out tasks that are both linguistically and cognitively complex is to deny the use of an important cognitive tool' (Swain & Lapkin, 2000: 269).

Codeswitching is a Part of Bilingual Interaction

Based on several decades of sociolinguistic research on bilingual conversation, it is abundantly clear that codeswitching is a characteristic feature of bilingual talk rather than a sign of a deficiency in one or the other of the languages (Li, 2000: 17). In bilingual communities, even the most fluent bilinguals sometimes switch into their other language at times when there is a momentary gap in their immediate access to the first one (Auer, 1984: 60; Zentella, 1997: 96), but it is also true that codeswitching can serve as a contextualization cue (Gumperz, 1982) that serves to organize and structure talk. Specifically, bilinguals may codeswitch when they are summing up the end of a narrative (Alfonzetti, 1998: 194–195; Zentella, 1997: 94), to set off an aside (Zentella, 1997: 94), to shift from one topic to another (Alfonzetti, 1998: 197; Zentella, 1997: 94), to demarcate quotations or reported speech (Alfonzetti, 1998; Álvarez-Cáccamo, 1996), to attract attention (Li, 1998: 160–161), and to organize turn-taking or speaker change (Auer, 1995: 120; Zentella, 1997: 95), among other discourse-related functions. All of these uses have been documented in second and foreign language classroom interaction as well (Gumperz & Cook-Gumperz, 2005; Liebscher & Dailey-O'Cain, 2004).

In addition to these organizational functions, codeswitching can also serve important identity-related functions in bilingual conversation. Codeswitching can serve as a means to construct a multilingual and multicultural space (DeFina, 2007), as a way of constructing interactants as either bilingual or as dominant in a particular language (Fitts, 2006; Fuller, 2007; Potowski, 2007a), as a means to express a struggle among competing identities (Heller, 2005), and to display relationships between language and social categories such as ethnicity and group membership (Auer, 2005; Cashman, 2005). Furthermore, just as with the ways codeswitching is used to structure talk, many of these identity-related functions can be found in classroom interaction as well (Fuller, this volume; Liang, 2006; Liebscher & Dailey-O'Cain, 2007). From this work, it seems clear that if we are to regard the language learner not as an imperfect monolingual speaker of the second language but as a budding multilingual whose model is the multilingual speaker, it therefore seems reasonable to expect and allow codeswitching to emerge naturally within second and foreign language classrooms.

Although the growing body of research opposing extreme versions of the virtual position – emerging from within foreign-language pedagogical, educational-psychological and sociolinguistic circles – has contributed to a weakening of the virtual position's hegemony among researchers, it is clear that these results have not yet filtered through to educators in communicative and immersion classrooms. Whether in primary, secondary or higher education, whether in Canada, the United States, Europe or Asia, it is clear that the virtual position still enjoys significant support. However, it is our hope that by condensing the arguments against the virtual position into one coherent whole, this volume will encourage more reflective and informed thinking on these issues, not just among researchers and policy-makers, but among classroom teachers and teacher educators as well. It seems clear that an extreme version of the virtual position are not theoretically or pedagogically tenable.

An Overview of this Volume

This volume includes nine chapters written by scholars from fields as diverse as language pedagogy, curriculum design and sociolinguistics. All describe empirical studies related to first language use in a variety of second and foreign language contexts. These studies draw on multiple theoretical frameworks and use qualitative and quantitative methodologies and focus on crucial aspects of theory, practice and policy in second and foreign language education contexts around the world. The overall goal of these chapters, as a collective, is to examine the optimal level of first language use in communicative and immersion classroom settings, how the optimal level of first language use might vary across different kinds of programs, and what kinds of uses of the first language are positive and effective in different contexts.

The first chapter, co-authored by Brian McMillan from Hiroshima Bunkyo Women's University and Kanda University of International Studies in Japan and Miles Turnbull from the University of Prince Edward Island, is a small scale qualitative study, informed by principles of grounded theory (Creswell, 2005; Glaser, 1992; Glaser & Strauss, 1967; Strauss, 1987) and narrative inquiry (Clandinin & Connelly, 2000). The overall aim of the chapter is to tell two participants' stories (Clandinin & Connelly, 2000) and describe and 'explain', at a broad, conceptual level, the participants' beliefs and attitudes towards codeswitching in French Immersion as well as their actual codeswitching practices. McMillan and Turnbull draw principally on theoretical discussions about teachers' beliefs, attitudes and knowledge or belief systems, and the ways in which these belief systems are formed, and how they influence teachers' intended and actual classroom practices. The authors also draw on Richards' (1996) notions of maxims or working principles as a way of understanding teachers' beliefs, decisions and actions in the classroom. In their data analysis, McMillan and Turnbull also draw on research on bilinguals that shows that codeswitching is natural and common.

This chapter includes a description and analysis of data collected in two different Grade 7 late French Immersion classes. Data collection included semi-structured interviews, classroom observations and stimulated recall sessions conducted immediately after the observations. Patterns of first language use were quite different in the two classrooms, especially during the beginning stages of the immersion program. The authors show how each participant's beliefs and practices are deeply influenced by their own bilingual identity and by the way they learned other second languages. McMillan and Turnbull call for a rethinking of the current target-language-only guidelines in late French immersion and recommend a model for professional development through which teachers can develop a personalized, yet pedagogically and theoretically principled approach to target and first language use.

The second chapter, written by Ernesto Macaro from Oxford University, flows nicely from the first since McMillan and Turnbull refer in significant ways to Macaro's important work relating to codeswitching in foreign language teaching. Macaro draws on two studies which have attempted to discover whether codeswitching contributes to better learning (in this case, vocabulary learning), either in the short term or the long term. Before describing the two studies that are part of the applied linguistics research agenda at Oxford University, Macaro provides his take on the theoretical substance of two existing positions on codeswitching (virtual position, maximal position) before defining what he terms 'optimal' use of codeswitching by second and foreign language teachers in 'broadly communicative classrooms'. The first study, conducted with 159 Chinese 16-year-olds who were learning to speak English in China, was quasi-experimental in nature (the only experimental study in the volume) and examined the differential effect of providing first-language, target-language or no explanations of unknown words in two different texts. In the second study, Chinese first year university students participated in stimulated recall sessions carried out in Chinese. The researcher videotaped sixteen 45-minute lessons in two different English as a foreign language classes. From the corpus of 700 codeswitch episodes, at least two medium-oriented episodes and two message-oriented episodes were selected for the individual learners to react to. While the findings of the two studies do not provide conclusive evidence that codeswitching is better than exclusive target-language use, Macaro argues convincingly that banning the first language from the communicative second language classroom may be reducing the cognitive and metacognitive opportunities available to learners.

Like Macaro, Michael Evans from Cambridge Universityalso draws on sociolinguistic theories to frame the third chapter in the volume. Evans describes the only study in the volume to analyze CS practices in a multi-media learning context. Evans analyzed data collected, over a four-year period, from asynchronous computer mediated communication involving 100 high school-aged learners (14–17 years old) of French as a foreign language in England or of English as a foreign or second language. This study is one of a handful of studies that has ever examined codeswitching in a multimedia learning context. Moreover, Evans' study examines codeswitching practices among younger learners than many studies from the literature. The objective of the project was to stimulate and examine genuine communication between peer native and non-native speakers of French and English in order to see how the learners interacted with each other, how they learned from one another and in which languages they interacted. Evans shows how 'naturalistic' codeswitching emerged among the study participants in this e-learning context corresponds to the categories of codeswitching identified in the sociolinguistics literature which has examined the phenomenon as it appears in bilingual speech. The data also include several examples of language play wherein codeswitching might serve as an effective mediating tool for learners engaged in genuine communication in the multimedia medium, at least. Evans argues that computer-mediated communication can serve as a suitable environment for naturalistic bilingual discourse in which codeswitching plays a significant role.

Chapter 4 also offers insight into a phenomenon only rarely discussed in the existing literature: codeswitching in second and foreign language classrooms in primary schools. Krisztina Nagy and Daniel Robertson from Stirling University present data from nonintensive English foreign language classes in Hungarian primary schools. Beginning and intermediate level classes were observed in order to assess the impact of students' proficiency level. The authors analysed the frequency of words spoken in Hungarian and English by the four teachers and the pedagogical functions associated with their use of the first language. The features of the pedagogical activities employed by the teachers were also examined in relation to their first language use. Data also included reflective interviews conducted with each of the four teacher-participants following the observations. Teachers used the first language for a variety of reasons but pressure from the learners, discipline problems and the need to save time in the infrequent and nonintensive classes were cited as the most common reasons for first language use. Nagy and Robertson call into question the target-language-only policy in Hungarian primary English programs. They also provide insights into the nature of pedagogical activities for primary aged learners that allow teachers to speak the target language more often. Although the authors do not directly refer to sociolinguistic or sociocultural theories, they do reflect on the historical and socio-economic realities of Hungary as factors in teachers' language choices and code-switching practices in primary English programs.

The following chapter, authored by Kim Potowski from University of Illinois at Urbana-Champaign also considers codeswitching practices among younger learners, but in a significantly different context than the Hungarian English as a foreign language situation. Potowski presents a quantitative study comparing the forms and functions of codeswitching among heritage language speakers and second-language learners in a Grade 5 (10–11 years old) Spanish-English dual immersion program in the United States. In dual immersion, two languages are used in the class-room starting from early childhood with the aim of transforming mono-linguals in each of the two languages into bilinguals. Spanish is the official language of the classroom and English is banned. One objective of the study is to determine whether second-language children in dual immer-sion programs begin to codeswitch, and whether their codeswitching practices resemble those of their heritage speaker peers. Drawing on socio-linguistics literature and theoretical lenses, and more specifically Myers-Scotton's (1993) language matrix model, Potowski finds that the heritage language speakers codeswitch in more structurally complex ways than do the second-language learners, suggesting that although both groups have a high level of Spanish proficiency, the heritage language speakers are still more balanced bilinguals. She then goes on to argue that second-language learners may well develop codeswitching skills more slowly than do heritage language speakers, in large part due to a differing amount of exposure outside of the classroom. Potowski is the only author in the volume to reflect on the influence of gender in learners' classroom codeswitching practices. Interestingly, students' first language was not correlated with their quantity of Spanish use whereas gender was more so. Girls used Spanish more often than the boys. This chapter includes intriguing reflections on the factors that lead girls to codeswitching less frequently than their male peers.

Janet M. Fuller from Southern Illinois University then reports on a fur-ther study from a dual immersion context. The data analyzed in Fuller's come from observations conducted in several 4th and 5th Grade classrooms in a German-English bilingual program in Berlin, Germany. Fuller draws on two different theoretical positions in her analyses: the sequential approach from conversational analysis (e.g. Auer, 1988) and a social constructivist perspective on language use (e.g. Mendoza-Denton, 2002). The sequential approach shows how codeswitching is a strategic, and not random, use of two languages. The social constructivist approach examines social identity construction through codeswitching. Fuller addresses the complex issue of why, even when language mixing is stigmatized within classrooms or even forbidden through specific classroom rules, speakers continue to codeswitch. Many readers will identify with this complex and puzzling question. Fuller's analyses show that bilingual children – both those who have learned English and German from early childhood, as well as those who have learned their second language in school – codeswitch to both structure conversation and construct social identities. Moreover, Fuller shows that overall codeswitching patterns remain the same regardless of proficiency levels in the two languages. Drawing on in-depth discourse analyses of particular examples, Fuller points to the notion that the motivation for learners' persistence to codeswitch is linked to social identity, and that just as with bilinguals in non-institutional contexts, language learners make use of their two languages in identity construction in classroom settings.

Chapter 7, written by Jennifer Dailey-O'Cain from the University of Alberta and Grit Liebscher from the University of Waterloo, also draws on conversational analysis and theoretical perspectives from the sociolinguistics literature. The authors provide detailed discourse analyses of interactions among intermediate and advanced university-aged learners of German and their instructors in two different German language classrooms at a western Canadian university. The first classroom is a content-based classroom, a third-year seminar on applied linguistics taught in German – a learning context that is not present in any other chapter in our volume. The second classroom is a more conventional second-year university intermediate-level German language class. The authors demonstrate that learners in both contexts develop naturalistic target language codeswitching practices even when teachers maximize their target-language use. Dailey-O'Cain and Liebscher argue that from the perspective of sociocultural theory (e.g. Lantolf & Thorne, 2006) it is important to consider not just whether and to what extent the first language is and should be used, but by whom. While they show that the teacher does not seem to have to model codeswitching behavior in order for students to use it naturally in the classroom, they argue that it is still possible that alerting students to the existence of codeswitching and its usefulness may have an impact on fostering these uses of codeswitching in the second and foreign language classrooms. Dailey-O'Cain and Liebscher suggest that learning how to use codeswitching to structure discourse in classrooms also promotes many language learners' goal of aspiring to bilingualism. Imitating natural bilingual CS practices allows learners to interact as fluent bilingual speakers do.

Chapter 8 is authored by Glenn S. Levine from the University of California at Irvine. Levine's chapter flows from Dailey-O'Cain's and Liebscher's; Levine draws on the tenets of sociocultural theory and his data come from university-level learners of German. Moreover, Levine also draws on an ecological perspective of language and learning (van Lier, 2004) – the only author to do so in this volume. Levine explores discursive functions of first language use in second-language interaction between two university-level learners of German who engaged in an interview and pedagogical tasks with one instructor. Levine distinguishes between the functions of a codeswitch in the organization of talk, and the enacting of what he refers to as 'big D' discourses through the participants' knowledge of external context. He finds that this shared contextual knowledge allows learners to use the first and second languages in creative and dynamic ways in the process of carrying out a language-learning task. Interestingly, Levine suggests that neither student was 'aware', in the sense of consciously attending to, their use of the L1 as they used it, despite the fact that they began the conversation knowing that it would be acceptable to codeswitch if need be. Levine discusses the importance of learners' awareness of codeswitching as normal verbal behavior for bilinguals and their awareness of the purposes of codeswitching in conversation. Levine offers several recommendations for classroom practice including the development of explicit, collaborative classroom norms for first language use and teaching the terminology and concepts to discuss bilingualism and codeswitching.

Finally, the volume comes full circle with another qualitative study of opinions about second-language use – a chapter by Carl S. Blyth from University of Texas at Austin who investigated 11 participants' reactions to a university-level French-as-a-foreign-language curriculum in the United States. This unique curriculum includes speakers with a much wider range of proficiencies than is typically found in commercially-produced materials, from fluent bilinguals to second-language learners, and perhaps most relevantly here, it deliberately sets out to increase learner awareness of authentic language use, including codeswitching. Participants were either native speakers of French and beginner and intermediate level university-aged learners of French. Participants viewed video and print segments from the new curriculum materials and were then engaged in a stimulated recall interview to assess whether participants notice the codeswitching included in the materials, their opinions on the codeswitching and the presence of non-native speakers within the materials. Blyth finds that this curriculum helps learners identify with the 'characters' in their course materials in a way that the stereotyped monolingual speakers in traditional course materials may not. He also finds that while learners notice the use of English in the discourse of the second-language learners in their curriculum, they do not notice it in the discourse of the native French speakers. In fact, Blyth argues that presenting non-native speakers to learners is more effective than presenting native speakers only. Presenting non-native target-language speakers may prove more relevant for the construction of a learner's projective identity than those of native speakers.

Taken as a whole, these chapters provide a wealth of information about actual classroom use of the first language and opinions about that use by both teachers and learners. The implications of this collection of findings for classroom language policy and for curriculum development are therefore unavoidable. Despite the persistence of policies that prohibit the use of the first language, both teachers and learners are in fact using the first language in cognitively and sociolinguistically productive ways, and in every kind of classroom imaginable. When confronted with the weight of the available information about these issues, it does not seem too bold to argue that a full-scale re-evaluation of the virtual position is in order, and that government policymakers, individual program developers or classroom teachers need to pay more attention to current theory and research. This reevaluation begins with the recognition of the benefits of principled classroom first language use for both learning and communication. This reevaluation should also include an exploration of additional kinds of learning tasks teachers might want to bring into their classrooms, as well as the kinds of course materials that would most successfully approach the ultimate goal of helping language learners develop into bilinguals. We are hopeful that the chapters and concluding reflections that follow will engage readers and lead to important and critical re-evaluation.

Chapter 1

Teachers' Use of the First Language in French Immersion: Revisiting a Core Principle

BRIAN MCMILLAN and MILES TURNBULL

L'apprentissage doit être intensif sans toutefois être une noyade. Les élèves doivent très tôt pouvoir comprendre le français et l'utiliser pour communiquer. Il est donc essentiel que la seule langue de communication dans la salle de classe soit le français. (La Fondation d'éducation des provinces de l'Atlantique, 1997: 9)
[Learning must be intensive, yet should not make students feel that they are drowning. From the early stages of the program, the students must be able to understand French and use it to communicate. It is therefore essential that French be the only language of communication in the classroom.[2]]
(Atlantic Provinces Education Foundation, 1997: 9)
French must be the language of communication in class.
(Ontario Ministry of Education, 1998: 8)

Introduction

As the above quotations clearly indicate, a core principle of Canadian French immersion is that learning is best achieved when teachers and students use French exclusively. While the exclusive use of the target language has been accepted as best practice in since its inception in 1965, first language use has long been a topic of much debate and controversy in many teaching and learning contexts beyond French immersion. Current thinking leans towards acceptance of judicious and theoretically principled L1 use (e.g. Cook, 2001; Levine, 2003; Liebscher & Dailey-O'Cain, 2004; Macaro, 2005; Turnbull, 2001). However, the results of this debate have generally been ignored by French immersion policy makers throughout Canada. Some researchers (e.g. Sanaoui, 2005; Skerritt, 2003; Walsh & Yeoman, 1999) suggest, nevertheless, that teacher codeswitching (CS)

15

practice varies significantly in French immersion. Swain and Lapkin (2000), Cummins (2000), Skerritt (2003), Sanaoui (2005, 2007) and Turnbull and McMillan (2006, 2007) have dared to wade into this controversy, but as of yet, calls for debate on this topic in Canadian French immersion programs have generally gone unheard. Moreover, curricula and policy across Canada do not reflect current thinking on first-language use in second and foreign language teaching and learning.

The strongly held position on exclusive target language use in French immersion persists, at least in part, because of the many accolades in the scholarly literature that promote Canadian French immersion – built on exclusive target-language use as a core principle – as 'the most effective approach available to second language teaching in school settings' (Genesee, 1994: 6). In 1987, Genesee argued that 'research has shown consistently that immersion students acquire functional proficiency in French, or in other second languages, that surpasses that of students in all other forms of second language instruction to which immersion has been compared' (Genesee, 1987: 10). Indeed, some even suggest that French immersion programs are the most studied language programs in the world, (Canadian Parents for French, 2003) and are held up as evidence of the power of communicative language teaching in which comprehensible input (Krashen, 1985) in the target language is foundational. Moreover, immersion programs have spread to many countries around the globe, particularly in Europe and the United States, often patterned on the Canadian model (Canadian Parents for French, 2003).

We agree that immersion programs are, in general, highly effective, providing many students with the opportunity to achieve a high level of proficiency in the target language. The success of French immersion is no doubt due in large part to the fact that the target language is the *main* language of communication and instruction in the classroom. However, Cummins (2000) and others (e.g. Genesee, 1994; Lapkin & Swain, 1990) argue that there is room for improvement in French immersion. These educators identify students' inaccurate productive skills as one of the main areas that need to be addressed in immersion pedagogy.

The use of the first language by students is seen (by teachers and policy makers) as contravening the basic premises of immersion. It rarely occurs to teachers to permit students to use their first language for discussion and initial draft purposes but to require that final drafts of writing or other project output be in the target language. The principle of language separation and vestiges of 'direct method' teaching approaches (i.e. remaining totally in the target language) in immersion programs thus sometimes results in pedagogy that is less cognitively challenging and creative than many educators would consider appropriate. The provision of *comprehensible input* in the second language is interpreted as the promotion of literal rather than critical comprehension (Cummins, 2000: 10).

Like Cummins (2000), we wonder if rethinking the inflexible and exclusive perspective on target language use may be one way to improve student learning in French immersion. We also contend that judicious first language use can help teachers and students comprehend and discuss cognitively challenging and age appropriate content. However, to advance this debate in Canadian French immersion, research is needed to understand the beliefs and practices of Canadian French immersion teachers – the overall aim of the study we report here.

Firstly, we give some background for French immersion in Canada. Secondly, we briefly review previous research on target language and first language use in French immersion. The main focus of the chapter is a small-scale study which examines the perspectives of two late French immersion teachers on their use of the target language and of their students' first language. We start by outlining the data collection methods, providing a detailed description of our two participants, and the theoretical lenses which guided our data analyses. We then describe our participants' beliefs and practices and the key factors that shaped and influenced these beliefs and practices. We conclude by proposing a model for professional development which will allow teachers to develop a personalized yet theoretically and pedagogically principled approach to target language and first language use.

French Immersion in Canada

FI is an optional program, designed for non-native speakers of French, which exists in all Canadian provinces and territories. Over 300,000 students are enrolled in FI, representing about 11% of the total school population in Canada (Canadian Parents for French, 2006). The growth in the first 30 years of the program (since 1965) can be attributed in part to federal government policy that offered grants to school boards who implemented immersion programs. This incentive program was viewed by the Canadian government as a way of promoting individual bilingualism in Canada's two official languages and, ultimately, national unity. There are many different types of French immersion programs in Canada, with the main differences being age of entry and intensity of the program.[3] The immersion curriculum is based on the principle of offering a variety of school subjects taught in the second language; French is therefore the medium and not the object of instruction. The expectations in school subjects (e.g. sciences, math) parallel those in the regular first language curriculum.

Given the official policy and widely accepted view that exclusive teacher use of the target language is the best practice, the issue of codeswitching by teachers rarely, if ever, enters professional discussions (even though it is common knowledge that some teachers use the first language at least sometimes). Consequently, late French immersion teachers (whether they use the first language to a certain extent or not) do not have a clear picture of what other teachers actually do. Thus one further goal of the present study is to demystify the issue of late French immersion teachers' target language and first language use. Teachers whose codeswitching is not in keeping with ministerial guidelines concerning target language and first language use may feel guilty, or may be viewed as not following 'proven' best practice procedures; target language exclusivity is taken for granted as the best practice, when the research literature, summarized in the following section, does not necessarily support this premise.

Previous research

Most of the previous work on codeswitching in French immersion has focused on *student* target language and first language use. For example, Behan *et al.* (1997: 41) tape-recorded Grade 7 late French immersion students working in groups; they concluded that 'L1 use can both support and enhance L2 development, [both languages] functioning simultaneously as an effective tool for dealing with cognitively demanding content'. Swain and Lapkin (2000) reported that Grade 8 Early French immersion students were able to complete a collaborative task more successfully by using some L1. While these students used some L1 in roughly 25% of the turns taken, only 12% of these were off-task; by far, most of students' first language use served important cognitive and social functions. Swain and Lapkin (2000: 269) conclude: 'Judicious use of the L1 can indeed support L2 learning and use. To insist that no use be made of the L1 in carrying out tasks that are both linguistically and cognitively complex is to deny the use of an important cognitive tool.' These studies show that that the communication that takes place amongst students during communicative cooperative learning activities, far from being target-language only, actually involves a good deal of natural first language use; furthermore student first language use would often seem to benefit and not hinder target language comprehension, production, collaboration, task management and performance.

We are aware of only two other studies that have examined teacher first language use in French immersion. Skerritt (2003) and Sanaoui (2005, 2007)[4] examined the amount and functions of English used by four Grade 3 Early French immersion teachers. Lessons were tape-recorded and teachers later reviewed their use of the target language and the first language. One teacher did not use any English, two used a limited amount, and the fourth used English considerably more. Skerritt and Sanaoui tentatively relate use of the first language to teachers' amount and type of teaching experience, their proficiency level, students' first language use and beliefs about the role of the first language in language learning.

Our Study

Our qualitative study was informed by principles of grounded theory (Creswell, 2005; Glaser, 1992; Glaser & Strauss, 1967; Strauss, 1987) and narrative inquiry (Clandinin & Connelly, 2000). The overall aim was to tell each participant's story (Clandinin & Connelly, 2000) and describe and 'explain', at a broad, conceptual level, the participants' beliefs and attitudes towards codeswitching in late French immersion as well as their actual codeswitching practices.

Research questions

(1) What are late French immersion teachers' beliefs and attitudes about the teacher's use of the target language and the first language in late French immersion?
(2) What are the teachers' codeswitching practices?
(3) Which factors contribute to these beliefs, attitudes and codeswitching practices? How and why?

Conceptual framework

Conceptually, this study was informed and guided by theoretical discussions about teachers' beliefs, attitudes and knowledge or belief systems, and the ways in which these belief systems are formed, and how they influence teachers' intended and actual classroom practices (e.g. Ajzen, 1991; Johnson, 1999; Kennedy & Kennedy, 1996; Nespor, 1987; Pajares, 1992; Richards, 1996; Woods, 1996, 2003). We drew on Richards' (1996: 282) notions of 'working principles or maxims which teachers consciously or unconsciously refer to as they teach'. Richards proposes that motivations for language teachers' decisions and actions can be understood by examining their guiding maxims. Moreover, we were influenced by research on bilinguals that shows that codeswitching is natural and common (e.g. Liebscher & Dailey-O'Cain, 2004; Myers-Scotton, 1993).

Context for this study

Data were collected in two late French immersion classes located in two different and relatively large intermediate schools in a semi-urban center in Prince Edward Island, Canada, where late French immersion begins in Grade 7 (age 13). In the first two years of late French immersion, French language arts, math, science, social studies and health are offered in French (representing about 80% of instruction). Prior to beginning late French immersion, students study French in short non-intensive periods of instruction (approximately 30 minutes per day) from Grades 4 to 6. Access to late French immersion is open to all students interested in enrolling; no aptitude or admission test is administered before the start of the program. In our study, students' first language was English in all cases. This is not necessarily the case in all French immersion programs due to increased immigration in Canada, including in French immersion programs, especially in urban centres (Swain & Lapkin, 2005).

Participants[5]

Pierre, a native French speaker, and Frank, whose first language was English, volunteered to participate in this study; both had been teaching late French immersion on Prince Edward Island for 10 years and were teaching Grade 7 late French immersion at the time of this study. Pierre taught math, sciences and social studies, while Frank taught math and health. As late French immersion teachers, both Pierre and Frank met the superior level of French proficiency required by the Prince Edward Island Ministry of Education.[6]

Data collection

After establishing a comfortable level of trust with Pierre and Frank, we conducted an initial one-on-one semi-structured interview with each participant.[7] Questions focused on their current teaching assignment, their experiences as a second language learner, teacher training and previous second language teaching experiences, and other important influences shaping their beliefs about target and first language use in late French immersion. We then conducted three classroom observations per teacher (approximately once per month), and a final one-on-one interview was conducted during the last month of the school year with each participant. Immediately following each observation, stimulated recall procedures[8] were used to review recordings of the class and discuss instances when the teacher used the first language (or perhaps could have, but did not). A final interview was conducted during the last month of the school year, which allowed for checking and further clarification of information collected during the previous rounds.

Data analyses

During transcription of the interviews, emerging themes and similarities or differences between Pierre and Frank's beliefs and strategies were noted. In keeping with grounded theory methodology, the research team met several times throughout the process to review transcripts and discuss additional questions which arose or statements that needed to be clarified in subsequent interviews. Field notes and interview transcripts were analyzed using systematic and thematic open coding techniques.

We now move to a summary of the findings from this small study. We first describe the participants' beliefs (and maxims) and their codeswitching practices. We then turn to an analysis of the factors that shaped and influenced these beliefs and practices. All English words used in the lesson are italicized; other reported speech (non-italicized) given in English here was actually said in French by the teacher or by students.

Frank and Pierre

Frank

Frank believed second language learning to be most effective when kept separate from the existing first language system, essentially equating second-language learning with first language learning. His beliefs were in agreement with the Atlantic Provinces Education Foundation guidelines and correspond to what Macaro (2001: 535) refers to as the virtual position: 'The classroom is like the target country. Therefore we should aim at total exclusion of the L1. There is no pedagogical value in L1 use'. Frank believed that trying to make connections between the first language and the target language most often lead to inappropriate transfers; students should therefore try to think in the target language and develop a separate target language system. While he knew of other late French immersion teachers who gave translation exercises to their students, Frank did not believe this to be helpful:

> I *do not* ask them to translate; I think that's a waste of time. You're activating part of the brain that you're trying to get them to forget about. I've always believed that. I know that kids need a French-English dictionary, but I don't ask for any translation because it's double-thinking and it's keeping the English in there.

Frank felt that any relationships drawn between the first and the target languages would only cause interference and confusion. In fact, Frank almost seemed to try to train students to forget about a part of their brain, rather than trying to establish explicit connections between students' existing first language knowledge and new target language words and structures. In the following quotation, Frank reflects further on his doubt regarding the effectiveness of pointing out similarities between French and English structures (e.g. the infinitives used in *je veux aller* = I want to go), or showing students that certain target language and first language structures are not directly translatable (e.g. I am 12 years old ≠ *je suis 12 ans*). His perspective is even somewhat in line with behaviourism:

> No, I would *never* do that. . . . Because I always put it down to how you learn as a child, from sheer repetition, right? Nobody sat down and said this works because, you know, these are the semantics of your mother tongue. No one ever really actually ever does that for you. You just learn how it all goes together and most of it's by ear.

Frank also believed that if he were to use English, his students, in turn, would likely increase their use of English as well. He expressed concern that codeswitching would therefore cause students to ignore target language input:[9]

> If they know that you're going to do this translation service, they're not going to buy into the French – but if they knew that you were going to, you know, as soon as someone wrinkled their brow, then you were going to say it in English, they'll just wait.

Frank's maxim for target language and first language use was therefore: *The Maxim of Target Language Maximization: Use French and strictly avoid using English in order to maximize students' exposure to target language input.* In following this maxim, Frank made a quick transition to near 100% target language use at the beginning of Grade 7, although he did find a need to use some English during the first two or three weeks of the year. However, he reported using English on the first day of school for dealing with administrative issues and explaining rules and procedures (Grade 7 students are not only new to being taught in French, they are new to the school). Following this, he tried to speak French as much as possible, as he indicates here:

> And September, granted, it's difficult to go in and do 100% right off the bat, but I go over all the school rules and all the homeroom stuff in the first week of school, and then I go right in and I do as much French as I can, and by October I really am speaking totally French.

Frank said that when introducing an activity at the beginning of the year: 'I might tell them, you know, "assemblage" is "matching" but then do the matching in French.' He said that he was able to avoid using English by speaking French 'in a very simplified way' at the beginning of the year; his French became more and more complex as students progressed.

In the three math classes we observed, Frank used target language synonyms and paraphrasing, along with pictures and gestures to convey the meanings of new French words and expressions. He did not provide or ask students for English equivalents to ensure comprehension, nor did he make comparisons between target language and first language structures.

For example, in one of the math classes we observed, Frank explained the word 'échantillon' (sample) by saying 'un exemple ou une partie pour tester (*an example or part to test*)'. Frank commented:

> Even if it's very simplified, like 'exemple' (for 'échantillon'), you know, that's how I keep it in French. They know enough to do that question, like they wouldn't know enough to obviously use that word themselves, but that's not where we are right now.

While Frank made no explicit references to first language equivalents, he made frequent use of French-English cognates to help students understand new words. For example, when several students had taken 'au moins' (*at least*) to mean 'less than', he asked the class if they had looked up the word: 'Nobody was giving me much feedback that way, so I thought well, they recognize "moins", and I just went on and told them "le minimum". You know, there are so many words that are so similar to English.' In another lesson, Frank used the French-English cognates 'partie' and 'portion' to explain the word 'segment' and used the target language synonym and first language cognate 'diagramme' to convey the meaning of the word 'schéma' (diagram).

On rare occasions, Frank did use a word or two of English later on in the year to help students to connect existing first language knowledge to important concepts in the target language. He told of an occasion in which he had used one English word in the weeks preceding our last final interview in June:

> In the last chapter, I was talking about integers and so I was telling them about 'nombres positifs et négatifs', and they were all looking at me, so I did say the word 'integer' at one point because they had had that in Grade 6. In that case I thought, I don't want them to think of this as something that they've never seen before, or take 20 minutes just to think – 'Wait a minute, we did this last year.'

Pierre

Pierre, on the other hand, believed that Grade 7 late French immersion students needed to relate new target language elements to their existing first language knowledge and used French-English translation as a means of ensuring or verifying comprehension, and of reducing any feeling students may have of being lost. He also made the telling assertion that unless a student can rephrase a target language statement in their first language, they haven't really understood it. Clearly, for Pierre, knowing that students have understood is an important benefit of codeswitching. He used lists at the beginning of the year to keep track of new words which students had learned and his tended to explain target language words and check student comprehension using the first language, which also indicated a strong desire to be sure that students had understood before moving on in the lesson.

Pierre's guiding maxim regarding target language and first language use could therefore be stated as: *The Maxim of Maximum Comprehensibility: Provide rich exposure to the target language by using French as the normal means of communication and instruction, but use the first language where helpful in order to ensure comprehension and scaffold target language production.* Following this maxim, Pierre (and his students) used English systematically over the course of the first two to three months of the year to ensure that everyone clearly understood new target language words and expressions; Pierre provided or asked students for first language translations each time new target language elements were introduced. Once students had become familiar with a basic start-up vocabulary, Pierre gradually reduced the amount of English he used:

> We start gradually in September. It's not 100%, it's far from it. In September, I speak English and the students speak in French. So I would start the class by saying 'Hi', and they would respond with 'Bonjour'. Then I say 'Today' and the students say 'Aujourd'hui' ... 'we're going to' – 'nous allons' ... I say 'work', and the students say

'travailler'. Then after that I ask them to repeat the sentence 'Bonjour, aujourd'hui nous allons travailler avec les nombres' *(today we will work with numbers)*. *They* speak French. I speak English, but my goal is to make *them* speak French, and to ensure comprehension. Then the next day when they arrive, it's 'Bonjour aujourd'hui nous allons étudier les sciences humaines' – boom, they know it. And then I can start with 'sortez vos livres' (take out your books), so, you know, we're always accumulating more and more new words. So the first six weeks, it's like that, and then they have a good base. It works really well.

Pierre's approach includes having students keep a running list of new words over the course of the first several weeks. At different intervals, students brainstorm all the new words they have learned, then add them to the list and study them for homework. Pierre then expects that students will know these target language words, and so codeswitching is no longer required for them.

Pierre had target dates for increasing his own target language use and that of his students. He said that he used 30 to 40% French in September and then made a gradual transition to around 80% to 90% French by the beginning of November:

The percentages really change from September to December, there's a big, big difference, but after Christmas, 100%, you know, as much as possible. It's just in September there a lot of people who think 'Oh, completely in French, completely in French' – it's impossible. You can do it, but it's very frustrating for the students, so for me, I like to show them a base, we do a lot of repetition, then every day I incorporate new words then eventually we're completely in French.

By January, Pierre used only isolated first-language words to ensure and to check comprehension. He explained why he continued to use first-language words beyond the first few months:

If I wanted to, I could teach completely 100% in French, but I just find it … good for the students. It helps me to know if they've understood what's going on and also to make them use French, which is the goal, to have them speak French. So if I ask them these questions and if they're able to answer with the word I'm looking for, they'll continue to use that word.

In January, Pierre posted a large sign on the board advising students that they must speak French and introduced a point system to encourage students to do so. However, students were also encouraged to use English words when asking how to say something in French ('Comment dit-on——en français?' *how do you say——in French?*) or when respond-ing to the teacher's request for an English equivalent ('Qu'est-ce que c'est en anglais?' *What is that in English?*). Pierre explained how he introduced his point system to ensure that students would 'buy in'; he stressed that he listened carefully and reacted dramatically to excessive first-language use by students (more than one or two words), especially during the beginning stages of implementation.

As in Frank's class, Pierre's students could consult French posters on the walls which featured key words and phrases. However, at the front of Pierre's room, the posters for the four most common verbs (*aller, être, avoir* and *faire*) also provided students with English equivalents (e.g. avoir – to have: j'ai – I have, tu as – you have, etc.). Pierre reflects on these posters and their usefulness in the following quotation:

> If everyone memorizes '*je fais, tu fais, il fait, nous faisons*' – well, it's important that students know that it's 'I'm doing, you're doing, he does' ... I think it's important when they're learning French that they know what they're learning, because if they're just memorizing and they don't know what they're memorizing they won't be able to put sentences together.

In the classes we observed, all of Pierre's first language use took place when new or difficult words or concepts came up during class discus-sions. Pierre explicitly and intentionally used a limited amount of the first language to ensure student comprehension and to move the activity along. For example, in one social studies lesson dealing with the topic of dis-crimination and racism, Pierre asked the class 'Qu'est-ce que c'est le mot en français pour *treat*?'[10] (What is the word in French for *treat*?). Several students knew, and replied with the French equivalent, 'traiter'. Further on in the lesson, Pierre asked students 'Qu'est-ce que c'est le mot en français pour *life*?' Again, several students answered with the French equivalent, 'vie'. Following the lesson, Pierre said that students had seen these two words in a previous lesson and that he wanted to test them to see if they had remembered them. Pierre said that he did this several times during an average lesson. He added that students who had not remem-bered would understand the word in English and would have another chance to learn the target-language word when they heard other students give the answer. Thus for Pierre, this use of the first language allowed him to check students' knowledge of vocabulary items and, for students who did not know the word, it ensured comprehension and helped them learn the word. On another occasion, a student was making reference to Martin

Luther King, and asked Pierre 'Comment dit-on *speech*?' Pierre gave the French equivalent, and the student then used the word, 'discours', to complete his sentence. Pierre said that encouraging students to use 'Comment dit-on——?' was very important because it enabled students to participate more fully, even when they did not know all the words needed to express their ideas.

Pierre sometimes asked students which English words they had looked up in their bilingual dictionaries. For example, while making a short presentation to the class, a student used the expression 'une foule fâchée'; Pierre asked, 'Quel mot as-tu cherché en anglais?' (Which English words did you look up?) and the student replied, '*angry mob*'. Pierre later asked the same of another student who had used the word 'grève' (*strike*) in his presentation. Pierre explained that his reason for doing this was to make these words comprehensible to students who would not have known them – in these instances most of the class. In addition, he sometimes asked students how they had used their dictionaries in order to clarify what they had attempted to express in French, and then making any necessary corrections.

What shaped and influenced Frank and Pierre's beliefs and codeswitching practices?

Both Pierre and Frank's beliefs regarding codeswitching seem to have been influenced considerably by their own experiences as second language learners (Lortie, 1975). Pierre's first language was French, but he grew up in a bilingual Acadian community and was fluent in both languages before he started school. In his school, the teachers and students would alternate between French and English, consistent with natural codeswitching amongst bilinguals. Frank, on the other hand, grew up in an Anglophone community with no exposure to French outside of his school's nonintensive French program. After completing his bachelor's degree, Frank spent two years in an immersion-type program at a French language university in Quebec. He acknowledged that he had been particularly influenced by one of his university professors during this time in Quebec:

> The program I took at university in Quebec was totally in French and I had a very strong teacher. You know, you model the way you were taught and I think that's what I did when I started as a Grade 7 late immersion teacher. Nobody was there to tell me what the program was, so I kind of based it more or less on the way I had been taught; you did the gestures, you did the visual, you did the audio-visual, you

did the reading, you did the acting, you did whatever you could to get the message across – but you did it in French.

Neither Frank nor Pierre had received any training with respect to target language and first language use; indeed, they had not undergone formal second language teacher training.[11] Pierre was trained to teach Francophone students in French-language schools. Before teaching late French immersion, he had taught in a variety of other French first and second language contexts at the elementary level. He began teaching Grade 7 late French immersion without having had the chance to observe late French immersion classes and, as a new late French immersion teacher, had little contact with other teachers in similar situations. Pierre thus developed his own approach to 'maximizing' target language use – both his own and that of his students – which included the use of codeswitching:

> I just developed my own style. I did whatever I needed to do and I tried anything I could to have as much French as possible. If something worked well, I used it again the following year and I made adjustments until, for me, it worked really well.

Teachers' preferred learning styles and perceptions of student target language anxiety

Frank and Pierre's beliefs also seem to have been shaped considerably by their own preferred learning styles and personalities, as well as their perceptions of student target language anxiety. Frank said that, as an adult learner, he was happy to have a global, overall understanding of things. He said that he was patient, had a high degree of tolerance for ambiguity and enjoyed figuring things out for himself. He hoped that his students would be motivated enough to figure things out while referring to the first language as little as possible, as he did when learning French in Quebec:

> I wondered what certain words meant but I wasn't upset about it, I was just trying to figure it out. It was just like a big puzzle to me. I was just trying to figure it out and *happy* to do that. And I would *hope* that the motivation of these kids is similar. I remember being somewhat frustrated that I couldn't express myself, but I just had to patiently bide my time and build on it, and then when I did it on my own it was such a sense of accomplishment.

Frank often expressed confidence in his students' ability to figure things out: 'They're like sponges at this age. As long as they're willing, it's quite doable.' Frank believed that even when students didn't understand completely, implicit learning was taking place.

> Well just the vacant look and you know they don't get it. But I firmly believe – well, next time around they will – so I'm very repetitive and I stick to key formats and key phrasings and I use them over and over the first few months and then I'll expand on them as the year goes on, because at least if they can catch those, they can catch the gist, which is all I'm expecting. I think you have to give kids that opportunity to figure things out for themselves, and that may not happen this *first* year, but this is just the foundational block, you know, it's going to build, progress as years go on, but I don't think you can baby them ...

Frank recognized that a French-only environment could be frustrating for students, but reassured them and prepared them for the ups and downs of the first few months in late French immersion:

> I tell them that right at the beginning and I tell their parents at Meet the Teacher Night, this is kind of like surfing, you're riding the wave and you're on the crest one day, but then the wave crashes and you bottom out, but you ride again and you bottom out, and you ride again. It takes a while for the waters to run still and smooth ... and certainly it takes until Christmas, and then they seem, after that two week break, to come back and they're refreshed again and they seem to understand *so* much more than before.

Pierre, on the other hand, identified himself as an analytic, detail-oriented learner who preferred to have things clearly spelled out. He stated that he could 'absolutely not' tolerate a large degree of ambiguity. Pierre felt that his students would become anxious and frustrated if he did not use some English, especially during the first three months of Grade 7. In the same way that Frank compared his students' experience in late French immersion to his own immersion experience in Quebec, Pierre pictured himself in his students' shoes:

> I want to avoid student frustration. I can't start off yak, yak, yak in French – the kids will panic. It would be much too frustrating. So I've found a method that works for me, and I find that the students feel much less frustrated. And the change from English to French is *very*, *very* gradual. So I do it the same way I would want to learn French if I were a student. If I were a student, how would I want to learn? With as little stress as possible ...

Did Frank and Pierre practice what they believed?

We identified three main factors which affected Pierre and Frank's ability to follow their maxims for target and first language use. However, because they were experienced and very resourceful teachers, and because of the strength of their beliefs, both participants felt they were able to follow their own ideas of best codeswitching practices.

Subject matter and resources

Both Pierre and Frank felt that math, as compared to other subjects, could be taught almost exclusively in French from the beginning. It was easier to use French almost exclusively for teaching math from the start of the year, citing the advantage of many French-English cognates (e.g. *addition, soustraction, multiplication, facteur*), and also because math can be represented in numbers and symbols. Pierre claimed that, for him, the transition towards maximizing target language use is more gradual in science and social studies due to the many difficult vocabulary items which can not be easily explained with French synonyms, French-English cognates or visual representations (e.g. 'l'azote' – nitrogen). Frank commented, however, that after completing the first unit in math, avoiding the first language became more of a challenge since there were more word problems.

Due to the relatively small numbers of students enrolled in late French immersion programs across Canada the textbooks used in science, math and social studies are not specifically written for late French immersion students. Rather, they are created for Francophone students, which means that there is no English within them, and the complexity of the language is often far beyond the limited reading skills of late French immersion students, especially in Grade 7. Pierre explained:

> The textbooks are too advanced for our students. If we had books that were a lot simpler, then we could read the instructions, you know, that would make a big difference. To tell the truth, we don't really start using the textbooks until April, and that's *serious* – except for the math exercises, you know, we can do the easier ones. But it would definitely be an advantage if we had books that were at an appropriate level.

Students requiring individualized instruction

Both Frank and Pierre noted that more and more students with learning difficulties were entering late French immersion (as compared to earlier in their careers, when a screening process had been in place). Frank saw a need to use English with students who were struggling, but this was done after school, enabling him to maintain a target language atmosphere during class:

> I do get around it though. Math is a core subject and sometimes it's not math, it's French that causes students difficulty, and that's just the reality of this program, so I offer after school math help and we do it in both languages – and that's the only time, because it's *after school* and it's a commitment beyond the in-class time. It's not like I would refuse to help a student who's not getting a math concept because I won't speak their mother tongue – I won't in class, not even at their desk – but I would once a week, after school.

Pierre was worried about his weaker students and said that he used codeswitching in order to help them understand what was being said, or to express their ideas. However, it seemed that Pierre's level of first language use with the whole class lessened the need for said use with individual students. Pierre's use of English was generally directed at the entire class and served several purposes: he could test students' knowledge; enrich the target language input – making the content more age and grade level appropriate; give students a clearer, more exact understanding of new target language words; and provide them with the means to express ideas which were beyond their own abilities in French.

Influence of significant stakeholders

Given the official policy and the accepted view of best practice in late French immersion teaching, we expected that teachers who used English, even judiciously, would be more likely to feel pressure to limit their first language use based on the reactions of 'important others' (Kennedy & Kennedy, 1996: 355) such as the students themselves, parents, colleagues, administrators and Ministry officials. It should be noted that late French immersion teachers in Prince Edward Island are generally not questioned about their use of the first language and can, in most cases, use a certain amount of English without suffering any adverse consequences.

Despite not following the guidelines – or perhaps because he was not completely aware of them[12] – Pierre was very comfortable with his level of first language use and did not report feeling any pressure to use less, or more, English. Interestingly, Frank, whose first language and target language use had been much more in keeping with the Ministerial guidelines, reported coming under pressure from 'important others' to use more English with his Grade 7 late French immersion students. However, his

ions to teach exclusively through the target language did not weaken
.te considerable pressure – in fact, Frank made the decision to trans-
te ٿ another school rather than increase his use of English. This suggests
that some teachers may be receiving mixed messages, with officials at
certain levels advocating target language exclusivity while at other levels
judicious L1 use may be supported.

Discussion

The fact that both teacher-participants used the students' first language
to some degree over the course of the first few weeks of Grade 7 late French
immersion is an important finding. Contrary to Ministerial guidelines
which state that immersion classes are to be conducted exclusively in the
target language from the first day of classes (Bajard, 2004; Calvé, 1993),
both Pierre and Frank reported conducting orientation sessions in English
during the first days and weeks of Grade 7 late French immersion classes.
Even Frank, who saw no real value in first language use, reported using
English to some extent during the first month of classes. Employing
codeswitching at this early stage may be of great benefit to learners who
otherwise may not have the chance to properly acquire the basics. However,
some subjects, such as math, may lend themselves to being taught more
easily through the target language from the outset, with the first language
potentially playing a more useful role later on as concepts and language
become more complex.

Codeswitching to promote maximum comprehension and target language use

Both Frank and Pierre recognized that Grade 7 late French immersion
students will sometimes feel the need to use English when their target
language vocabulary and mastery of French syntax are insufficient for
expressing complex ideas, or when the cognitive demands of the material
or task are too great (e.g. Brooks & Donato, 1994; Swain & Lapkin, 2000),
but they take different approaches in trying to encourage students to use
as much French as possible. Over the course of his career, Frank had tried
various ways of encouraging students to use French (point systems,
'dollars français') but in recent years has come to view a certain amount of
L1 use during student interaction as natural and, to some extent, unavoidable. Here, Frank explains his expectations with regards to student target
language use:

> Just kind of easing them into it without being the language police,
> right? And even now, I know some teachers really have a lot of angst

over hearing the kids talk English amongst themselves, well I don't think you can take that away in a few months or a year. As long as they're not talking English to *me*.

Yet Frank also sees student target language use as closely tied to his own. Here, he expresses how he views his role as the ultimate linguistic model for students, explaining why he accepts student use of the first language amongst themselves but never with him, as native speaker model. Even though he is a near balanced bilingual, Frank denies this with students and believes that modeling exclusive target language use is necessary to ensure maximal target language use in his class. He elaborates on his expectations in the following quotation:

> I think they have to know what my expectation is. So as long as I'm doing 100%, or 99.9%, then they'll come up to meet me. Whereas I think if you brought in any little bit of English then their French is going to fall back. That's always been my philosophy.

While Pierre made more extensive use of the first language, especially during the first two to three months of the year, he also took a more active role in promoting student target language use. Beginning in January, Pierre used a point system to encourage student target language use, with impressive results. Based on the three lessons observed, it seemed that Pierre's use of English lead to further target language exposure, intake and use of French by students. His use of English did not open any floodgates, probably because, overall, Pierre's first language use did not exceed what Macaro (2005) suggests as a threshold (around 10–15%)[13] beyond which teacher use of the first language may begin to have a negative impact on student learning. While providing large amounts of rich target language input, the teacher can model appropriate and beneficial first language use and at the same time teach students to persist in the target language when the first language is not helpful or necessary. Contrary to the commonly held notion, and Frank's beliefs, that more teacher use of the first language leads to more student use of the first language, we observed that Pierre's students made a consistent effort to speak French with their teacher and also among themselves. Indeed, the only time Pierre's students were heard using English was when asking for help in expressing their ideas in French by using '*Comment dit-on*——?' Therefore, we argue that Pierre demonstrated that teachers can use the first language *judiciously* without it becoming excessive; first language use can generally *decrease* as learners' target language proficiency *increases*. These observations support the findings by Butzkamm (1998), Liebscher and Dailey-O'Cain (2004), Macaro (2005), and others – judicious use of the first language does not sarily lead to increased student use of the first language, rather it can aid comprehension and increase and improve students' target language production.[14]

Our findings also support the idea, as suggested by Macaro (2001: 545), that target language exclusivity can sometimes result in language being overly simplified, with an over-reliance on cognates. We suggest that codeswitching can be a valuable teaching strategy for words having no first language cognates, especially if the words can not be easily explained by paraphrasing or represented through gestures or pictures. Limited, judicious codeswitching may indeed help to make lessons more cognitively challenging and improve student target language production (Cummins, 2000).

Future work in this area

This modest case study has proven effective for shedding some light on a complex issue, however larger scale and more intensive work is necessary. We advocate future research that adopts a professional development or action research approach, affirming teachers' ability to develop their own strategies for maximizing student comprehension and use of the target language. Through reflective activities, such as keeping a journal, using video and stimulated recall, reading current research on the topic, and sharing ideas with colleagues, immersion teachers can become more aware or their own target language and first language use in different situations and possibly identify the overuse of a particular strategy. Rather than blindly following official policy, or feeling guilty for adopting pedagogically principled codeswitching, teachers can gain confidence in their beliefs and practices and 'may come to experience and enjoy a new level of self-articulated professionalism' (Farrell, 1998). Frank's simple words reinforce the importance and relevance of our suggested research model:

> Well it makes you reflect on what it is you do on a daily basis, because you don't sit around and think about these things very much, and we don't actually have a whole lot of professional discussion about it. I'm glad somebody's looking at it, I really am. And you know, it's something that's been very near and dear to my teaching experience and the mission I guess behind my teaching. I'm not a big theorist, to tell you the truth, like I just kind of do what I feel is right and the most reflection I've done about it in years is talking to you ... because you kind of teach in a vacuum.

Chapter 2

Teacher Use of Codeswitching in the Second Language Classroom: Exploring 'Optimal' Use

ERNESTO MACARO

Introduction

In the early 1990s a government agency in the English education system made a number of policy statements (for a selection see Macaro, 1997, 2001) which amounted to an affirmation that, to all intents and purposes, the first language of the students in a foreign language classroom should be banned and that teachers should use the target language exclusively. As someone who had recently completed some 16 years of language teaching in secondary schools and was now attempting to explain my ideas to student-teachers, I was shocked and disoriented by these (what appeared to me) dogmatic and prescriptive declarations. I was shocked because I certainly had been using small (and what I considered 'justified') quantities of the first language in the classroom and I was disoriented because I was certain that I had used my first language (Italian) to assist me in learning my second language (English) without any apparent damaging effects.

These largely emotional reactions led me to carry out the TARCLINDY research project (Macaro, 1997). The name is important as it stood for the three inter-related issues I wanted to explore: whether exclusive use of the target language was the best teaching approach, how this approach might affect collaborative learning, and whether exclusive use by the teacher promoted or hampered independent learning. The project included surveys and interviews of teacher beliefs and attitudes with regard to first language use. From the findings I concluded that teachers held three quite distinct personal theories.

Some believed that the second language could only be learnt through that language, and that exclusive use of the second language provided a kind of 'virtual reality' classroom which mirrored the environment both of the first language learner and the newly arrived migrant to the target language country. I labelled this position the 'virtual position' (see case study 'Frank' in Turnbull & McMillan, this volume).

Some believed that the second language was only really learnt through the second language but that this was an unattainable ideal because in second language classrooms the perfect learning conditions did not exist. One therefore had to use the second language as much as possible. However, since with each use of the first language the ideal was 'tainted', a sin was being committed and, as many people know, sinning leads to feelings of guilt. I labelled this position the 'maximal position'.

Some believed that there was some recognizable value in first language use. That at certain moments during the teaching and learning process the use of the first language might actually enhance learning more than by sticking to the second language. I labelled this position the 'optimal position' (see case study 'Pierre' in Turnbull & McMillan, this volume).

These theoretical positions were then confirmed in a study with beginner teachers (Macaro, 2001) who could also be divided into these categories of belief systems. This study also found that teacher use of the first language did not lead to student use of the first language, and that teacher use of the second language did not lead to student use of the second language.

I am therefore grateful to the editors of this volume for giving me the opportunity to explore the notion of optimal use some ten years after the publication of the TARCLINDY data. I will do so first by exploring the theoretical substance of these three positions and then by describing a research agenda currently operating in the Applied Linguistics area at the University of Oxford on this theme. Included in this description will be a summary of data gathered by a number of my collaborators, and I am grateful to them for their permission to present it here.

Theoretical Underpinnings for Teacher Theories

The theoretical framework that might support the 'virtual position' can probably be found in the huge body of literature on input and interaction which was carried out in the 1980s and 1990s. With the overarching theory that language learning derives from innate properties and functions in the brain (Chomsky, 1965), researchers provided evidence that aspects of the second language were acquired by premodified input (Krashen, 1985), by interactionally modified input (Ellis *et al.*, 1994; Long, 1981) and by interactionally modified (or forced) output (Ellis & He, 1999; Swain, 1985). During the same period research into feedback to learner error (Dekeyser, 1993) also proposed that the second language is acquired by negative evidence as well as positive evidence. These authors do not explicitly state that the first language should therefore be banned from the classroom. Rather, the first language is considered unnecessary to acquisition, or its role is simply ignored. Little wonder then that practitioners might assume that there is no evidence to support first language use.

Theories providing evidence of a facilitative effect of the first language come from three sources. The first of these is cognitive processing theory (see e.g. Ellis, 2005) which predicts that the way that language is perceived, processed and stored is done so (essentially) in the same way as other types of information and that working memory and long term memory interact in order to allow these processes. Most importantly, this theory claims that the first language and the second language are not contained in separate conceptual stores and that the mental lexicon is best represented by an increasing number of connections (and therefore potential activations) which are not language specific until they are required to be so by the processing function needed (Ellis, 2005; Kroll, 1993; Libben, 2000). In other words, both first and second language lexical items, in long term memory, are activated when a bilingual speaker is trying to process language. Since connections with the first language (especially in nonbalanced bilinguals) are going to be much stronger than connections with the second language, then to ignore the first language during the process of second language learning is to ignore an essential tool at the learner's disposal.

The second theory supporting an first language facilitative effect is sociocultural theory, and this is documented elsewhere in this volume (but see also Antón & DiCamilla, 1998; Brooks *et al.*, 1997). In brief, this theory would suggest that inner voice and private speech are essential contributors to the way we think and act, and that they are almost always performed in the first language (see e.g. Brooks & Donato, 1994).

The third theory supporting facilitative effect of the first language is that of codeswitching in naturalistic environments (language alternation which occurs in nonformal, noninstructional contexts) and this too is extensively discussed in this volume. However, to use it as an argument related to optimal teacher use of the first language, we have to explore a number of avenues. The most important of these is whether naturalistic codeswitching is similar to teacher codeswitching in 'broadly communicative' classrooms (see further explanation below) where the primary objective is the promotion of second language proficiency. What I mean here is that in these classrooms, a teacher codeswitches in order to put across message-oriented information to students [following Häkansson & Lindberg's (1988) distinction] certainly resembles naturalistic codeswitching. In these utterances the teacher's main intention is for learners to focus on the content of the utterance and, usually, to act upon it (e.g. 'look at page 10; you have 2 minutes left; you've done well; the match has been cancelled'). However, whether a teacher codeswitches in order to focus on the language itself (medium-oriented) is like naturalistic codeswitching, is less certain. Do speakers in the naturalistic context switch in order to provide information *about* meaning, or *about* form or *about* form–function relationships (e.g. 'raze is different from raise; not all past tenses end in "ed"; "could I possibly" is a request')? There is no reason why these codeswitching practices might not exist in naturalistic settings and a continuing search for similarities is important if, as the authorship of this volume generally wants to claim, we want to remove, from certain types of teacher use of the first language, an essentially negative connotation of 'unfortunate recourse to first language' and replace it with the more positive image of 'codeswitching'.

I can find no theoretical underpinnings for the 'maximal position'. If a theory's functions are to explain phenomena and to predict their occurrence in specified circumstances then I can find no theory which explains second language acquisition through the use of the 'second language as much as possible'. Nor can I find a theory that predicts that if the second language is used 75% in one set of circumstances but 85% in other circumstances it will lead to similar levels of acquisition. A maximum use theory would have to include 100% teacher second language use, but there would be no way of testing such a theory. Put differently, if a teacher was able to maintain 100% second language use through sheer willpower and exuberant personality, how would they know that their learners could not have learnt better through, say, 5% first language use?

This leads me to my advocacy and working definition of 'optimal use' of codeswitching which is:

> *optimal use* is where codeswitching in broadly communicative classrooms can enhance second language acquisition and/or proficiency better than second language exclusivity

In other words, optimal use of codeswitching by the teacher involves a judgement to be made about the possible detrimental effects of *not* drawing the learners' attention to aspects of their first language, or *not* making comparisons between the first and second languages. It involves a principled decision regarding the effects of *not* conveying important information simply because this might be too difficult for the learners to understand in the second language – a teacher avoidance strategy. It involves decisions about the relative merits of second language input modification as opposed to activating first language connections. These judgements, of course, have to be informed judgements, and there are virtually no studies which have demonstrated that switching to the first language as opposed to maintaining second-language discourse, in specific circumstances, actually leads to better learning whether in the short term or the long term.

I should stress that the above definition of optimal use only works in 'broadly communicative' classrooms, where predominantly the focus is on communicating meaning through the target language. For example, a broadly communicative classroom would be one where the *predominant* objective of a listening comprehension task would be to understand what the speakers are saying, not the acquisition of the vocabulary or the grammatical structures the text contains. Moreover, it makes very little sense to talk about optimal use in classrooms where the focus is on extensive use of translation in both directions. This idea needs a little further explanation when applied to research on codeswitching.

Lack of controlling of the type of instruction that is intended by the teacher is a problem to be found in the previous literature on teacher first language use. For example Duff and Polio (1990: 157) report a huge variance in teacher use of the first language from a few classes when it was never used to extreme amounts of first language use. However, we are not given a clear picture of the types of activities the students experienced, or the general type of instruction intended by the teacher. Even in studies where a link is made between amount of teacher first language use observed and the functions to which it was put (Kharma & Hajjaj, 1989; Liu *et al.*, 2004), it is not clear to the reader what the underlying teaching approach is. What are we to make, for example, of a teacher who reports that s/he 'often' uses the first language for explaining grammar, or a researcher who reports that 66% of teachers used the first language for explaining grammatical points (Kharma & Hajjaj, 1989: 228)? How long was the explanation and did it dominate the lesson? If the grammar explanation in the first language came after a considerable period of second-language communication where acquisition of the element in question had been pursued by inductive means, then we may be able to consider it a prolonged codeswitch in a predominantly communicative environment. If the first-language explanation of grammar came at the beginning of a lesson followed by extensive practice of the element using a comparison between the first and the second languages, then clearly we are not in a communicative environment and the primary objective is not to develop language skills or to put across content information.

We will therefore now look at two studies which, in their different ways, have attempted to discover whether codeswitching does or does not lead to better learning but which are squarely set in classrooms where meaning is central to the pedagogical objective. Before we look at the two studies, though, we should note that a lot of classroom codeswitching research has centred on lexical items, usually content words (see e.g. Evans, this volume). This is not surprising as vocabulary features prominently in interlocutors' quest to achieve communication (Nation, 2001) and that a very high percentage of vocabulary in a text needs to be known before comprehension of the remaining vocabulary can take place by inference. I use 'text' here in its broadest sense to include teacher input. So, what do we know about vocabulary acquisition research that might inform the current discussion on codeswitching by the teacher?

The majority of vocabulary studies comparing incidental learning with intentional learning have shown the superiority of the latter (Hulstijn, 2001; Laufer, 2005). Relatively few studies, however, have compared different types of intentional learning. Kim (2006) drew readers' attention to unfamiliar items in a text by inserting an second-language paraphrase immediately after the item or by putting the word in bold type and found that this elaboration of the text did facilitate vocabulary acquisition. The study did not, however, compare the effects of providing the learners with the first-language equivalent. Jacobs *et al.* (1994) did provide university students with glosses in either the first or the second language whilst reading, but no significant differences were found between the two conditions. The only study to find a positive effect for providing first-language equivalents of new words was by Laufer and Shmueli (1997).

Readers will no doubt now be asking themselves what all this research on written texts has to do with teacher codeswitching. Well, given the absence of experimental or quasi-experimental studies in classroom-based teacher codeswitching, research on reading at least provides us with some relevant insights. In other words, we can draw a parallel if we consider teacher-learners oral discourse as text, that is if we consider the language of the classroom as text from which learners can learn vocabulary as well as text for communicating information, instructions, and so on. The 'drawing of attention to vocabulary' via ways of highlighting unfamiliar words in a written text is not that dissimilar to codeswitching in oral interaction. Yet it appears fairly legitimate, as the above studies seem to show, for a teacher to insert first-language glosses in a written text in a student-centred activity but (so far) not legitimate to insert an L1 gloss in his or her discourse.

We also have evidence that bilingual dictionaries are preferred by learners to monolingual dictionaries in the majority of cases (Nation, 2001). Is this just laziness? Does it get the dictionary writer to do the hard work for the learner? Or is it that the learner has concluded that they can make more felicitous concept-word connections by obtaining a precise first-language equivalent rather than by pondering over the second-language definition?

There is also fairly secure evidence that the keyword strategy (e.g. Lawson & Hogben, 1998) is an effective way of storing and recalling new words, especially difficult words. This involves making a form connection between the first and the second languages (tappo [Italian meaning 'cork'] and the English 'tap') and then making some kind of mental image that brings the two together (e.g. a cork stuck in a tap, the tap bulges and is about to burst 'oh' dear!).

In summary, there is a wealth of evidence to suggest that in all sorts of circumstances we find the use of our first language facilitative in learning and recalling second-language vocabulary and there is further evidence of the facilitative effect of the first language in reading (Kern, 1994) and in writing (Kobayashi & Rinnert, 1992; Qi, 1998). There seems to be evidence in all circumstances except one – during oral interaction between teacher and learners. We will now consider a study which explored the effect of teacher codeswitching on vocabulary acquisition.

Study 1 (in collaboration with Qingtao Meng[15])

In this study a sample ($n = 159$) of Chinese learners of English, aged 16, were randomly allocated to two different conditions. The context chosen was an oral interaction session between the teacher and the whole class. The interaction centred around two challenging (as determined by the teacher) English texts about the ubiquitous nature of sport and a biographical account of Walt Disney. There were two sessions, each with a different text, and the conditions were rotated with each text.

In the first condition, the teacher provided a first-language equivalent of words contained in the text that she knew the students were unfamiliar with as determined by a pre-test of vocabulary knowledge. In the second condition, the same teacher provided learners with second-language definitions of the same unfamiliar words. Put differently, students in each condition were given different *types* of information about unknown words.

A third group was an intact class that operated as a form of control. We were not able to operate a classic control group in which the students would not have been given any information at all about the unknown words. This would have been unsustainable, would have upset the learners, and anyway seemed unethical. An alternative was found by providing *both* types of information (codeswitch and paraphrase) and, in addition, the new word was contextualized for them in a different sentence to the one in which it appeared in the text. In this way we would be able to determine not only which condition was more effective for learning vocabulary (conditions 1 or 2), but also if learning vocabulary was merely a question of how much time and salience was given to a lexical item (control condition).

A pre-test of receptive vocabulary showed that (a) the students in the three different classes did not know the 24 target words and (b) there were no significant differences between the three different classes in a further 24 words (some of which were known). Additionally, the classes were specifically chosen because they did not differ in proficiency according to their general school proficiency tests.

The students were given a vocabulary test immediately following the session in which the different types of interaction around the texts had occurred, and a delayed test two weeks later. The following is a selection of the results of these tests, ones which relate directly to our discussion.

In text 1 (the text about sport) the students who had been provided with a second-language definition scored significantly higher in the immediate post-test of receptive vocabulary than the students who had been given a first-language equivalent and also significantly higher than the control. However, two weeks later this advantage had disappeared and there were no significant differences.

In the case of text 2 (the text about the life of Walt Disney) there were no significant differences between the three conditions, neither at immediate post-test nor at delayed test.

In all three conditions there was significant forgetting of words learnt between immediate and delayed test, as one might expect given that these were fairly low-frequency words. But this forgetting did not interact significantly with the condition in which the teacher had first presented the words.

So, what can we conclude from this study? Do we conclude that, because there were virtually no differences in learning resulting from the way the students were taught, the study offers no pedagogical implications? If the study were purely about vocabulary learning, then it might well be a conclusion that one could draw. But I would argue we are not dealing here purely with vocabulary learning. The teaching activity had two objectives: comprehension of the text *and* the acquisition of vocabulary, and optimal codeswitching needs to be considered within this context. That the results show that it does not appear to matter what type of information is given by the teacher (i.e. a first-language equivalent or a second-language paraphrase) suggests that in a comprehension led activity, a teacher may consider it legitimate to code-switch in order to provide a first-language equivalent for a selection of lexical items. There appears to be no harm being done at least in terms of vocabulary acquisition and clearly no harm in terms of comprehension of the text. One might hypothesize that, given processing limitations, providing a first-language equivalent lightens the cognitive load freeing up processing capacity to focus on the meaning of the text as a whole. We now turn our attention to a different kind of study.

Study 2 (in collaboration with Tao Guo[16])

In this second study the research question which is most pertinent to this chapter is similar to the one in the first study but approached from a different perspective. Instead of asking how teacher codeswitching *directly* affects vocabulary acquisition, we ask: What are the strategic reactions of learners to teacher codeswitching, particularly with regard to medium-oriented lexical items? Space does not allow discussion of learner strategy theory (for recent reviews see Cohen & Macaro, 2007; Macaro, 2006) but by 'strategic reaction' here I intend the cognitive and metacognitive processing which occurs in working memory in connection with second-language material of any kind. Thus 'strategic reaction to a teacher's lexis-related codeswitch' might be said to be the cognitive mechanism the learner employs in order to comprehend and acquire the lexical item highlighted by the teacher.

The study was again set in China, in two universities (one teacher in each university), and involved first year students. Once again the teacher-class interaction centred around the comprehension of a written English text.

The researcher videotaped sixteen 45-minute lessons of a number of these English as a foreign language classes and then, immediately following the lesson, asked individual learners ($n = 32$) to take part in a stimulated recall session carried out in Chinese. He chose, from a total collected corpus of some 700 codeswitch episodes at least two medium-oriented episodes and two message-oriented episodes for the individual learners to react to. In this chapter we will only examine a small selection of the medium-oriented episodes where the switch occurs around a lexical item that the teacher appears to want the learners to make a mental note of. Recall that in our earlier discussion these were the most controversial switches in terms of comparison to naturalistic codeswitching theory.

Episode 1

Teacher: ... For instance, adolescence is the transition between adulthood and childhood, childhood and adulthood ... do you know what adolescence means? adolescence? ... 青少年, 青春期, [TEENAGER, ADOLESCENCE, ADOLESCENCE, ADOLESCENCE, ADOLESCENCE ...]

In this extract the teacher is discussing the various stages in a person's life. She pre-emptively (because there is no evidence on the video of students asking for a clarification) decides that the students have not understood the word 'adolescence' and carries out a target-language comprehension check in line 2 ('Do you know what ...') followed by an elicit in line 3 ('adolescence?'). This is then almost immediately followed by a switch to Chinese where the information provided is more than a one-to-one lexical match. One student's strategic reaction is as follows (students' use of English words are in italics):

Feng Tao: When she mentioned 'adolescence' ... it was new to me ... at the beginning I felt confused and guessed it was 'puberty' when I heard *childhood* and *adulthood* ... my guess was confirmed by her Chinese.

What appears to be happening in this student's reaction is, first, an attempt to relate the target-language word to a known semantic framework and then an attempt at an first-language equivalent guess which is close to the second language (although not quite). The teacher's switch to the first language provides confirmatory evidence that the guess is on the right lines as well as providing a better Chinese equivalent. In the above episode it is the teacher who makes the learner selectively attend to a lexical item, encourages cognitive processing through hypothesis generation, and then provides (at least so it seems) helpful additional information about the item.

Episode 2

Teacher: you may find that your values, your prejudices are challenged ... values here means, in Chinese, means 价值观, 价值观 [VALUE, VALUE], ok. Normally we know what's the value of

> this product 这个东西的价值是多少 [WHAT'S THE VALUE
> OF THIS PRODUCT], well, here values means 价值观
> [VALUE] … ok, paragraph twenty …

In this extract, the teacher does not attempt a comprehension check but rather provides an immediate Chinese equivalent (twice) of the word 'value' followed by a contextualization in lines 2–3 and a first-language equivalent of the contextualization. In other words, given that the English word value has other meanings (the quantitative worth of material objects), there is an attempt by the teacher to demonstrate that it also has a figurative meaning. One student's strategic reaction is as follows:

Gu Xin (a female student):   When she spoke (in English), I was thinking
of the meaning of *value*, then the teacher
said '价值观', then, I placed the meaning of
'价值观' into the sentence and had a go at it
quietly to myself.

It is unclear which meaning of 'value' Gu Xin was thinking of before the codeswitch. Perhaps it was the more common 'value of material objects'. The interesting result of the switch is that she then attempts to process the word for recall by placing the word in a contextualizing sentence, an important vocabulary strategy in the literature (Nyikos & Fan, 2007). Whether this is a sentence of her own or the sentence provided by the teacher ('your values are challenged'), is not clear. However, it is clear that the reaction to a teacher codeswitch is not passive. There is potential for some important cognitive processing to occur.

Episode 3

Teacher: You may say, if you don't have a favourite food, I like all kinds
of food. I'm not particular about food. Right, I'm not particular about food, 我不挑食 [I'M NOT PARTICULAR ABOUT
FOOD]. Ok, I like everything …

In this extract, once again there is no apparent comprehension check of the phrase 'I'm not particular about food'. It should also be noted that it follows a student contribution (or presentation) where she apparently said the phrase 'I like all the food in the world' as this reaction by Li Na shows:

Li Na: I was thinking whether or not she was correcting [my] sentence,
or whether she was trying to give me a new expression. When
doing the presentation, I said '*I like all the food in the world*'. [……]

However, another student reacting to the same switch offered the following:

Zhang Fan: Her use of Chinese is reassuring and familiar to me.....
however, one thing worth mentioning here is that I often
go blank for a moment when a Chinese word or a sentence
pops up in this English dominated class ... as I'm tuned
into the English .... when Chinese pops up, at first, I treat it
as English, and then, once I realise it is Chinese, I get to
know the Chinese meaning of the word.

What is interesting about the impact of this teacher codeswitch is the very different reaction of these two students. Li Na is so concerned with whether the teacher's English phrase is a correction of hers or a new one that she does not appear to even notice the switch to L1 which literally translates as 'I'm not picky on food'. For Zhang Fan, on the other hand, the switch is reassuring in its provision of semantic information even though there appears to be some kind of processing perturbation when the switch occurs ('I go blank for a moment'), so much so that at first she appears to treat the first language as the second language before starting to make connections between the two languages.

The potential for a codeswitch to have either a positive or negative impact on vocabulary processing is provided in the next example.

Episode 4

Teacher: Can you tell me the meaning of 'fruitful'? (One student
answered '成果' [FRUITFUL]) Yeah, 硕果累累的, 有成果的
[ABUNDANTLY FRUITFUL, FRUITFUL], ok, with research
environment ...

In this interesting extract, there is a teacher elicit for the English 'fruitful' which provides a first-language response from one of the learners. This response ('成果') can roughly be translated as 'good outcome'. However, the teacher provides additional information in Chinese roughly equivalent to adding 'abundant'. We should note that the Chinese character for 'fruit' (果) is the same as the Chinese character occurring in 'fruitful'. In other words there is some semantic equivalence for 'fruitful' in both languages. This connection between the two languages and the two words appears to trigger some confusion in one student:

Chen Qi: When she was speaking English and translating her English
into Chinese ... I felt suddenly slightly confused ... I won-
dered what the word meant ... if she had spoken a Chinese

> word that was not linked in meaning to the preceding English word, I would not have been confused [......].
> When .. for example, she said '今天早上 [THIS MORNING]' in a flow of words and I thought about '今天早上 [THIS MORNING].

What appears to be happening here is that because there is a cross-over in form–meaning connections in both languages between two related words, the amount of processing that a learner has to do is in fact increased rather than decreased. Whether this leads to better opportunities for recall we don't know but there is a suggestion that the strategic reaction is more intense (i.e. more cognitive processing takes place) and may have afforded deeper processing opportunities than a second-language definition. For example, a second-language definition of fruitful might be 'producing good or helpful results' (*New Oxford Dictionary of English*). This definition, however, does not make a connection to the equivalent form–meaning relationship in Chinese which links the concept of bearing fruit (in the botanical sense) to the figurative concept of results. Given that form–meaning relationships will have been established first in the first language, the switch to Chinese may provide a stronger trace back to that established relationship than a definition which does not include the botanical sense of fruit. Of course this is only speculation or an attempt to interpret what Chen Qi said and it may be possible that what she simply meant was that she remained confused.

However, what even these few examples show is the complex inter-relationship between the first and second languages and that these teacher codeswitches are far from being easy ways out of semantic difficulties or lazy solutions to lexical problems. In these examples the codeswitch triggers a number of strategic reactions which appear to confirm students' hypothesis generation, lead to contextualization and provide information used in additional processing.

As a result of these two studies, a number of issues are being explored in follow-up research at Oxford and the following are among a number of further research questions we would like to find answers to:

(1) Would the same outcomes (as in the two studies above) be obtained if the text had been presented orally (via a tape recording or video) rather than in written form?

(2) Does limited teacher switching lead to different levels (or different dimensions) of comprehension of a text than providing definitions and/or contextualization in the second language?

(3) Do adults benefit more from a codeswitch around a lexical item than young children?

(4) Are abstract words learnt better than concrete words via a codeswitch and vice versa?

(5) Are some words in English which are represented by only two Chinese characters learnt differently (via first-language equivalents or second-language definitions) than those represented by five or more characters?[17]

Discussion and Conclusions

This chapter has attempted to explore what we might mean by 'optimal use of codeswitching' by the teacher. That is, in those classrooms where the teacher has at least some proficiency in the first language of the students (or indeed where s/he shares their first language), in what ways might the first language be used in order to enhance learning? To do this, codeswitches have, for example, to assist the learner in building up linguistic knowledge (e.g. vocabulary) without being detrimental to the development of their linguistics skills. To re-emphasize, optimal codeswitching can only be examined against the background of a 'broadly communicative' language classroom as described above.

In the exploration of optimal use of teacher codeswitching I have limited myself to its impact on vocabulary acquisition. It is a measure of the complexity of the issue of whether codeswitching can be of benefit in the classroom that the studies presented here only scratch the surface even of this limited area of enquiry. This chapter did not intend to provide definitive answers to the question of first language use. Rather, it has tried to demonstrate ways in which the question is currently being explored and how it might be explored in the future. Although there is no question here of having found the 'optimal' formula, the evidence presented above, I would argue, at least opens the door to a more informed discussion set against a background of a rigorous research agenda.

Previous research has concentrated too much on people's opinions of what is right and what is wrong and on practitioners' reports of their quantity of first language use. Observation studies which have described the function to which first language use is put, or have measured the amount of target language used, have failed to control for the type of learning environment that the teacher was trying to create.

In the two studies described above, teachers were involved essentially in communicative activities involving the second language, they were trying to arrive at a shared understanding of a second-language text. The focus was on the meaning contained in the text. Simultaneously, they were trying to ensure the comprehension of certain potentially difficult lexical items and promoting the acquisition of those items. Codeswitching was put in the service of these last two objectives but with the intention of not damaging the first.

The findings of the two studies do not provide conclusive evidence that codeswitching is better than trying to achieve comprehension by remaining in the second language, but there is no evidence so far that teacher codeswitching is detrimental to lexical acquisition. What emerges is an increasing possibility that banning the first language from the communicative second language classroom may in fact be reducing the cognitive and metacognitive opportunities available to learners. We have some evidence that some items of vocabulary might be better learnt through a teacher providing first-language equivalents because this triggers deeper semantic processing than might occur by providing second-language definitions or paraphrases.

Finally, I would like to return briefly to my link made in the introduction to this chapter between exclusive use of the second language and learner autonomy. It may simply be the case that learners want to learn (and perhaps will only learn!) in ways that they think best suits them, regardless of the teacher's pedagogical approach. Given that there are differential success rates, and rates of progress among learners, it is of vital importance that teachers create the kind of strategic classroom that permits a shared understanding of the processes involved in second-language learning, and one which encourages an exploration of the self such that teaching may lead to greater learner independence.

Chapter 3

Codeswitching in Computer-mediated Communication: Linguistic and Interpersonal Dimensions of Cross-National Discourse between School Learners of French and English

MICHAEL EVANS

Introduction

It is understandable, given that the study of codeswitching has its roots in the analysis of bilingual speech within the framework of the discipline of sociolinguistics, that the study of language learner codeswitching has mostly focused on oral production in the classroom. The rare studies that have been conducted on codeswitching in written discourse have examined occurrence of the phenomenon in exchanges of personal letters between students (e.g. Montes-Alcalá, 2005). What has been almost entirely neglected so far by researchers (with the exception of Kötter, 2003), both in the fields of codeswitching research and of computer-related discourse analysis, is a consideration of this phenomenon in the textual exchanges of language learners communicating within the e-learning environment. Yet the acknowledged hybrid nature (e.g. Belz & Reinhardt, 2004: 349–350) of this medium is potentially generative of codeswitching as a feature of communicative interaction. In his study of real-time negotiation of meaning and codeswitching by university students in Germany and the United States using synchronous computer-mediated communication (CMC), Kötter found that most of the participants 'were willing to find a solution to the dilemma of wanting to use their second language, having to use their first language, and the challenge of having to achieve a stable balance between these competing goals over the course of the project' (Kötter, 2003: 24–25). The aim of this chapter is to interpret the practice of codeswitching by younger language learners than those in most existing studies by defining its characteristics and functions in the CMC exchanges of pupils learning each other's language.

The asynchronous computer mediated communication project, called *Tic-Talk*, which is at the centre of the study reported in this chapter, took place mainly over a period of four years (2001–2005) involving each year approximately 100 pupils either of French as a foreign language in schools in England or of English as a foreign or second language in francophone countries including France and Canada. Each year a different cohort of pupils was involved in the project which lasted from October to May. The participants were allocated to a group (as shown in Table 3.1 below), consisting of approximately 10 pupils, and only had access to messages within their group.

The pupils were mostly native speakers of English or French and were members of particular classes rather than interspersed across different classes within the school. In this way there was a degree of control over participation, as in most cases the pupils accessed the forum on a weekly basis within the context of their foreign language lesson. In addition they were able to access the forum independently from home or elsewhere via the internet. Whilst participation was thus framed within the context of school-based classroom access, it was not tied formally to any summative assessment of their work.

The explicit objective of the project was to stimulate genuine communication between peer native and non-native speakers of French and English (aged 14–17) in order to see how the pupils interacted with each other and how they might learn from one another. They were required to engage in

Table 3.1 Tic-Talk corpus

Year of project	No. of pupil participants	No. of groups	Approximate no. of pupil messages
2001–2002	152	24	2000
2002–2003	134	20	1600
2003–2004	100	15	1000
2004–2005	94	10	885
Total corpus	480	79	5485

two strands of interaction on the bulletin board: one strand consisted of an open-ended 'conversation' in which they were asked to introduce themselves, talk about their daily lives and communicate with one another on a personal basis, choosing their own topics of discussion. The second, or 'discussion', strand required the pupils to engage with a particular topic (such as 'the war in Iraq' or 'Does the devil exist?'), which varied on a weekly basis, and which was introduced by the project coordinator. The nature of the discourse that was elicited could be described as 'naturalistic' or 'free' in the sense of representing the independent expression of the participants' thoughts rather than the controlled production of language within the tight constraints of more didactic language learning exercises. However, although the coordinator's interventions were minimal and although the teachers attached to the participants' classes did not intervene at all on the bulletin board, it is undeniable, and reflected in several pupil postings as well as in comments at interview, that underlying pedagogical expectations at times influenced aspects of the pupils' discourse. One such aspect was the issue of language choice, and in order to pre-empt pedagogical assumptions about the use of the first or the target language by the pupils in their postings, the matter was explicitly addressed in my opening message for each strand. In the case of the conversation strand, my guidelines to the participants on which language to use were as follows: 'Try to do as much as you can in the foreign language but don't worry if you switch into your own language – the main thing is to communicate.' In the case of the discussion strand, my own weekly messages alternated between French and English and the pupils' use of their first language was openly sanctioned.

Before proceeding with the analysis of the codeswitching data it is worth clarifying the parameters of these data further as this will impact on the validity and generalisability of the findings. An accurate interpretation of these data needs to take account of extraneous features relating to the participants in order to avoid sweeping generalizations about e-discourse and the significance of codeswitching within it. These parameters influence the hypotheses one can make about the likely nature of the discourse produced. Firstly, unlike bilingual speakers, the majority of the language learners on this project did not have equal access to both linguistic systems; codeswitching decisions would therefore at least sometimes be related to learning issues such as second-language vocabulary gaps or re-use of phrases learnt in the classroom. Furthermore, there was a wide spread of proficiency in the second language between the different participants, with some demonstrating a high level of fluency while others still operating at a very basic beginner level. This may have impacted on the discourse and on the pupils' response to it in different ways. Greater proficiency sometimes resulted in more sustained and more extensive use of the second language by individuals. Greater proficiency was also accompanied in some cases by more dominance in the interactions (through steering discussions by using questions and other strategies in the second language). Secondly, the temporal dimension of the asynchronous interaction may have implications for the nature of the codeswitching produced. The interaction produced constituted a form of deferred communication whereby messages were replied to several days after they were sent, and whereby the reader could take time in prior reflection as well as in the composition of his or her reply. As Warschauer (1999) has pointed out, asynchronous CMC users are able to 'notice input' from others' messages and to incorporate it into their own messages.

Language Choice or Language Switch

There is insufficient space here to situate my broad use of the term 'codeswitching' in the context of the rich body of literature in which different definitions and models of the concept and practice have been elaborated. A useful critical overview, including the debates surrounding 'codeswitching' as language alternation or lexical borrowing, is provided by Gafaranga and Torras (2002). What I do want to delineate here is a distinction between 'code choice' and 'code switch'. By the former, I am referring to an overall decision taken, in this context, by the CMC user as to which language to write either all or a particular message in. As researchers of bilingual discourse have pointed out (Brown & Levinson, 1987; Burt, 1992; Myers-Scotton, 1983) code choice is 'potentially pragmatically ambiguous' (Burt, 1992: 183) in the situation where 'a speaker is a learner of the other's native language', since choosing the second language (the interlocutor's first language) may be interpreted as an act of deference and choosing to use one's own first language (the interlocutor's second language) may be seen as an indication of inadequate proficiency. Some of the *Tic-Talk* participants I interviewed on completion of the project provided similar socio-pragmatic explanations of their code choices, as in the following example:

R: What about the idea of writing in English or French? I know your teacher always wanted you to write in French. Is that a good idea?

L1 English pupil: Yes it's a good idea. But I thought English as well. Because at the end of the day, if we were to write in English and French they could learn because they

> speak French most of the time they could learn
> English as well. So in response they'd also write to
> me in French and in English so I'd be able to under-
> stand what they say.

Though the issue of code choice plays an important role in the analysis of the data that follows, I shall primarily focus on the concept of 'codeswitching' which implies a research focus on the movement from use of one language to another. In order to analyse the characteristics and functions of codeswitching in this context one must begin by identifying how and where to locate this form of linguistic alternation.

The Locus of Codeswitching

Between-post switching

The textual and temporal fragmentation that characterizes the structure of asynchronous CMC means that codeswitching can take place on two planes of the discourse: between posts and within posts. Between-post switching is explicable in terms of the socio-pragmatic considerations referred to above, as in the following example taken from the 2003–2004 corpus. Each of the messages in this sequence represents a separate posting with a few days' interval between each message.[18]

Annabelle: Hello everybody!!! /How are you? me fine. I'm fed up because you don't answer me. I EXPECT YOU TO ANSWER ME!!!!!!!!!!!!!!! /Bye ....

Jeffrey: bonjour annabelle quelle age a tu? est-ce que vous fumez,

Annabelle: Salut Jeffrey!!
Comment vas-tu? Moi super ! J'ai 14 ans (-4 jours) et toi? Tu me demande si j'ai déjà fumé. Ce n'est pas la première question qui me viendrai à l'esprit. Pour te répondre, j'ai déjà fumé mais je ne fume plus. Et toi? A plus tard ....

P.S.: je ne m'appelle pas Annabella, mais Annabelle. Byeee

Jeffrey: moi je ne pas le fume je destest le fume

Annabelle: OK but you hasn't smoke once? i think it's good to try, to know it's very bad.

A quick reading of this sequence of exchanges would pick out the fact that Annabelle, a francophone pupil, switches from English (her second language) in message 1 to French (her first language) in message 2 to English in message 3. Jeffrey, an anglophone pupil, writes both messages in French (his second language). However, beneath the surface of this textual behaviour, it is possible to detect an underlying tension or dynamic that is motivating this particular instance of between-post codeswitching. To support such an interpretation one must turn to Burt's (1992) discussion of the relevance of Speech Accommodation Theory and 'complementary schismogenesis' on code choice in speech.

As Burt points out, 'Speech Accommodation Theory' refers to the behaviour whereby interlocutors 'welcome speakers' attempts at convergence or, making one's speech more like that of one's interlocutor' (Burt, 1992: 170). The *Tic-Talk* data contains many apparent instances of this behaviour which is indeed explicitly acknowledged in some of the pupil interviews, as in the following comment from a Canadian participant: 'je faisais comme quelqu'un qui parlait en anglais, je lui répondais en anglais juste pour la rendre plus confortable'.

However, the codeswitching in the above example suggests that a more discordant and less stable impulse is influencing the verbal behaviour, which is more explicable in terms of complementary schismogenesis. According to this theory, 'each speaker (or actor) models the type of behaviour which she would like to see her interlocutor display, but since the two individuals differ on the values assigned to the behaviours in question, each continues to behave in precisely the opposite fashion to that which her interlocutor wishes' (Burt, 1992: 175). Here Annabelle begins by writing a message to the group as a whole in English either, one can speculate, as a friendly gesture to the English speaking members of the group or because she enjoys the opportunity to communicate in the foreign language. Jeffrey replies to her in French. Annabelle replies to Jeffrey by switching to French: the tone is friendly, his question answered, more personal details are provided. One could say that Annabelle's text is accommodating both interactionally in the sense of a friendly, open manner that seems to reach out to her interlocutor and linguistically in the sense of complying to the interlocutor's choice of language by switching to French. The brief switch back to English in the final word of the message ('Byeee') suggests that despite this compliance, her preference is to communicate in English. Jeffrey's reply remains intransigently in French; he does not reciprocate Annabelle's accommodating moves and he sticks to his original theme of smoking rather than looking for alternative topics to develop the personal contact. As a result, Annabelle switches back to her seemingly preferred medium of communication (English) and the exchange ends. This example suggests that between-post codeswitching can be an expression of the same interactional and psychological processes that are found in spoken dialogue. The medium of communication (French or English) becomes a tool for interpersonal give-and-take.

The pedagogical context is probably also a factor triggering this pattern of dialogic interaction: Jeffrey's apparent inflexibility reflects his compliance with his teacher's request to make exclusive use of the target language, and his focus on smoking coincides with this being a recent topic in his French lessons.

Within-post switching

The majority of codeswitches in bilingual asynchronous CMC between language learners are located within posts; more specifically, locatable as either intersentential or intrasentential switches. As with dialogic, between post switching, discussed above, this form shares characteristics with codeswitching in bilingual speech. In her study of speech by Puerto Ricans in New York, Poplack (1980: 603) found that nonfluent bilinguals mainly codeswitched between sentences, as this avoided the possibility of violating a grammatical rule of either of the two languages which would be risked in intrasentential switching: 'full sentences are the most frequently switched constituent, making up 20% of the data'. Though at first glance the summary of the *Tic-Talk* data (see Table 3.2) suggests a more or less even rate of occurrence of inter and intrasentential switches, a closer analysis will indicate that intersentential switches do in fact predominate.

The first point to note is that the majority of intrasentential switches are switches to the first language and in most cases can be interpreted as representing recourse to the first language due to a gap in knowledge of the second language, as in the following examples:

- It is the history about three <u>orphelin</u> who rae adubtuded by teir <u>oncle</u>.
- Can you <u>devine</u> what is this?
- La guerre n'etait pas justifier, Saddam Hussein n'avais pas des <u>weapons</u>.

Ignoring, for our purposes, the question as to whether 'history' is a confused use of the English word 'story' or a borrowing of the French 'histoire' transliterated into English, the words I have underlined are instances of codeswitches in that they are words which belong to a different language to that of the remainder of the sentence in which they have been inserted. If one subtracts these types of first-language borrowings then, as we shall see later, the ratio of inter to intrasentential switches is very much in favour of the former. However, ascertaining whether or not a sentence boundary exists between two segments of text is not always

Table 3.2 Breakdown of codeswitch occurrences in four cohorts of Tic-Talk pupil messages totalling 5485 postings

	2001–2002	*2002–2003*	*2003–2004*	*2004–2005*
Total codeswitches count	77	70	64	39
Total codeswitches L1 → L2 count	22	23	29	12
Total codeswitches L2 → L1 count	55	47	35	27
Lexical borrowing from L1 count	17	8	18	14
Intrasentential codeswitches L1 → L2 count	6	3	5	5
Intrasentential codeswitches L2 → L1 count	29	20	18	17
Percentage of total codeswitches as intrasentential	45.4	32.8	35.9	56.4
Percentage of total codeswitches as intersentential	54.6	67.2	64.1	43.6

straightforward despite the presence of punctuation. In the following example, a francophone pupil switches into and out of French apparently in mid-sentence:

> Personally, I love this photo and I think it's very similar to the painting, au hazard, je dirais que le tableau a été fait par léonard de vinci, ou un autre artiste connu, but i'm not sure …

A closer reading of the text will indicate that the degree of syntactic distinctness differs at either end of the intercalated French segment. Although 'au hazard' is preceded by a comma and therefore ostensibly part of the earlier text, it is in fact syntactically separate from it. There is a punctuation error here, perhaps caused by the speed of keyboard use, as there is a clear break in the referential focus of what comes before and after 'au hazard'. The end of the French segment, on the other hand, presents a more blurred transition between the two languages: 'but i'm not sure' can be read as part of the French sentence that preceded it. In sum, the message, with its embedded structure, can be read as consisting of an intersentential switch from English to French and then back again, intrasententially, to English.

The second issue related to these data relates to the definition of what constitutes an intrasentential codeswitch. Traditionally this is defined as a mixing of two languages within a sentence where the joins between the two (or more) different language segments are subject to syntactic, semantic and discourse constraints (Pfaff, 1979). In our data, which consist of chunks of text serving as messages in a diachronic chain of interaction, the length of text in a switch can be an indicator of the degree to which the writer/speaker has made a significant cognitive switch from one language to another. Single word occurrences of the first language, such as 'Maybe in a few year' times we will work on computers at all times to redige lessons ... but in the other hand professor must stop to enseigne because the computers is going to do that at it place' [my underlinings] do not interrupt the flow of the main language of the text which in this case is English. On the other hand, longer intercalations of codeswitched text do suggest a more sustained mental switch, however temporary, to a different linguistic system, as in the following example: 'hello it's Maureen I don't have the time for reply but je suis contente que vous ayez repondu ya pas assez d'ordi alors je repondrais vendredi a+'. The two halves of this sentence, with the conjunction 'but' facilitating the switch to French, do represent consecutive processing in two languages, in the way that single word borrowings do not. The difference between the two perspectives of intrasentential codeswitching in oral speech has been described by Muysken as 'insertional' ('the insertion of alien lexical or phrasal category into a given structure') and 'alternational' (Muysken, 1995: 180). From a language learning point of view this distinction (if corroborated in learner discourse) can provide a framework for investigating the cognitive basis of the codeswitching output. Does the pupils' thinking alternate between the two languages or is there a more integrative impulse at work? If such a distinction can be identified, and if the relative acquisitional benefits of either impulse are identified, then appropriate pedagogical strategies would arguably need to be developed.

A third criterion which is relevant to the analysis of intrasentential codeswitching is the direction of the switch, since in learner discourse switching to the second language in mid-sentence, even if it takes the form of a single word insertion, is likely to be serving a function other than that of vocabulary gap filling. But before proceeding to examine what this function might be, it is worth looking at a summary of all the intrasentential switches that took place in two cohorts of the project.

Table 3.3 lists the actual words used in the inserted switch and gives a count of the types of words and structures involved.

Poplack (1980) noted in her study that 'the two most frequently recurring switch points among 681 tokens of intrasentential codeswitch and preceding category were between determiner and noun, and between verb phrase and object noun phrase' (Poplack, 1980: 604). We can see from Table 3.3 that the most frequently recurring intrasentential switches in these four years of *Tic-Talk* involved nouns and most of the phrases were lexical units (noun phrases, adjectival phrases) or set phrases such as 'bûche de noel' and 'VIVE LES DIFFERENCES!'. There were relatively few instances of verbs or prepositions being borrowed from the first language. The primary linguistic function of the switches to the first language in mid-sentence was therefore *lexical support* whether provided by a noun 'royaume', a verb 'redige', an adjective 'pants', or a phrase 'la marche de la croix'. The main purpose of these inserts is to keep the message rolling rather than to interrupt or deflect the discourse. Occasionally, the switch had the function of *marking a shift in addressee*. This was evident in the codeswitches involving 'everyone' or 'tout le monde', as in the following from an English participant: 'salut Marion, and everyone else too' which by switching to English seems to be serving the purpose of addressing the anglophone members of the group in particular. This use of codeswitching to mark a shift in 'addressee specification' (Gumperz, 1982: 77) is more frequently apparent in intersentential codeswitches within the corpus. The overall framework of communicating within a group of interlocutors requires speakers/writers to make a special discursive effort to refer specifically, usually by name, to individual addressees, and in a bilingual discourse context such as *Tic-Talk* this was sometimes accompanied by a codeswitch, as in the following from a Canadian participant:

> Mais felicitations à toutes deux de nous écrire dans des langues secondes que vous semblez très bien maitriser! Où as-tu appris ton anglais Lenaïg? And you, Amanda, we rarely see british people speaking French so well!

A third discernible function of the intrasentential switches was that of *triggering a more global switch* within the message as a whole, as in the following example:

> Je crois que la guerre d'Irac n'est pas justifié car si il y a une guerre ca n'arrangera rien au contraire ca aggravera le cas. JEMIMA pourquoi personne n'écrit except Jemina and me? So what's up? Where are you? What are you doing? What do you enjoy? What about the holidays?

Table 3.3 Instances of intrasentential codeswitching

2001–2002	2002–2003	2003–2004	2004–2005
and co (L2)	except Jemina and me (L2)	les reality shows (L2)	le vacances (L2)
moi (L2)	la belle Cambridge (L2)	downloads (L2)	avec ma famille (L2)
phil going back	so much (L2)	listening to (L1)	mais (L2)
2 france (L2)	seigneur (L1)	grand-parents (L1)	avec ma copines (L2)
time (L2)	the royal family (L1)	stage (L1)	tres (L2)
my poem (L2)	love (L1)	(for half term) (L1)	orphelin (L1)
each to his own (L2)	praticant (L1)	VIVE LES DIFFERENCES (L1)	oncle (L1)
'délire' (L1)	Pâques (L1)	(eg premiere et terminale) (L1)	devine (L1)
'hors piste' (L1)	paques (L1)	(la prophétie des pierres) (L1)	existe (L1)
'poudreuse' (L1)	US army (L1)	'bûche de noel' (L1)	raison (L1)
in (L1)	queen (L1)	happy new year (L1)	by (L1)
prie (L1)	championat (L1)	dommage (L1)	weapons (L1)
'professional-computer' (L1)	'brevet des colleges' (L1)	'paque' (L1)	meritent (L1)
tout le monde (L1)	'la marche de la croix' (L1)	'in' (L1)	génie (L1)
les amis (L1)	and everyone else too (L1)	everybody (bilingual Can)	au hasard, je dirais que le
redige (L1)	everyone (L1)	(is that the right word) (L1)	tableau a été fait par
enseigne (L1)		'un procès international' (L1)	Léonard de vinci, ou un
'patinoire' (L1)		'peine de mort' (L1)	artiste connu (L1)
'les mots en entier' (L1)		(sorry I can't say this in French)	'genre' (L1)
tres moche (L1)		'industrialized' (L1)	laic (L1)
'amener' (L1)		'stressant' (L1)	serie (L1)

	'tenebre les lier' (L1) 'ombres' (L1) cauchemar (L1) personnage's (L1) 'pas à temps plein' (L1) 'au moins' (L1) 'porte-key' (L1) Paques (L1) avril (L1) baptem (L1) royaume (L1) republique (L1) 9th (L1) je suis contente [.] (L1) look notre photo (L1)	christmas holiday (L1) turkey (L1) martial arts (L1) pants (L1) april (L1) view (L1) homeworks (L1) until (L1)	(that would make – ferait faire!?!?! My french better) (L1) the best singer (L1) 'a snow day' (L1) (quel baratin!!!) (L1)	'un sucker' (L1) 'les chick-flicks' (L1) (spelling?!?!) (I1) holdays (L1)
Grammatical features of codeswitch	Single nouns – 12 Verbs – 4 Adjectives – 1 Prepositions – 1 Phrases – 15 Longer segments – 3	Single nouns – 10 Adjectives – 1 Adverbs – 1 Phrases – 8 Longer segments – 2	Single nouns – 5 Verbs – 1 Adjectives – 3 Phrases – 11 Longer segments – 2	Single nouns – 10 Verbs – 3 Prepositions – 1 Adverbs – 1 Phrases – 5 Longer segments – 1

Aren't you happy to be able to correspond with teenagers from other countries? Hope you'll read this message and have nice holidays? And write back!!!

As with almost all the intrasentential switches, slipping into the new language (here English, the second language) is done without disturbing the syntax of the sentence ('pourquoi personne n'écrit except Jemima and me?'). The sentence codeswitch mirrors the broader codeswitch within the message as a whole which consists of two linguistically separate parts. Semantically the onset of the switch is again a case of shifting the addressee focus (albeit implicitly in this case) of the message: it is clear, however, that the words 'except Jemina and me' and the rest of the text are directed at the silent anglophone members of the group and not at Jemima herself even though the sentence in fact begins by addressing her.

Switching into the second language midsentence was extremely rare and mostly done by fluent bilinguals in the Canadian schools. As stated earlier, unlike switches into the first language these forms of codeswitches cannot be said to have the function of supporting gaps in the user's vocabulary, apart from the use of technical or specialist terminology that are more common in the second than the first language. The few cases of second-language intrasentential codeswitching in *Tic-Talk* were mostly performed by the more fluent Canadian bilingual in the groups, thus suggesting that this form of discourse behaviour requires a degree of confidence and proficiency in the two languages. However, there were a few examples of much less proficient users of the target language spontaneously trying this out, as in the following example from an anglophone pupil:

Hi
I am soooooo excited about <u>le vacances</u> but I am not doing anything <u>avec ma famille</u>. <u>Mais</u> I may do something <u>avec ma copines</u> like punting.
<u>Au revoir</u> [my underlining]

Second-language intrasentential switching then seems to suggest the beginnings of a bilingual discourse in which the speaker/writer is switching between the two languages for interactional or playful purposes. The 'language play' (Cook, 2000; Warner, 2004) exhibited here is similar to the sort of verbal behaviour described by Belz and Reinhardt (2004) in relation to advanced foreign language learners who were seen to use CMC as a 'mediator of foreign language play' (Belz & Reinhardt, 2004: 347). In the

Tic-Talk example English remains the matrix language of the message, but the French words and phrases are not inserted for 'lexical borrowing' purposes. For a discussion of the pupils' post hoc explanations of their codeswitching in the *Tic-Talk* project see Evans (2009).

The Interpersonal Function of Learner Codeswitching

'Longer code-switches are motivated by discourse considerations (parenthetical comments, asides, framing, metaphor, etc.) rather than lexical ones' (Pfaff, 1979: 315). Poplack categorized these features of the discourse as 'extra-sentential codeswitching types [e.g. interjections, quotations, idiomatic expressions]' and noted that they required less knowledge of two grammars. The concept of 'discourse-related codeswitching' referred to by these writers, theorized by Auer (1984: 32–46) and applied to the context of language learner oral codeswitching by Liebscher and Dailey-O'Cain (2004, and in this volume), is a useful label with which to interpret a large portion of the codeswitching events in the *Tic-Talk* corpus. These data are best understood from three interlocking perspectives: form, function and addressivity. The textual form in which this use of codeswitching appeared in the data can be described as 'highlighting' and appeared in various guises in the corpus: within brackets [e.g. 'j'aurai une semaine de vacances (for half-term)']; in capital letters (e.g. 'so VIVE LES DIFFERENCES!!!'); and, most commonly, in quotation marks (e.g. 'It's 'stressant'!) The functional objectives of this type of codeswitching are related to both form and content of the discourse. Regarding the former, the visual form of the highlighting serves a similar paralinguistic purpose as that of facial gestures, tone of voice in adding expressive emphasis and meaning to the codeswitched speech. The behaviour may be comparable to the 'flagging' of codeswitching noted by Arnfast and Jørgenson (2003: 46) in the speech produced by the students of Danish elicited at individual interviews. In terms of content, these highlighted switches tended also to have a clearly defined expressive purpose: as a request for help [e.g. 'Pardon, mais je dois quitter (is that the right word) l'internet maintenant']; as an ironical aside [e.g. 'I have two brothers ... I have a cat too. Its name is Roucky (un peu banal mais bon) And what do you like in life?']; or as a metalinguistic comment on the writer's own use of language [e.g. 'Vous connisez (spelling?!?!?!) le film en anglais??']. Finally, these types of highlighted codeswitched interjections can be analysed from the point of view of inclusivity/exclusivity of the identity of the implied addressee. Three main types of interlocutors are invoked in the corpus. The first-language discourse community is sometimes implicitly or explicitly drawn in by the aside, as in:

salut! ecole est tres tres enneyeux! Ca va?

Are there no other english people on this thing?

Whether deliberate (as in this case) or subconscious, the above example of an aside appeals exclusively to the francophone members of the group. In other cases, such as the spelling query above written in the second language, the discourse-related switch would seem to be addressed primarily at the second-language members of the group who are appealed to as 'teachers' to help with the language production. Finally, at other times the codeswitched interjection seems aimed mainly at the writer him/herself as in the following self-deprecatory metacomment:

Finaly, they mustn't be endanger since more culture can give to the world more intresting.
Bye (quel baratin!!!!!).

From a language learning point of view, different aspects of this discourse feature are interesting. Firstly, the e-medium seems to have the advantage of encouraging a degree of metalinguistic self-reflection which might otherwise not have opportunities for expression in other forms of language activities. This reflection can relate to the form of the second-language output (as in the spelling example above), or to its meaning, often framed as a translation query as in the following example of a switch within a switch:

Parce que ça rendrait mon français plus mieux, (that would make – ferait faire!?!?!?! my French better,) j'espère que vous me comprenez!

A second interpretation that one can make of this discourse feature, particularly with reference to the frequent use of quotation marks around inserted codeswitched words or phrases, is that this reflects an awareness by the pupil that what they are doing does not correspond to normative behaviour. At times this awareness seems to take the form of a hesitation or a reluctance, as if they feel that what they are doing is taboo rather than a natural part of the language learning process. Paradoxically, the fact that the medium allows this (even if the dominant pedagogy may seem not to) results in some second-language output at least which may, in different situations (such as classroom oral interaction), have resulted in silence or total communicative breakdown.

Conclusion

In this chapter I have indicated how 'naturalistic' codeswitching between young learners of each other's language corresponds to the categories of codeswitching identified in the sociolinguistics literature which has examined the phenomenon as it appears in bilingual speech. This is important in the context of the second-language discourse of language learners in that firstly it provides a degree of validation of the status of the linguistic data produced. Secondly, it means that pupil data of this sort can (and arguably should) be included in the corpus of the sociolinguistic research into codeswitching. Finally, and perhaps most importantly from a language learning point of view, it means that as an alternative to face-to-face bilingual interactions (notoriously problematic to arrange in the school context), the CMC platform can serve as a suitable environment for naturalistic bilingual discourse in which codeswitching plays a significant role.

We have also seen how the structure of asynchronous CMC impacts on the use of codeswitching by the participants. I have argued that interpretation of these linguistic events should be based on a consideration of key syntactic factors such as location and linguistic direction of switch as well as of meaning-related and sociopragmatic functions.

It is also clear that the codeswitching elicited through this medium and in this context has considerable implications for language learning and pedagogy. For the learner, the codeswitching option does not always represent a 'dilemma' of language choice, as Kötter argued, but is also an opportunity for language learning through playful, experimental combination and sequencing of the first and second languages. More broadly, the occurrences of codeswitching in the corpus were also instances of pupils focusing on their language use, thinking about the accuracy, appropriateness or the communicative effects of their language production. In other words, while the act of codeswitching may not necessarily always be self-reflexive, the evidence here suggests that the linguistic behaviour is closely interlinked with the pupils' reflexive gaze at the communicative frame in which they were operating. The basis of this linkage between codeswitching and the reflexive focus in CMC participation by language learners requires further research.

From the pedagogical perspective, many of the examples of codeswitching in the *Tic-Talk* project were an expression of the role of peer learning. Pupils often switched language, as we have seen, either as a way of sharpening the interpersonal edge of a particular message or as a way of appealing for help with the language. For the language educator, the question that arises is the following: how can formal instruction capitalize on this natural overlap between language learning and real communication that is often the play of codeswitching in CMC?

Chapter 4

Target Language Use in English Classes in Hungarian Primary Schools

KRISZTINA NAGY and DANIEL ROBERTSON

Introduction

This chapter presents evidence from an observational study of English language classrooms in primary schools in Hungary. The focus of the chapter is on the use of Hungarian, the teachers' first language, in the classroom. In foreign language classrooms where the teacher shares the mother tongue with the students the use of the mother tongue has always been controversial (Cook, 2001; Medgyes, 1994; Turnbull, 2001). As part of the communicative approach (Breen & Candlin, 1980; Canale & Swain, 1980; Littlewood, 1981) to foreign language teaching, the teacher is usually expected to use the target language as much as possible to provide comprehensible input (Krashen, 1982) for the learners. This emphasis on maximum exposure to the target language is especially important in foreign language teaching contexts where there is little opportunity for exposure to the target language outside the classroom, as is the case with the teaching of English in Hungary.

The Hungarian National Core Curriculum for primary schools which was current at the time when the data for this study were collected (NCC, 2004) takes a pragmatic approach to the use of the first language in the foreign language classroom, acknowledging that it is unrealistic to expect young learners not to use the first language, while at the same time implying that the teacher is expected to use the target language most of the time:

> The language required from the students (in Year 4) is one word answers ('yes', 'no', names, colours, numbers, etc.) or longer, memorised chunks

of language (greetings, songs, games, rhymes). The students naturally ask and answer in Hungarian during the English lesson [...] at the same time (as) the teacher is using the TL. (NCC, 2004: 27)

Despite this expectation, the evidence suggests that teachers of English in Hungary still use the first language extensively in class (Lugossy, 2003; Nikolov, 1999). One approach to understanding the reasons for this mismatch between policy and practice is to look at what happens in the classroom. Most of the research on target language use in foreign language classrooms has been undertaken in the secondary and tertiary sectors, and there is a comparative lack of information about practice in primary schools (Cameron, 2001: 200). This chapter attempts to fill in some of the gaps by providing evidence from an observational study of a number of Year 4 (average age 9–10) English classes in Hungary. The focus of the study is the teachers' language choices. The ultimate aim of this research is to contribute to our understanding of the factors which affect the language choices made by teachers and learners in the primary foreign language classroom.

This chapter begins with a brief description of the political, social and educational factors which are relevant to an understanding of the primary English language curriculum in Hungary. This is followed by a review of research studies on the use of the first language in primary foreign language classrooms in a number of widely differing contexts. The review serves to underline the fact that empirical evidence in this area is patchy and unsystematic, and therefore provides a limited basis for theory-building and policy-making. The review is followed by the main body of the chapter, which presents a quantitative and qualitative analysis of the transcripts of audio-recordings of four lessons. The chapter concludes with an analysis of the various factors which influence the language choices made by the teachers in this study, and some suggestions as to how these factors may interact.

The EFL Curriculum in Hungary

Hungarian is not widely spoken beyond the borders of Hungary, so Hungarians have always needed to learn other languages for the purposes of international communication.

Throughout its history, the teaching and learning of foreign languages in Hungary, like anywhere else in the world, has been deeply rooted in, and determined by, the political and economic structure of the country. (Medgyes & Miklósy, 2000: 184)

During the period of Soviet influence, the foreign languages curriculum was dominated by the teaching of Russian, virtually to the exclusion of other languages, including English. The coursebooks in use in the Russian classroom were full of Soviet writers and poets, stories about Lenin and other communist heroes and pioneers. The methodology was based on traditional decontextualized grammar exercises, with an emphasis on rote-learning and memorization. Written tests and graded oral recitation were in everyday use and little attention was paid to oral communication skills, since few of the students or their teachers would ever need to communicate with a native speaker of Russian (Medgyes & Miklósy, 2000).

After 1989, Hungary became a free, democratic country, and compulsory Russian language teaching stopped almost overnight. Following recent trends in globalisation, English language learning has become increasingly popular and important. The value placed on English is all sectors of Hungarian society is clear from the following:

> ... in just a few years English has become an essential tool for modernisation and economic development and a significant medium in the tourist and entertainment industries as well as education, and [that] the need for the use of English in the workplace has had a major impact on its learning, especially in Budapest. (Petzöld & Berns, 2000: 113)

The Hungarian education system has been struggling to accommodate these rapid changes. In 1989 there were large numbers of redundant teachers of Russian and a shortage of teachers of English. The solution to this imbalance was to retrain the teachers of Russian as teachers of English. Sixty-five percent of the foreign language teachers now teaching at primary level used to be teachers of Russian or other subjects apart from English (Nikolov, 2000: 8). The same teachers who themselves learnt and taught Russian mainly through the grammar-translation approach were suddenly required to teach a language for communication (NCC, 2004).

The Hungarian Core Curriculum for English has the explicit aim of teaching the language for communication (NCC, 2004: 31). Attempts have been made to implement this aim in stages from 1998 (Medgyes & Miklósy, 2000: 192), but some aspects of the curriculum have been slow to respond to these initiatives. In particular, exams still play an important part in the curriculum. There has long been a tradition of using oral examinations in Hungary to assess most school subjects, including foreign languages. The traditional oral examinations in English were primarily tests of the ability to memorise and recite factual information or to deliver a prepared monologue. Very little provision was made for the assessment of the use of the spoken language in spontaneous communication (Alderson & Szollás, 2000). The school-leaving exam (typically taken at the age of 18) underwent a major reform in 2006, with more emphasis on communicative language use, but it is not likely that the backwash effect of these reforms will be felt in the primary schools for some time to come.

In Hungary children attend primary school between the ages of six and 14, and secondary school between 14 and 18, although some secondary schools now offer to take pupils from Year 7 (age 12). Pupils must learn at least one foreign language from Year 4 (age nine) until the end of compulsory education. Pupils can study additional languages if there are suitable teachers available in the school (NCC, 2004). Although Year 4 is the official starting age for learning a foreign language in Hungary, many schools offer an earlier start in English, often from Year 1. Parents can choose which school their children will attend, and schools advertise their English language achievements prominently to make the school attractive to parents (see e.g. Nagy, 2006).

This brief description of the context for English language teaching at primary level in Hungary highlights the fact that the English language curriculum in Hungary is going through a period of rapid change. Because English has replaced Russian as the foreign language of choice, teachers have been retrained to teach English, and to adopt a methodology which emphasizes the use of the language for communication. In this context of rapid curriculum change, the use of the first language in the classroom becomes a matter of important and legitimate debate.

Research on the Use of the First Language in the Primary Classroom

As we have indicated above, research on the language choices made by teachers in primary school foreign language classrooms is sparse; what there is presents a picture of varying attitudes and practices. The early research tends to focus on the frequency of target and first language use. A representative example is a study of elementary core French classes in Western Canada (Shapson *et al.*, 1978). The study shows that only 26% of the teachers used the TL for at least 75% of the time. This early research tends not to look in detail at the functions associated with the use of the first language, so it fails to provide an explanation of why the teachers used the first language to the extent that they did. This question is addressed by Lai's (1996) study of first language use by trainee teachers in upper primary and junior secondary schools in Hong Kong. This study showed that the four trainees in the study used the first language more than 30% of the time. A functional analysis of the first-language utterances and interviews with the trainees suggest that the main reasons for the use of the first language were pressure from the learners, discipline problems and the need to save time.

There is some evidence that it is possible to sustain the use of the target language with young learners. A study in a Swedish-immersion kinder-garten in Finland with six-year-olds found that the teachers used the target language almost all of the time (Vesterbacka, 1991). This was achieved largely through the frequent use of formulaic utterances in situations where the use of language was routine and predictable. In a study in Hong Kong, Carless (2004) examined the interaction of one teacher with a class of six-year-old Year 1 learners. The teacher succeeded in sustaining the use of the target language almost all of the time. This was achieved through the use of short simple sentences, visual support and avoidance of diffi-cult vocabulary. The teacher focused on concrete situations, controlled the input carefully, provided motivating activities and involved the pupils through the use of choral and individual repetition, whole class and indi-vidual questioning and activities with movement. This teacher had been educated in an English-medium school and had taken her undergraduate degree in English at a university in the UK. She was very confident in her use of English and was committed to sustaining the use of English in the classroom as much as possible.

The Present Study

As we have indicated, the present chapter is based on evidence from an observational study of English language classes in Hungarian primary schools. As we have also suggested above, the foreign language curricu-lum in Hungary is passing through a period of transition. One of the man-ifestations of this ongoing change is that there is strong pressure on the teacher to move from the traditional grammar-translation approach which was typical of the Russian language classroom towards the more commu-nicative approach which is considered appropriate in the teaching of English. One of the principal objectives of this study was to determine how the teachers were responding to this pressure. In this chapter we focus on the use of the first language in the classroom in the belief that this feature of the classroom is a particularly sensitive indicator of the extent and nature of the changes we refer to above.

Research questions

This study addresses the following questions:

(1) How often do the teachers use the target language and how often do they use the first language?
(2) What are the functions associated with the teachers' language choices?
(3) What are the factors which affect teachers' language choices, and how do these factors interact?

Data collection

The data collection for this study took place in Budapest during April and May 2004. Four teachers in four schools took part. Twelve lessons in total at levels from Year 3 to Year 6 were observed and audio-recorded. The researcher (the first author of this chapter) was present during the recordings and made hand-written notes about the activities, timings, use of materials, and incidents which seemed at the time to be significant to an understanding of what was happening in the classroom. Brief informal interviews were conducted after each lesson with the teacher, and the researcher took notes after the interviews. These notes provide some evidence relating to the teachers' thinking in relation to particular incidents observed during the lesson. For the purposes of this chapter, the four lessons with Year 4 classes were selected for analysis. Two of the classes were in their fourth year of the study of English, and we refer to these classes as the 'intermediate' classes. The remaining two were in their first year of English, and we refer to these classes as the 'elementary' classes. Thus although the pupils were at the same level in terms of their year group, they were at different levels in terms of their exposure to English. We make extensive use of this comparison in the analysis of the data to come. The teachers of the elementary classes are identified here by the pseudonyms 'Etelka' and 'Sára' and the teachers of the intermediate classes are referred to as 'Katalin' and 'Ibolya'.

Data analysis

Each of the four lessons lasted approximately 40 minutes. The recordings were transcribed and analysed both quantitatively and qualitatively. In an attempt to estimate the relative frequency of use of the target language (English) and the first language (Hungarian) by the teacher in each lesson, a frequency count of words in the lesson transcripts spoken by the

Table 4.1 Number of words of TL (English) and L1 (Hungarian) spoken by the teacher in four 40-minute lessons (two elementary and two intermediate)

Level	Teacher	TL	TL (%)	L1	L1 (%)	Total
Elementary	Etelka	2364	90.6	245	9.4	2609
	Sara	1980	72.3	759	27.7	2739
	Total	4344	81.4	1004	18.8	5338
Intermediate	Katalin	1532	52.5	1386	47.5	2918
	Ibolya	1533	59.1	1059	40.9	2592
	Total	3065	55.6	2445	44.4	5510

teacher in English and Hungarian[1] was carried out. For convenience we use the number of words spoken as a measure of the amount of time spent using the two languages. The results are shown in Table 4.1. As the table shows, the teachers in the elementary classes used the target language more frequently (relative to their use of the first language) than the teachers in the intermediate classes. The elementary class teachers Etelka and Sára used the target language 91% and 72% of their total speaking time while the intermediate class teachers Katalin and Ibolya used the target language 53% and 59% of their total speaking time.

In order to reach an understanding of this result, two lessons were chosen for a more in-depth analysis: the lesson with the elementary class conducted by Etelka and the lesson with the intermediate class conducted by Katalin. These two lessons were selected for comparison because they had the lowest and highest amount of first language use of the four lessons. These lessons are not intended in any way to be representative; the expectation is, rather, that an in-depth examination of the transcripts of these two lessons would provide insights into the reasons for the use of the first language by the teachers which might be applicable in other situations. The transcripts were segmented into episodes, with each episode characterized according to the predominant activity type. The number of words used in English and Hungarian[19] was cross-tabulated with activity type. We consider first the total number of words in both languages considered together according to activity type. This number provides a means of comparing the amount of time given to each type of activity by the teachers. The results are shown in Table 4.2, with the activities sorted roughly in descending order of the number of words spoken by the teacher.

Table 4.2 Number of words spoken in English (TL) and Hungarian (L1) in the two lessons according to type of activity

	Etelka (elementary)		Katalin (intermediate)	
	Number of words (English and Hungarian)	Percent of total	Number of words (English and Hungarian)	Percent of total
Use of textbook	454	17.40	2015	69.05
Work in notebooks	978	37.49	–	–
Homework check	342	13.11	–	–
Warm up	328	12.57	91	3.12
Game	229	8.78	187	6.41
New homework	114	4.37	360	12.34
Pictures	103	3.95	–	–
Collecting notebooks	24	0.92	–	–
Farewells	24	0.92	9	0.31
Greetings	13	0.50	23	0.79
Pronunciation	–	–	129	4.42
Evaluation	–	–	73	2.50
Real communication	–	–	31	1.06
Total	2609	100.0	2918	100.0

In Katalin's lesson the activity involving the use of the textbook resulted in more spoken language use by the teacher, by a considerable margin, than any other kind of activity (69.0% of the total number of words spoken in English and Hungarian considered together). In Etelka's lesson, the activity which accounted for most spoken language use by the teacher was 'Work in notebooks' (37.5% of the total number of words spoken), with 'Use of the textbook' the next most frequent (17.4%).

In order to begin to understand the reasons for the difference in the frequency of use of the target language and the first language by these two teachers, we look now at their use of the two languages according to activity type. Table 4.3 shows a breakdown of the number of words in the

Table 4.3 Number of words spoken in English (TL) and Hungarian (L1) in the two lessons according to type of activity

		Etelka (elementary)			Katalin (intermediate)		
		TL	L1	Total	TL	L1	Total
Use of textbook	Frequency	439	15	454	1189	826	2015
	Percent	96.7	3.3		59.0	41.0	
Work in notebooks	Frequency	840	138	978			
	Percent	85.9	14.1				
Homework check	Frequency	341	1	342			
	Percent	99.7	0.3				
Warm-up	Frequency	324	4	328	83	8	91
	Percent	98.8	1.2		91.2	8.8	
Game	Frequency	166	63	229	31	156	187
	Percent	72.5	27.5		16.6	83.4	
New homework	Frequency	113	1	114	151	209	360
	Percent	99.1	0.9		41.9	58.1	
Pictures	Frequency	80	23	103			
	Percent	77.7	22.3				
Collecting notebooks	Frequency	24		24			
	Percent	100.0					
Farewells	Frequency	24		24	6	3	9
	Percent	100.0			66.7	33.3	
Greetings	Frequency	13		13	23		23
	Percent	100.0			100.0		
Pronunciation	Frequency				49	80	129
	Percent				38.0	60.0	
Evaluation	Frequency				73		73
	Percent				100.0		

(Continued)

Table 4.3 *Continued*

		Etelka (elementary)			Katalin (intermediate)		
		TL	*L1*	*Total*	*TL*	*L1*	*Total*
Real discourse	Frequency					31	31
	Percent					100.0	
Total	Frequency	2364	245	2609	1532	1386	2918
	Percent	90.6	9.4		52.5	47.5	

target language and the first language according to activity type for the two teachers. The table shows very clearly that the difference in the proportions of overall first and target language use by these two teachers derives primarily from the first two listed activities: 'Use of textbook' and 'Work in notebooks'. In the category 'Use of textbook', the proportion of target language use in Katalin's lesson was 59.0%; in Etelka's lesson, in contrast, the target language was used 96.7% of the time in this activity. In the activity 'Work in notebooks', the proportion of target language use in Etelka's lesson was nearly as high, at 86%. The picture is clear: in the two activities which account for most of the spoken language use in the two classrooms ('Use of textbook', and 'Work in notebooks') the proportion of target language use in the elementary classroom was much higher than in the intermediate classroom. In order to understand why this might be so, we now look more closely at the activities and at the texts which form the basis for these activities.

The activity 'Use of textbook' in the intermediate class was based on an audio-cassette recording of a textbook dialogue (Holderness, 1990). The textbook dialogue consisted of a strip cartoon with speech bubbles about the adventures of a group of children and their dog. The teacher played an extract from the tape and then nominated individual students in turn to read aloud from the textbook and to translate the English text into Hungarian. In the elementary class, in contrast, the activity 'Use of textbook' was based on a black and white line drawing of a house in the textbook, with no text. The teacher used the drawing as the basis for a series of question and answer drills concerning rooms and objects in the house. The activity 'Work with notebooks' in the elementary class was similar, using pictures drawn by the learners themselves in the previous lesson as the basis for controlled practice activities of grammar and vocabulary. In both of these activities, the teacher used pictures without text to provide the context for controlled practice of familiar structures and vocabulary. The practice routines were devised by the teacher, not taken from the textbook.

In the intermediate class, the teacher acted as a mediator between the target-language text and the learners. The target-language text consisted of dialogue in speech bubbles with linking narrative and the teacher's mediation consisted largely of translations of the target-language text into Hungarian. It is not clear why the teacher felt the need to mediate between the text and the students in this way, but there are a number of possible reasons. First, the text was the primary source of input for the learners, and often contained new words; the teacher needed to make sure that the learners understood these new words. Secondly, and perhaps more significantly, the extended nature of the written text presents a challenge to the processing capacities of the learners which is different from the challenge presented by the use of short, repetitive spoken exchanges used in the elementary class. It is likely that the teacher's use of the first language was intended to make the text more accessible to the learners. In the elementary class there was very little target-language text in the textbook, so the teacher was more in control of the target language input than her colleague and so in a better position to avoid the use of the first language.

One further comparison in Table 4.3 is of interest, and that is in relation to the activity 'Game'. The term 'game' is used here to refer to an activity where there is an essential element of competition, and a routine which provides a context for the learners to participate using the target language. Both teachers used a game in their lessons but the elementary class teacher used the target language 83% of the time during the game in her lesson while the intermediate class teacher used the target language only 17% of the time. The difference is accounted for by the different character of the two games. The game in the elementary class was a repetitive drill; the game in the intermediate class, in contrast, was a complicated word game requiring a good deal of explanation in Hungarian before the learners could understand the procedure. In the drill, the use of language is routine and predictable, and this makes it easier to use the target language. Where language use is not routine (as was the case with the explanation of the game in the intermediate class), the tendency is to use the first language. One implication which might be drawn from this is that in order to maximize target language use at lower levels one key strategy is to ensure that the use of the target language is routine and predictable.

Qualitative Analysis

The analysis to this point has been based on comparisons of the frequency of target and first language use in different activities in the two classrooms. The analysis helps us to understand the major differences which are apparent in Tables 4.2 and 4.3, but it does not provide much insight into the *reasons* for the teachers' language choices in particular instances. For this kind of insight, we need to use a qualitative approach to the analysis of the data. Our approach is based on the assumption that particular 'critical' episodes can be revealing as to the reasons for the use of the first language in general. This is especially the case where the speaker switches from the use of the target language to the first language or vice versa, since it is in the context surrounding such episodes that the factors influencing language choice are most likely to be apparent.

In what follows it will help to understand how the particular episodes fit into the general pattern of the lesson if we outline the structure of a typical lesson. Table 4.4 shows the structure of a typical lesson in a primary school in Hungary.

The early and closing stages of the lesson are the most regular and predictable, since they function to set a frame around the main content of the lesson and to help the students with the transition from the world outside to the microcosm inside the classroom. In order to fulfil this function it is necessary that the activity be familiar and recognised for what it is, so that the children know what is expected of them and behave appropriately. The first two stages of the lesson ('Greeting' and 'Reporting') are part of the routine of almost every lesson in all subjects throughout the school system in Hungary. These activities are rituals with which every student is familiar. Where language use is familiar and predictable it is easier to use the target language. It is therefore not surprising that these activities are typically conducted in English. In the 'Greeting' stage of both lessons, the target language was used by both teachers and students 100% of the time.

At the beginning of the lesson the students are expected to stand up when the teacher enters the room, and the 'Greetings' are accomplished. The students remain standing for the 'Reporting' stage, when one student at the front of the class reports on attendance. Since this is a routine activity the students can be trained to conduct it in English. The first two stages in the typical lesson (as shown in Table 4.4) are exemplified in Example 1. (The caret symbol '^' is used to indicate rising intonation at the end of an utterance, used as an elicitation device by the teacher. Pauses are marked in seconds and tenths of a second in round parentheses. Further details of the transcription conventions are given in the Appendix.)

Example 1: Greeting and reporting (Katalin, intermediate)

1 **T:** Good morning students.
2 **Ss:** Good morning teacher.
3 **T:** So what's the date today?

Table 4.4 The structure of a typical lesson at P4 in Hungary

1.	Greeting	The students stand up and greet the teacher.
2.	Reporting	A student, chosen beforehand for this purpose, gives a report on the date and attendance. The report may include information about the time and the weather.
3.	Homework check	A student reports on who has/has not done the homework. Alternatively, the teacher may ask about this.
4.	Warm-up	A transition from the routine activities at the start of the lesson to the main content of the lesson. This stage is used for revision, to relax the students (by playing a game or singing a song, for example) and to establish the mind-set of 'speaking English'.
5.	New lesson content	The activities in this stage of the lesson are the most varied and unpredictable. A wide range of different types of activity is used, usually involving the introduction and/or practice of new material.
6.	New homework	The homework for the next lesson is set.
7.	Evaluation	The teacher gives praise (or blame, if appropriate) to the students for their performance and/or behaviour during the lesson.
8.	Closure	Students stand up and take leave of the teacher.

```
4   S:   Today is Monday for (2.0) twenty-eight.
5   T:   The twenty-eighth.
6   S:   The twenty-eighth of (1.0) April (2.0). No ...
7   T:   Nobody^
8   S:   Nobody is (2.0)
9   T:   is^
10  S:   is (1.0)
11  T:   is absent
12  S:   is absent
13  T:   Okay, thank you, sit down.
```

Although all of this exchange was conducted in English, the student needed a good deal of prompting from the teacher in order to complete the routine. The failure of the student to complete the familiar routine without help prompted the teacher to admonish him for his poor performance, as we see from Example 2. (In this example Hungarian is printed in bold, and an English gloss of the Hungarian is provided in italics, surrounded by angled brackets):

Example 2: Greeting and reporting continued (Katalin, intermediate)

13 T: Okay, thank you, sit down. **Jövő héten ki lesz a hetesünk? Jövő héten? Jövő héten? Vivien után?** [STUDENT PUTS UP HIS HAND] **Akkor Bálint úrfi már elkezdi tanulni a jelentés szövegét jó? Már most.** <*Next week who will be the person to report? Next week? Next week? After Vivien? Well Mr Bálint is to start learning the words of the report right now okay?*> Right. Now Kata.

The teacher's utterance in this episode is one of only two examples of the category 'Real communication' (Table 4.3) in the transcripts of the two lessons. The reference to 'Bálint úrfi' ('Mr Bálint') is ironically formal and deferential in this context, and is intended as a mild reprimand to this student for his poor performance of the reporting ritual. This illustrates very clearly the contrast between the use of the target language in situations where language use is ritualized and formulaic and the use of the first language which occurs when language use departs from the routine and becomes spontaneous and unpredictable. This example is also a striking illustration of the fact that the use of the TL is something into which the students have to be enculturated, in the sense that they have to learn the appropriate modes of language behaviour which are expected in different familiar situations. We can think of this set of expectations about appropriate modes of behaviour as being part of the 'culture of the classroom' (Jin & Cortazzi, 1998). Where the process of enculturation has not yet been successfully accomplished by the pupil, it becomes an occasion for comment and admonition by the teacher. The teacher's main purpose here is to shape the behaviour of the pupil according to the expectations that she has established about appropriate modes of behaviour, and it is likely that she uses the first language for this purpose because the need to reinforce the social norms of the classroom takes priority over the need to use the target language.

Example 2 is not an isolated incident: a similar switch from the target to the first language happens a little later in the Homework check, as we see in Example 3 (continuation from Example 2).

Example 3: Greeting and reporting continued (Katalin, intermediate)

13 T: Right. Now Kata [THIS IS ANOTHER CHILD WHO CHECKS HOMEWORK AND ALL THAT IS NEEDED BEFORE THE LESSON STARTS AND REPORTS]

14 S: Everybody ... mmm ... ha

15 **T:**   has got
16 **S:**   has got, e, everything
17 **T:**   Okay **kivéve ugye azokat akiknek nincs itt a piros könyve**
            <*except those who have not got the red book*> [THEY ARE JUST
            STARTING THE NEXT BOOK] Now I would like you to open
            your books please at Page One, Unit One.

The teacher says 'Okay' in turn 17 to signal the end of the Homework
check episode in turns 14–16, but, as with the first reporting ritual, there is a
departure from routine at this point and she switches into Hungarian to
comment on this. The students had been expecting to have a test in this lesson before beginning a new book (the 'red book') and some of them had not
brought the book. So when the student says 'Everybody has got everything'
this is not actually true. The reason for the change in plan was the presence
of the researcher. The teacher had discussed this with the students before-
hand and had explained that because of the researcher's visit they would
start the new book instead of having the test. The point of interest here is
that the student is still required to perform the ritual of reporting that 'everybody has got everything' (and is assisted in doing so by the teacher), even if
it is not true. The ritual has become an end in itself. The teacher feels obliged
to comment on this (indirectly), and in the circumstances it is not surprising
that she does so in Hungarian. Pennington (1995) has argued that the use of
language in the foreign language classroom can be seen as being constrained
by different 'frames', including a 'Lesson frame', where the business of the
lesson is conducted, an 'Institutional frame', where the teacher makes reference to circumstances outside the classroom but within the institution (such
as when e.g. she talks about examinations) and a 'Commentary frame',
where the teacher steps outside the Lesson frame to comment on what is
going on, perhaps so as to provide a justification for her actions to the students or an explanation of an incident to an outsider. In this instance, the
teacher is commenting, perhaps for the benefit of the researcher, on the fact
that some of the pupils have forgotten to bring their books.

The next activity is the 'Warm-up'. This comes before any new material
is introduced. It is not simply revision, and may contain songs and games
learned in previous lessons. The two teachers differed in how much time
they gave to this activity and also how much target or first language they
used. Etelka took a relatively long time with her elementary class over this
activity, asking the students to practise conversational exchanges they had
already learnt. She also had the students take on the role of the teacher as
the initiator in these exchanges, thus decreasing teacher talking time. She
achieved 99% use of the target language in this activity.

Example 4: Warm up (elementary)

3	**T:**	So Szabi, what's your name?
4	**S1:**	My name is Alexander Szabó.
5	**T:**	Ask Niki.
6	**S1:**	What's your name?
7	**S2:**	My name is Nikolett Kovács

Other routines practised in this session included the following:

- Where do you live?
- How old are you?
- When were you born?
- Alphabet
- Say words with letter ...
- What month is it?
- What season is it?

The 'Warm-up' stage in the intermediate class was different. The teacher concentrated on the textbook from the beginning of the lesson. The class was using the third book in the 'Chatterbox' series (Holderness, 1990). The series has the same characters and a continuous detective story throughout the four books. Katalin introduced the new book by asking two questions about the picture on the first page (Example 5, turn 15: 'Who are the children' and turn 19: 'What animals can you see in the picture?').

Example 5: Warm up (intermediate)

15	**T:**	Now I would like you to open your books please at Page One, Unit One. Okay, so (xxx) so this, mmm, new unit is about friends and we are going to learn about the children. Who are the children? In the story? Who are the children? **Kik a gyerekek akiket már eddig is ismertünk?** <*Who are the children we have met before?*> Anna.
16	**S:**	Katalin, Caroline, Ken.
17	**T:**	Katalin, Caroline and Ken. And who is this man? Martin?
18	**S:**	(unclear)
19	**T:**	Yes, he is uncle John. Very good. Okay, what animals can you see in the picture? What animals? Viki?

It is likely that the teacher uses the first language in turn 15 in order to ensure that all the students in the class have understood the question 'Who are the children?' Perhaps she feels that the students will not be able to assimilate the new material which is coming unless the context has been clearly established in their minds.

Having established the context, the teacher moves on to the text itself. Her routine practice in dealing with new text was to get the students to underline the unknown words before listening or while listening to the conversation on the tape (Example 6).

Example 6: Warm up (intermediate)

21 **T:**   and a dog and, and a^ ... rabbit, yes. Great. Okay, now I would like you to listen to the cassette, okay? And take your pencil and underline the new words in the text. Underline the new words in the text.

[TEACHER PLAYS THE TAPE]

After the students had listened to the tape, the teacher asked for the new words (Example 7).

Example 7: Use of textbook (intermediate)

23 **T:**   ... okay then **jó akkor nézzük hogy az első részben milyen** <*good let's see if in the first part what kind of*> In the first speech bubble what new words have you found? Okay? Anna?

24 **S:**   **nincs új szó** <*no new words*>

25 **T:**   no new words? What is 'remember'? Zsolt?

26 **S:**   **emlékezni** <*remember*>

27 **T:**   **emlékezni** <*remember*>, yes, very good.

After going through the new vocabulary in this way, the teacher gets the children to copy the new words into their exercise books. In this lesson the teacher used Hungarian extensively, both for translating new words, but also for giving instructions and encouragement. The teacher's immediate purpose in this episode is to ensure that the students have underlined the new words, and it is likely that her use of the first language in turn 23 is intended to check that this has been done. It is interesting that she begins this check in the first language but breaks off before she has finished and gives the same instruction in the target language. The use of the target language is possible because it is part of a familiar routine that she has established for dealing with new text. The text was the focus of the lesson and the priority for the teacher was to ensure that the text had been understood, and the need to use the target language has lower priority. The codeswitching at this point is evidence, however, that the teacher is not entirely confident that the students will be able to follow her instructions in English, even though the activity of underlining the new words is a routine part of the classroom culture.

As we have seen in the analysis above, a departure from routine activities may trigger the use of the L1 by the teacher. Thus the pressure of the immediate interactive context may over-ride the expectations associated with the wider context of the activity. More generally, the Institutional context serves as an ever-present constraint which affects the teacher's language choices. The teacher's extensive use of Hungarian at this stage of the lesson can be understood partly as a response to the external pressures of the curriculum. The students' progress in English is monitored regularly each week by means of a vocabulary test, a sentence translation test and a text to be memorised and repeated orally. Parents want their children to perform well in these tests. Entry to secondary school, and in particular to the prestigious bilingual secondary schools, is competitive and selection is based on tests set by the schools themselves. The child's chances of getting into the school of his/her choice may depend on getting good results in the English test. Later on, students at university may have to pass an English test before they can graduate. Given these external pressures it is understandable that 'covering the syllabus' (which, in effect, means getting through the textbook) becomes an over-riding priority for the teacher, and if it is necessary to use the first language to accomplish this, this is a price worth paying.

The pressure of impending exams is not a factor in the elementary classes. Instead of *Chatterbox* (the textbook used in the intermediate class) the teacher used a textbook (*Practice Together*) published in Hungary (Sződy, 2001). This book is a picture dictionary with images grouped around topics such as the house, the family, pets and hobbies. The illustrations are line-drawings in black and white, so the students can colour in the pictures and thereby personalise their book. The book uses very little text (either TL or L1), so the language input depends primarily on the teacher.

Example 8 is representative of the elementary teacher's style when using the textbook:

Example 8: Use of textbook (elementary)

276 **T:** Yes, thank you very much. I would like you to open your books at page, on page, mmm, hundred and thirty-four, hundred and thirty-four. [...] What you can find in the house? Where is the shower? Where is the shower? Yes?

277 **S:** In the bathroom.

278 **T:** It is^ [WRITING ON BOARD]

279 **S:** It is in the bathroom.

280 **T:** It is in the bathroom [WRITING ON BOARD]. Thank you very much. Where is the fridge? Yes ...

281 **S:** It is in the kitchen.

282 **T:** [WRITING ON BOARD]
[...]

301 **T:**   I have got a question. What colour is your TV set, Viki?
302 **S:**   It is mm . . .
303 **T:**   Just a moment [WRITING ON BOARD]. Mmm, my question
         is, listen: what colour is your TV set? So, it's your, so . . .
304 **S:**   (xxx)
305 **T:**   No, okay. So look at my question [WRITING ON BOARD].
         What colour is your TV set, okay? So how can you start the
         sentence?

In Example 8 the teacher provides the language input with the help of
the pictures. Because she has control over the input she is free to decide on
the mode of interaction with the learners according to their needs and
capabilities. She uses the familiar I-R-F 'triadic dialogue' (Mehan, 1979;
Nassaji & Wells, 2000; Sinclair & Coulthard, 1975) Exchange structure
(Initiation–Response–Feedback) as a way of managing the interaction
with the students. This mode of interaction requires only short responses
from the learners, using familiar material, and as a result makes it possible
for the teacher and the learners to sustain the use of the target language
throughout the episode. In this activity, the teacher used the target language 97% of the time. In the intermediate class, the teacher is not in control of the input and her priority is to make the target-language text
accessible to the learners, and the strategy she uses requires translation of
the target language into the first language. The differences in the use of
language between the two classes in this category of activity derive primarily from differences in the nature of the texts used in the two classes.
The 'text' in the elementary class is, in effect, the set of lexical items in the
picture dictionary together with a familiar spoken language repertoire of
question and answer exchanges. The text in the intermediate class is written language consisting of dialogue and interlinking narrative. The intermediate text imposes more severe demands on the processing capacities
of the learners and requires a different strategy from the teacher.

Conclusion

Any serious attempt to explain the language choices made by teachers in a foreign language classroom has to start by recognising that a
multitude of factors is potentially relevant. In this complex situation, it
is helpful to distinguish between factors which are external to the classroom and those which are internal. Of those which are internal, some
relate to the teacher, others to the learners, the nature of the situation or
the extent to which the use of language is formulaic or predictable. As a

first attempt to identify the factors influencing language choice in our data, we propose the following:

External factors: The curriculum, examinations, expectations in the school, the attitudes of the head-teacher, colleagues, parents and the political context.

Internal (teacher-related): Professional experience, training, proficiency in the target language, self-confidence, beliefs about and attitudes towards the target language.

Internal (learner-related): Age, ability, proficiency level, motivation, attitude towards the target language.

Internal (context-related): The stage in the lesson and the nature of the task or activity.

Internal (use of language): The extent to which language use is formulaic or predictable in the context.

We consider first the external (or, as we have referred to them earlier, the 'Institutional' factors). The Institutional factors should be seen as always potentially relevant in any of the classrooms in our study, but their effect is not uniformly in the same direction. The pressure of impending exams and the perceived need to complete the syllabus may make the teacher more inclined to use the first language in order to save time in giving explanations of unfamiliar classroom procedures. Pulling in the opposite direction is the Hungarian National Curriculum, and the beliefs and aspirations of parents, which promote the use of the target language in the classroom where this is possible.

In relation to the internal factors, we consider first the teacher-related factors. The evidence of our study suggests that the personal beliefs and preferences of the teacher may have an influence on his/her choice of language. In particular, it is likely that teachers who are confident in their use of the target language will be more inclined to use it. We don't have any information on the beliefs or level of self-confidence of the teachers in this study, so the effect of these factors must remain a matter for speculation.

In relation to the learner-related factors, the evidence of this study suggests that these learners are not inhibited in using the first language if they need to. They are not, in any case, given much opportunity to exercise choice in whether to use the target or the first languages, since their contributions are usually constrained by having to respond to an Initiating move from the teacher, and the nature of the activity will usually make it clear whether the first language is permissible or not.

Our analysis in this chapter has focused primarily on the last group of factors, those related to the stage of the lesson and the nature of the task or activity. Typically, activities where the use of language is repetitive, formulaic and predictable will allow the use of the target language, whereas any communication which is not routine will usually be carried out by the student in the first language. As we have seen, routine formulaic use of language is typical at the beginnings and ends of lessons and at familiar transition points between different activities. In relation to the type of activity, we have seen that short question-and-answer conversational routines will require, and allow, the use of the target language. In activities requiring the processing of extended text from the textbook, the teacher acts as a mediator between the target-language text and the student, and often feels compelled to use the first language in order to facilitate this process of mediation. Cameron (2001: 27) has pointed out that young learners in foreign language classrooms are faced with a range of demands, both cognitive and linguistic, which require different levels of support from the teacher. We suggest that use of the first language by the two teachers in our data is strongly influenced by the teacher's assessment of the cognitive and linguistic processing demands made on the learners by the texts used in the classroom (see also Behan *et al.*, 1997; Swain & Lapkin, 2001).

In our data the factors which have the strongest influence on the language choices made by the teacher are the type of activity (and, contingently, the extent to which the use of language in the context is ritualized and formulaic), the control the teacher can exercise over the input, and the teacher's assessment of the cognitive and linguistic demands made on the learners by the texts used in the classroom.

Appendix: Transcription Conventions

T	teacher
S	student
Ss	students
igen	utterance in Hungarian
<*yes*>	English gloss of Hungarian original
(1.0)	pause in seconds
^	rising intonation, cue
WRITING ON THE BOARD	researcher's comment
xxx	not audible

Chapter 5

Forms and Functions of Codeswitching by Dual Immersion Students: A Comparison of Heritage Speaker and L2 Children

KIM POTOWSKI

Introduction

This chapter examines a corpus of codeswitches produced by fifth graders in a dual immersion classroom. Given the proliferation of terminology in the field, a clarification of terms will be useful at the outset. Montrul (2002) uses the following terms for Spanish-English bilinguals in the United States: *simultaneous bilingual* for children that learned English and Spanish at the age of early syntax, between 0–3 years of age;[20] *early child L2 learners* for children who began acquiring English after the age of first syntax but between the ages of 4–7 years; and *late child L2 learners* for those children who begin acquiring English between the ages of 8–12 years. In addition, all three of these groups are typically referred to as heritage Spanish speakers. Montrul (2002) found linguistic evidence that these distinctions are valid. The simultaneous bilinguals had less knowledge of Spanish preterite/imperfect distinctions than did early child second-language learners, who had less knowledge of this distinction than did late child second-language learners. These findings suggest that age of onset of bilingualism leads to different underlying grammatical knowledge, with earlier age of exposure to English being correlated with weaker Spanish systems. Other work by Montrul (2005) has looked at knowledge of unaccusativity, comparimg heritage speakers who had acquired Spanish before the age of seven to adult second-language learners. In that study, she found that even when matched on a general proficiency measure, the heritage speakers had better knowledge of unaccusativity than did the adult second-language Spanish learners. Again, these findings suggest that age of onset – this time the onset of learning Spanish, not English – leads to differences in underlying grammatical knowledge.

However, in addition to age of onset of bilingualism, the context of input must be considered when seeking to understand individuals' language abilities. Consider two children in the United States, one who comes from a monolingual Spanish-speaking home and one who comes from a monolingual English-speaking home. In kindergarten, they both begin attending a dual immersion school, where both languages are used for substantial portions of instruction. Both children are *early child L2* learners according to Montrul's (2002) classification. When both children are in 5th Grade, they will have had six years of intense exposure to their second language. However, in addition to exposure to English at school, the child with Spanish as the first language has received extensive input in English every day through television, movies and interactions with monolingual English speakers. In fact, children who begin school monolingual in Spanish are often English dominant by third grade. The children with English as their first language, however, typically are exposed to Spanish only during those portions of the schoolday that are taught in Spanish. In addition, the vast majority of social exchanges among dual immersion students are in English (Potowski, 2007a). Therefore, in dual immersion, the Spanish of the first-language students is usually stronger than the Spanish of the second-language students, although the English proficiency of both groups is fairly equal – and stronger than either group's Spanish. Some students in dual immersion who have Spanish as their second language do achieve high levels of oral fluency, although they evidence persistent grammatical inaccuracies not present among the students who have Spanish as their first language (Potowski, 2007b).

The context of English acquisition of the heritage speaker, then – that is, a child from a minority language background – is very different from the context of Spanish acquisition of mainstream children. The difference has been referred to as additive versus subtractive bilingualism (Crawford, 1995). Hispanic children living in the United States experience enormous daily pressure to acquire English, typically at the expense of their Spanish, while English-speaking children at a dual immersion school can get by with surprisingly low levels of Spanish (Potowski, 2007a) while incurring no cost to their English. Although I agree that second-language learners are 'incipient bilinguals' (Byram, 1997; Kramsch, 1993), their underlying grammatical systems (Montrul, 2002, 2007) and pragmatic performance (Potowski, 2007b) are shown to differ from those of heritage speakers. Therefore, in this chapter I use the term *second-language learner* to refer to the mainstream child from a monolingual English-speaking home who is acquiring Spanish at school – even if their age of onset of Spanish was in preschool at age four or five – and *heritage speaker* or *native bilingual* to refer to simultaneous and early child bilinguals (ages 0–7) from Spanish-speaking homes. I shall now review studies about codeswitching by bilingual children and by second-language adults, in order to set the framework for the present study that will compare the codeswitching of heritage bilingual children to that of their second-language classmates in a dual immersion setting.

Research on Codeswitching by Heritage Bilingual Children and Second-Language Adults

Research on codeswitching began with native bilingual adults, showing that codeswitching is generally rule-governed behavior that fulfills pragmatic and social functions (diSciullo *et al.*, 1986; Myers-Scotton, 1993; Poplack, 1980; among others). Research with native bilingual children revealed similar patterns and, in addition, some studies suggest that children's codeswitching patterns change over time, with early codeswitching consisting mainly of lexical items and later codeswitching consisting of longer constituents (McClure, 1981; Meisel, 1994; Zentella, 1997). For example, Zentella (1997) found that older children seem to manipulate their linguistic codes for a wider variety of stylistic purposes and situational demands than younger children. Patterns were related to age and to English proficiency, which in fact were related to each other: the younger children were Spanish-dominant, and the older children were English-dominant. Similarly to McClure (1981), Zentella (1997) posited that it is the greater English proficiency of older children that is responsible for their different codeswitching behavior, although there were also some identifiable personal preferences among the children. In general, the younger children's codeswitching was dominated by lexical gaps and translations, while the older girls' codeswitching consisted predominately of realigning the conversation by breaking into narratives and shifting roles.

Reyes (2004) studied the codeswitching forms and functions of two groups of Spanish-dominant students at age seven and 10. Studying only switches consisting of more than one word, she found that the 10-year-olds codeswitched more frequently, and for a wider range of functions, than did the seven-year-olds, which she argues is indicative of a developmental trait. That is, similarly to Zentella's (1997) findings, as children's English (and hence their bilingual communicative competence) got stronger, they more frequently used codeswitching as a strategy to meet their conversational goals.

Chinese-speaking children living in England began incorporating single English lexical items – all of which were content morphemes – by age three years and three months.[21] Six months later, however, not only were the children much more reluctant to speak Chinese, their codeswitching consisted mostly of English EL islands. The authors argue that this qualitative change in codeswitching, while indicative of growth in English proficiency, may also be the first sign of first language attrition.[22]

Although McClure (1981), Zentella (1997) and Reyes (2004) suggest a developmental pattern of codeswitching, Cantone (2007) argues that child codeswitching can be analyzed in the same way as adult codeswitching, because the quantity of mixing among children depends on an individual choice, not on language development, language dominance, or other factors. Note that Zentella (1997) did find individual preferences for codeswitching among the five children she studied, although the overall patterns in her data did prompt her to suggest an age-based difference.

Before reviewing the research on codeswitching by second-language adults, it is useful to understand that the work just summarized codifying the functions of codeswitching has utilized different categories. Furthermore, it is notoriously difficult to determine with certainty the function of a codeswitch. For example, Zentella (1997) was able to attribute only 48% of the codeswitches in her corpus to one of her categories. Thus, it becomes nearly impossible to reliably compare data on codeswitching functions across studies.

There has been one study of codeswitching by second-language adults, that of Liebscher and Dailey-O'Cain (2004), who studied advanced German students in a content-based college course about linguistics. They argued that learner codeswitching in their corpus served not only participant-related functions, such as when they did not know how to say something in German, but also served discourse-related functions that 'contextualize[d] the interactional meaning of their utterances' by indicating changes in their orientation toward the interaction and toward each other.[23] A principal factor that complicates these findings, though, is that there were heritage speakers in this German classroom, and the present study suggests that the distinction between heritage speakers and second language learners is relevant regarding codeswitching. In addition, although second-language adults may be able to codeswitch for conversationally similar functions as bilingual adults, as yet we have no comparison of second-language and native bilingual production of codeswitching on lexical, semantic and syntactic levels. More generalizable conclusions about second-language adult codeswitching could be drawn from a quantitative analysis of linguistic structure as well as data collected in additional classrooms and within non-classroom settings. For example, a recent study (Potowski & Lee, 2009) suggests that heritage speakers and L2 learners differ in their grammaticality judgements of codeswitched sentences, with the L2 learners more apt to reject well-formed codeswitches. Thus, although second-language learners and heritage speakers are increasingly compared to each other, particularly regarding the comprehension, production and instructed acquisition of grammatical features (Montrul, 2002, 2005; Montrul & Bowles, 2009; Potowski *et al.*, under review), research comparing second-language and native bilingual codeswitching is still in its infancy.

Having established that some adult second-language learners codeswitching phenomena may resemble those of native bilingual adults, the question arises whether second-language children codeswitch similarly to native bilingual children. This issue is more complex when we consider that codeswitching among children appears to be developmental, changing as they get older (as reviewed above). Dual immersion is an ideal environment to compare heritage speaker children with second-language children because both types of children are studying Spanish and English in the same classrooms. The heritage speaker children are most probably native codeswitchers like those studied by McClure (1981), Zentella (1997) and Reyes (2004), while the second-language children, by virtue of lengthy and significant immersion in Spanish, may also engage in codeswitching similarly to the second-language adults studied by Dailey-O'Cain and Liebscher (2006). In fact, given the nature of dual immersion programs, these second-language children are probably among the most proficient second-language speakers at this age in the United States, and thus are ideally suited for a study of this nature. The present study seeks to shed light on several issues, including whether second-language children in dual immersion acquire codeswitching at all, and whether it is similar to that of their heritage speaker peers. This would constitute additional evidence that second-language codeswitching shares features with bilingual codeswitching, as well as evidence that dual immersion programs can promote native-like bilingual proficiency in Spanish.

Although there has been ample research in dual immersion contexts (including Carranza, 1995; Christian, 1996; Fortune, 2001; Lindholm Leary, 2001; Potowski, 2007a; Valdés, 1997), surprisingly few have carried out linguistic analyses, and even fewer have examined codeswitching. I have separated these studies from the previous review of codeswitching among children in naturalistic contexts (Zentella, 1997) and in bilingual classrooms (McClure, 1981; Reyes, 2004) because the sociolinguistic context of dual immersion classrooms, particularly the presence of both heritage speakers and second-language learners as well as the expectation for Spanish use during large portions of the school day, render them sufficiently different from the other two contexts.

Fuller *et al.* (2007) examined codeswitching among native Mexican Spanish-speakers in a Midwestern dual immersion school using both the Markedness Model (Myers-Sctton, 1993) and the Sequential Approach (Li, 1988). Since the students were Spanish-dominant, Spanish was the unmarked choice for their interactions, especially interactions that were non-academic in nature. The authors proposed that the codeswitches in their corpus could be explained by both models – within the Markedness Model, the switches indicated a shift in alignment between speakers or a switch in RO sets, while within the Sequential Approach, the switches were contextualization cues for different functions of the turns. However, when codeswitching itself was actually the unmarked language choice, the Sequential Approach was more useful in analyzing the switches sequentially as markers of conversational structure.

Fuller (this volume) again examined dual immersion students' talk, this time in a German-English school in Germany. She found that German was used primarily for off-task topics, and many codeswitches to German could be analyzed as contextualization cues that signaled off-task talk. Other instances of codeswitching, the author argues, were used as a means to construct social identity. Again, German was used to index peer relationships and also to construct an international identity. Sixteen of the 27 children in the focus classroom claimed a multiple or hybrid identity as German plus something else (English, Indian, etc.), and the author notes that codeswitching is a means of expressing such a dual identity.

Finally, Rubinstein-Avila (2002) found that Portuguese-English dual immersion students engaged in codeswitching games which for the boys 'may have served to relieve stress or tension and affirm group membership and solidarity' and allowed the girls to be the center of attention, play out family anxieties resulting from social demotion upon arrival in the United States, underscore the socioeconomic differences among them (Rubinstein-Avila, 2002: 79).

In summary, Fuller *et al.* (2007), Fuller (this volume) and Rubinstein-Avila (2002) analyzed the pragmatic and social functions of codeswitching by dual immersion students. To date, no study has examined whether second-language children codeswitch, or compared the forms or functions of codeswitching between second-language and heritage speakers, which is the focus of the present study.

Methodology

Source of language data

The data for the present study come from a fifth-grade dual immersion classroom of 10 and 11-year-old students in Chicago, Illinois. A total of 53 hours of classroom instruction were collected during 22 different lessons between December 1999 and May 2000. For the present study, I examined 16 Spanish lessons totaling $12\frac{1}{2}$ hours of data. There were four focal students selected out of the 20 students in the class, two girls and two boys, one from each language background, from the pool of students whose parents had granted consent and who had at least average grades and classroom participation levels in both languages. Between $6\frac{1}{2}$ to $8\frac{1}{2}$ hours of data were recorded for each of the four students, and a total of 2203 turns transcribed and coded. Table 5.1 shows that all four students were proficient in oral Spanish, receiving ratings of a 3.3 or higher on a modified Student Oral Proficiency Assessment administered and rated by researchers from the Center for Applied Linguistics (CAL). The teacher also rated students' Spanish at 3 or higher on a scale of 1–5. Matt (a first-language speaker) was not evaluated by CAL, but the teacher rated his Spanish proficiency.

Spanish language arts, math and half of the social studies curriculum were taught in Spanish in the morning. English language arts, science and the other half of the social studies curriculum were taught in English each afternoon. The same teacher taught the students the entire day in both languages. When students spoke to the teacher in English during Spanish lessons, she sometimes required them to repeat themselves in Spanish, but often allowed English use to go uncommented. When I asked her about this, she commented on the challenge of balancing curricular with linguistic goals: whether to pause a lesson to focus on the language of a student's response, or whether to accept the English response in order to move the lesson forward. Other teachers I interviewed at the school expressed the same challenge, an issue that I will return to in the conclusions.

Table 5.1 Students' Spanish proficiency (maximum score = 5)

	Name	*CAL*	*Teacher*
L1 Spanish	Carolina	4.9	5
	Matt	n/a	3+
L1 English	Melissa	4.6	3+/4–
	Otto	3.3	3

Coding procedures

The main unit of analysis of students' speech was the *turn*, which has been defined as when an interlocutor stops talking and thus enables another interlocutor to initiate a turn, or when the interlocutor is interrupted by another who initiates another turn (Ellis, 1994; Levinson, 1983). In Example 3, each numbered line represents a separate turn. Matt was assigned a total of four turns in this exchange. Transcription conventions (outlined in Appendix) were adapted from Hatch (1992).

(3)

1	**Ms Torres:**	¿De qué otros lados vienen las historias y los cuentos?
2	**Matt:**	Oooh!
3	**Ms Torres:**	Matt.
4	**Matt:**	De ... cosas que existen y/
5	**Ms Torres:**	De cosas que existen pero ¿dónde?
6	**Matt:**	... y que no existen. Como/
7	**Ms Torres:**	De cosas que existen/
8	**Matt:**	Uh ... como ... um ... como ... son como ... como una leyenda, dice de, del sol, *and how it was made and*, y cosas así.

1	**Ms Torres:**	Where else do stories and tales come from?
2	**Matt:**	Oooh!
3	**Ms Torres:**	Matt.
4	**Matt:**	From ... things that exist and/
5	**Ms Torres:**	From things that exist but where?
6	**Matt:**	... and that don't exist. Like/
7	**Ms Torres:**	From things that exist/
8	**Matt:**	Uh ... like ... um ... like ... they're like ... like a legend, it tells about, about the sun, *and how it was made and*, and things like that.

I utilized the matrix language model of Myers-Scotton (1993) to code the codeswitched forms. The matrix language is the language with more morphemes and is the expected, unmarked language for a specific interaction (Myers-Scotton, 1993: 6). Once the matrix or base language has been established, there are three categories of codeswitches: intersentential switches, intrasentential embedded language morphemes and intrasentential matrix or embedded language islands. Intersentential codeswitches consist of language changes at the sentence boundary, such as 'Oh, yo sé. I have it in my notes.' Given that oral speech does not come with punctuation marks, at times it is difficult when transcribing to determine whether a new sentence is intended, but every attempt was made to code turns consistently.

The first type of intrasentential codeswitch, an embedded language morpheme inserted into a matrix language frame, contains morphemes from both the matrix and the embedded language. The embedded language content morpheme is congruent with the morphosyntactic specifications of the matrix language and is typically a singly occurring embedded language lexeme (Myers-Scotton, 1993: 77) – thus I refer to them simply as embedded language lexemes. The second type of intrasentential codeswitch is called a matrix or an embedded language island. An island is a switched portion of language that conforms internally to the specifications of the language it is in. That is, an embedded language island conforms to embedded language specifications, and a matrix language island conforms to matrix language specifications. Singly occurring lexemes are excluded from this category (Myers-Scotton, 1993: 83) – thus, an island by definition has more than one lexeme. Returning to Example 1, the portion 'and how it was made and' is an English island embedded in the Spanish matrix language. Finally, there were four codeswitched turns in which a student was reading aloud a portion of text in the embedded language, such as, 'OK, then this one, wouldn't it be, [*student reads from paper*] "Al norte, al norte, vamos a mudar"? (to the north, to the north we are going to move)' Because the embedded language was entirely read, and no reading was involved in the production of the other codeswitches, these four turns were eliminated from the corpus.

After coding the data for these three forms of codeswitching, I then assigned each codeswitch one of seven functional categories: lexical gap, discourse marker, repair, translation, fixed vocabulary and word focus. Turns that did not fit any of these categories were labeled 'other'. These categories were based principally on the functions present in my data – 68% of all codeswitches fulfilled one of these six functions – but also on past work on child codeswitching. Examples of all six functions will be presented with the findings.

(1) *Lexical gap* indicated that the inserted lexeme or island was preceded by the word 'um', a repetition, or a pause, indicating that the English word filled in a lexical gap for another word that the student probably did not know in Spanish.

(2) *Discourse marker* included expressions such as 'yeah', 'wait' or 'right'. There were no instances in the corpus of Spanish discourse markers inserted into English turns.

(3) *Repetition* refers to instances in which a student started a turn in one language but then partially or totally repeated what s/he had said in the other. Given that all data were collected during lessons in which Spanish was the expected language, repetitions were often attempts by students to recast their English utterances in order to conform to the Spanish language use expectations. In this sense, it was much like a repair.

(4) *Fixed vocabulary* refers to words that, according to my observations, were used routinely and only in one specific language to refer to school-related topics and items. For example, students volunteered each quarter to carry out a classroom 'job' such as erasing the board after school or collecting lunch money. These jobs were always named in Spanish – such as *pizarrón* (board) and *almuerzo* (lunch), even when speaking in English. Another example is the word *Mississippians*, a Native American group that was always referred to in English, even in the Spanish-language social studies textbook. Fixed vocabulary items, therefore, functioned almost as loanwords when they were inserted into the opposite base language.

(5) *Word focus* is similar to *fixed vocabulary*. A word focus took place when a student was referring to a particular word that had recently been uttered or read in a particular language. What distinguishes word focuses from fixed vocabulary is frequency: fixed vocabulary was used many times throughout the year, while a word focus was a unique instance of a particular word.

(6) *Translation* could be either a request for a translation, such as '¿Cómo se dice *man* en español?', or a response to such a request.

(7) Other was used to code codeswitches whose function was not clearly determinable.

Of these seven categories, only (1) through (3) plus (7) 'other' are similar to those found in naturalistic child codeswitching corpora (McClure, 1981; Zentella, 1997). Therefore, in my analysis I will pay particular attention to the categories *lexical gap*, *discourse marker*, *repetition* and *other*.

Findings

Before analyzing and comparing the students' codeswitching, I will present several brief analyses of monolingual turns, which will be helpful in interpreting the codeswitching data. When monolingual turns are considered by themselves (Table 5.2), we see that the students used Spanish for 56% of their turns,[24] far less than the 100% officially expected during

Table 5.2 Monolingual turns by speaker's first language

	Spanish L1		Spanish L2		
	Carolina $n = 562$	Matt $n = 499$	Melissa $n = 311$	Otto $n = 565$	Total $n = 1937$
Spanish	67% (376)	47% (234)	64% (199)	47% (265)	56% (1074)
English	33% (186)	53% (265)	36% (112)	53% (300)	44% (863)

these Spanish lessons, and English 44% of the time. In addition, the students' first language was not correlated with their quantity of Spanish use. Carolina (a first-language speaker) and Melissa (a second-language speaker) used Spanish for monolingual turns between 64–67% of the time, while Matt (a first-language speaker) and Otto (a second-language speaker) used Spanish for monolingual turns just 47% of the time. Therefore, gender was more correlated with language choice than was the first language, with the girls using Spanish more often than the boys. Elsewhere (Potowski, 2007a) I have speculated that a gendered explanation might be found in other elementary school classroom research showing that girls are generally more willing to conform to the teacher's expectations and invest in identities as good students. In this case, following the rules meant using Spanish during Spanish lessons. However, it must be noted that there were also some girls in this classroom who resisted using Spanish and boys who seemed to enjoy it.

In addition to gender, Spanish use was correlated with the topic of the turn, which entailed three possible classifications. *On task* turns were directly related to the academic content of the lesson. *Off task* turns were not related to the lesson in any way. *Management* turns were not related to academic content, but served to manage the completion of an on-task activity, such as asking a classmate how to do something or requesting to borrow an item necessary for completing the task. Turns that were inaudible or impossible to categorize with certainty were excluded from this analysis. Table 5.3 shows that when students were on task, Spanish was used 68% of the time. Viewed another way, 88% of all monolingual Spanish turns in the data were on task, suggesting that the more students stay on task, the more Spanish they will use. On the other hand, students overwhelmingly preferred English for off-task topics (83%). Management turns, too, were in English the majority of the time (57%), suggesting the discursive similarity between management and off task turns (and justifying the separation of management turns from on task turns). There were

Table 5.3 Monolingual turns by topic

n = 1937	Spanish	English
On task n = 1334 (67% of corpus)	68% (907)	32% (427)
Management n = 299 (16% of corpus)	43% (128)	57% (171)
Off task n = 274 (15% of corpus)	17% (47)	83% (227)
Unknown n = 30 (1% of corpus)	30% (9)	70% (21)

Table 5.4 Monolingual turns by interlocutor

	Spanish	English
To teacher n = 911 (47% of corpus)	82% (747)	18% (164)
To peers n = 1026 (53% of corpus)	32% (328)	68% (698)
Total n = 1937 (100% of corpus)	1075	862

no major differences between bilingual and second-language students' language use according to topic.

This presentation of monolingual turns concludes with a consideration of the interlocutor. Two interlocutors were identified: *teacher* when students answered questions aloud during teacher fronted lessons or spoke to the teacher when she was near their desks, and *peers* when students directed turns to their classmates only. Table 5.4 shows that when speaking with the teacher, students used Spanish 82% of the time. This is a fairly good adherence to the language expectations during lessons taught in Spanish. As was mentioned in the introduction, however, students' language use with other students was mostly in English (68%).

In summary, of all the monolingual Spanish turns in the data, the majority were on task and directed to the teacher. In practically a mirror image of the Spanish data, students used the most English when off task and when speaking to peers. As was the case with the topic of students' turns, there were no major differences between first and second-language students' language use according to interlocutor.

Intrasentential codeswitches

Now I will turn to the intrasententially codeswitched turns. Table 5.5 shows that just 6% of the turns in the corpus (128) contained an intrasententially

Table 5.5 Intrasentential codeswitches by type and base language, all students

Base language	Codeswitched		Monolingual
	Single lexeme from other language	Island from other language	
Spanish	61	44	1074
% of column	75%	93%	56%
% of corpus	3%	2%	
English	20	3	863
% of column	26%	7%	44%
% of corpus	1%	0.1%	
Total	81	47	1937
% of corpus	4%	2%	94%
	128 (6%)		

codeswitched element, although this is slightly more than the 2% found by Broner (2000). Sixty-three percent of these (81 out of 128) contained a single lexeme inserted from the other language, while the other 37% (47) contained embedded language islands. This finding is in line with other findings that single lexemes are the most commonly codeswitched items (e.g. Zentella, 1997). In addition, the majority of intrasentential codeswitching occurred when Spanish was the base language: 75% of lexical insertions and 93% of embedded language islands had Spanish as the base language with an English lexical or island insertion. This information is displayed visually in Figure 5.1.

Next, the overall amount of intrasentential codeswitching produced by each student was compared. Table 5.6 shows that there was no relationship between the percentages of intrasentential codeswitching and first language or gender. All students produced between 5% and 7% of their corpus in intrasentential switches. This is in line with the premise that the frequency of codeswitching is primarily dependent on community norms (Meisel, 1994: 418) and suggests that both types of students exhibit linguistic behavior of a sole classroom community. The first-language students produced a total of six more intrasententially codeswitched turns than

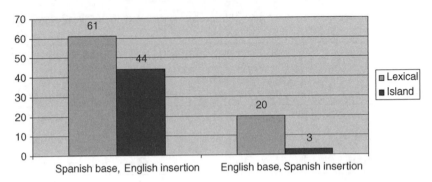

Figure 5.1 Intrasentential codeswitches by type and base language, all students ($n = 128$)

Table 5.6 Intrasentential codeswitching (lexical and island insertions) by student

Spanish L1	Carolina	5.8% (34/590)	5.9% (66/1117)
	Matt	6.1% (32/527)	
Spanish L2	Melissa	5.2% (18/340)	6.3% (59/933)
	Otto	7.3% (41/593)	
Total			6.1% (162/2050)

did the second-language students (66 vs. 59), for which no explanation is readily apparent.

Of perhaps greater interest is the fact that the first and second-language students did not show major differences in the proportion of lexical versus island intrasentential codeswitches in both languages (Figure 5.2). Both groups of students produced almost identical numbers of English lexemes inserted into a Spanish base and Spanish lexemes inserted into an English base. However, regarding the insertion of embedded language islands, heritage speakers used almost twice as many English islands inserted into a Spanish base than did the second-language students (27 vs. 17). This may find an explanation in arguments that codeswitching patterns are connected with bilingual proficiency. As suggested by Zentella (1997), children who are more proficient in both languages take more risks when codeswitching and switch larger constituents of speech. Embedded-language islands are syntactically more complex than single

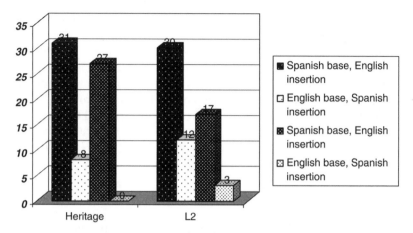

Figure 5.2 Intrasentential codeswitching forms by type, base language and first language

lexemes – which are typically nouns – to and therefore require a higher level of bilingual proficiency to switch without violating the rules of either grammar. Thus, even though some second-language students received similar ratings as heritage speakers on overall oral Spanish proficiency (Table 5.1), other measures including grammatical and written production (Potowski, 2007a) showed the heritage speakers in fact possessed

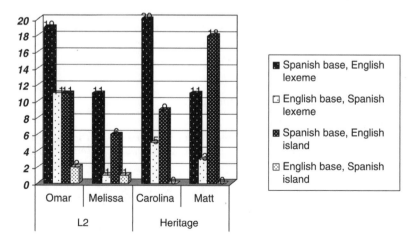

Figure 5.3 Intrasentential codeswitching type and base language by student

stronger Spanish systems. These codeswitching findings are further evidence that this is the case.

Unlike monolingual language turns, which we saw in this sample was correlated with gender, intrasentential codeswitching forms showed no correlation with gender (Figure 5.3). We see a fair amount of individual variation in codeswitching forms, which was also found among the children studied by McClure (1983) and Zentella (1997). I will now present a more detailed analysis of the single lexeme borrowings and of the island borrowings in an attempt to explain their functions. Finally, I will present the data on intersentential codeswitches.

Single lexeme insertions

As was shown in Table 5.5, there were 78 cases in the corpus of single lexeme insertions, and the majority of these consisted of an English word inserted into a Spanish base (57, or 74%). Table 5.7 shows that approximately one-third of these English lexemes (21 of 77) were due to lexical gaps, as suggested by the word 'um' or a long pause preceding the English word (see Examples 4 and 5). Such uses of English undoubtedly serve to promote learning in that they move a lesson along by allowing the student to focus on content rather than struggling to find a particular word. Three of the four students – the two second-language students and one heritage speaker – were very similar in their use of single word English insertions to fill a lexical gap, each producing between five and eight codeswitches of this type. Matt had only one example in the corpus of a lexical gap. We also notice from Table 5.4 that there were no cases of a Spanish lexeme being used to fill in for an unknown English word. This is not surprising given that English is the students' dominant language.

Table 5.7 Functions of single lexeme insertions

Language of inserted lexeme	Lexical gap	Other	Discourse markers	Word focus	Fixed vocabulary	Transla- tions	Repeti- tion
English *n = 61*	21	18	12	0	4	4	2
Spanish *n = 20*	0	0	0	12	6	2	0
Total *n = 81*	21	18	12	12	10	6	2

Single lexeme-level lexical gaps

(4)

Teacher:	¿Saben lo que es una hoguera de leña? [six second pause]. Vean la parte de en frente.
Carolina:	Es como una, como, es como, um, uno, um, *fire* … que tiene palitos para sostener la olla.
Teacher:	Do you know what a bonfire is? [6 second pause] Look at the front part.
Carolina:	It's like a, like, it's like, um, a, um, *fire* …. that has little poles to hold the pot.

(5)

Teacher:	¿Qué celebramos el cinco de mayo?
Melissa:	Cuando los franceses, um, vinieron a México y, um, como tenían un, una guerra<, y, y um, los mexicanos no tenían muchos, um, *weapons*.
Teacher:	Armas.
Teacher:	What do we celebrate on May fifth?
Melissa:	When the French, um, came to Mexico and, um, like they had a, a war<, and, and um, the Mexicans didn't have many, um *weapons*.
Teacher:	Weapons.

A fifth of the English lexical insertions – 18 out of 78, or 23% – were categorized as 'other' because they did not fit well into any of these six functional categories. Based on my extensive observations of these students during the course of the year, I am fairly certain that most of these words were, in fact, not known to them. However, due to the lack of clear hesitational pauses or markers of uncertainty such as 'um', I could not code them as lexical gaps. The inserted lexical items included 'wrestling', 'cartoon', 'tape', 'alleys', 'research' and 'bookmark'. If, on the other hand, the Spanish equivalent of these words were indeed known to the students, these lexical insertion codeswitches would be fulfilling some pragmatic or discursive function like those proposed by McClure (1981), Zentella (1997) and Reyes (2004).

The next largest functional category of English lexemes, discourse markers, consisted of 12 tokens but only two types of discourse markers – 'yeah' and 'wait' – and all 12 tokens were produced by the two heritage students. That is, the second-language learners did not produce any English insertions of discourse markers into Spanish speech. No student in this corpus inserted a Spanish discourse marker into an English base.

Fixed vocabulary items (Examples 6 and 7) accounted for 43% (10) of all lexical codeswitches, and were almost evenly divided between Spanish insertions into an English base and English insertions into a Spanish base.

Single lexeme fixed vocabulary

(6)

[*The teacher regularly gave students marbles* (canicas) *as prizes for good behavior*]

Carolina: I got two *canicas*! Yay, I got two *canicas*!

(7)

[*The teacher was soliciting student volunteers to carry out a classroom 'jobs', one of which was collecting money for lunch* (almuerzo).]

Otto: I shoulda raised my hand on *almuerzo*.

The next category, word focus (shown in Examples 8 and 9) accounted for 60% (12) of the Spanish lexical insertions into an English base. There were no English items inserted into a Spanish base with this function of word focus.

Single lexeme word focuses

(8)

Emily: What rhymes with *educación*? [Education]
Carolina: Hold it, I have that word. *Migración*. [Migration]

(9)

Teacher: Continúa leyendo, Matt. Esta vez no vas a salir del ... vas a leer y vas a explicar.
Student: He can't find his place.
Matt: I just heard Emily go to *cimar*.
Teacher: Empieza aquí.
Teacher: Keep reading, Matt. This time you're not going to get away with ... you're going to read and explain.
Student: He can't find his place.
Matt: I just heard Emily go to *reach the top*.
Teacher: Start here.

Translations accounted for relatively few of the lexical insertions – four English insertions and two Spanish insertions (Examples 10 and 11). Finally, there was only one lexical item repetition, an English lexeme inserted into Spanish (Example 12); we will see that there were many more repairs at the island insertion level.

Overall, Examples 6–12 – fixed vocabulary, word focuses and translations – demonstrate that these types of lexical insertions are qualitatively different from the codeswitching functions proposed by McClure (1981), Zentella (1997) and Reyes (2004). That is, these three functions make codeswitching practically obligatory, not a communicative choice that carries any conversational meaning. Therefore, they merit less attention as indicators of codeswitching behavior.

Single lexeme translations

(10)

Otto:	¿Heno es un comida?
Carolina:	No, heno es *hay*.
Otto:	Hay is a food?
Carolina:	No, *heno* is hay.

(11)

| Lorenzo: | How do you say background? |
| Carolina: | Background … [2 sec] *Antecedentes*. |

Single lexeme repair

(12)

Teacher:	¿A quién enviaron el dinero? [To whom did they send the money?]
	[*Multiple answers shouted out, one of them being 'Russia'*]
Teacher:	Pero Rusia tenía mucho poder … so[25] ¿quién ustedes creen? [But Russia had a lot of power … so who do you think?]
Matt:	*Russia*. Rusia.

Island insertions

As was shown in Table 5.5, the overwhelming majority (93%, or 44 tokens) of island insertions consisted of a Spanish base with an inserted English island. Table 5.8 displays the functions of all the island insertions. As was the case with lexemes, the two most frequent functions of island insertions were that of fulfilling a lexical gap – all of which were Spanish gaps filled in with English (Examples 13 and 14) – and 'other' (Examples 15–18). I have included four examples in the category labeled 'other', one for each student. We can see that these 'other' codeswitches, unlike those

Table 5.8 Functions of island insertions

Language of inserted island	Other	Lexical gap	Repeti- tion	Transla- tions	Fixed vocabulary	Discourse markers	Word focus
English $n = 44$	17	12	8	3	3	1	0
Spanish $n = 3$	3	0	0	0	0	0	0
Total $n = 47$	20	12	8	3	3	1	0

I coded as lexical gaps, translations and word focuses, are voluntary in nature and thus carry out some pragmatic function. I could not discern any further categories, however, to code these turns in greater detail beyond 'other'.

Interestingly, these 20 tokens were equally distributed among Carolina, Matt and Otto (Melissa only produced one), indicating that both heritage and second-language students engaged in this type of codeswitch, and that the second-language student Otto did so just as frequently as the heritage speakers.

Island lexical gaps

(13)

Carolina: Cada vez que un dios moría, o un rey, lo enterraron. Y despúes *he um, they kind of like shoot him up in the air.* [Each time that a god died, or a king, they buried him. And then ...]

(14)

Melissa: Es como una guerra, pero es que como, um, estaban, um, como se dice, *like fighting each other.* [It's like a war, but it's like, um, they were, how do you say ...]

Island 'other'

(15) *L2 student; base language = Spanish*

Teacher: Si no entienden una palabra, vamos a volver a leer. Se acuerdan del método de.../

Otto: ¿Puedo ir a la baña *before we start reading*?

Teacher:	¿Qué?
Teacher:	If you don't understand a word, we'll read it again. Remember the method of …/
Otto:	Can I go to the bathroom before we start reading?
Teacher:	What?

(16) *L2 student; base language = English*

Melissa:	We're getting a Playstation.
Joaquín:	From who?
Melissa:	Well, maybe. Last year, mi hermanito y yo estabámos selling chocolate bars para su baseball team, mi hermanito, y después, y, we sold the most and so we're getting a Playstation.

[My little brother and I were selling chocolate bars for his baseball team, my little brother, and then, and …]

(17) *Heritage speaker; base language = Spanish*

Teacher:	Los cinco sentidos. También dibujen lo que se puede oír …/
Carolina:	Pero si usted, um, si usted lo está dibujando, you can't, like, taste it.
Teacher:	No, pero de todas maneras …
Teacher:	The five senses. Also draw what you can hear …/
Carolina:	But if you, um, if you are drawing it, you can't, like, taste it.
Teacher:	No, but in any case …

(18) *Heritage speaker; base language = Spanish*

Teacher:	A mí me tienen que pagar para subirme en esos aviones. Ok, um …/
Matt:	Mi hermana le gusta ir en avión. Yo tengo miedo de los aviones, porque … y ella siempre, she looks out the window every five seconds.
Teacher:	Sí, pero sabes que …
Teacher:	They have to pay me to get on one of those airplanes. Ok, um …/
Matt:	My sister likes to go on planes. I'm afraid of planes, because … and she always, she looks out the window every five seconds.
Teacher:	Yes, but you know what …

The next largest functional category for island insertions was repetitions (Examples 19 and 20), which consisted of eight cases in which a student had begun to speak in English, but quickly shifted to Spanish.[26] These are cases in which students seemed to repair the language of their turns in an attempt to conform to the Spanish language use expectations of the lesson.

Island repairs

(19)

Carolina: Is there a ri .., ¿hay un río en la pelicula? [Is there a river in the movie?]

(20)

Matt: We don't have to do it exactly like she did.
Melissa: Ya sé, pero tengo que hacerlo [*inaudible*] un poco. [I know already, but I have to do it (inaudible) a little]
Matt: No, couldn .. po .. podemos hacer otro, otro *board*. [can we do another, another]

There were just three cases of island insertions that constituted fixed vocabulary items (Examples 21 and 22) and only one discourse marker, 'I mean', inserted into a Spanish base.

Island fixed vocabulary

(21)

Melissa: Yo quiero reconocer a todos que, um, trajeron la comida del *bake sale* en, el viernes, porque tenemos mucho dinero ahora para personas que// [*inaudible*]
I want to recognize all those who, um, brought food to the bake sale on Friday, because we have a lot of money now for people who//

(22)

Teacher: Y me van a encontrar tres diferentes tipos de montículos.
Otto: Para *silent reading*?
Teacher: And you're going to find for me three different types of mounds.
Otto: For silent reading?

To conclude this section, Table 5.9 offers a combined presentation of the functions of all intrasentential codeswitches. As mentioned earlier, of these seven categories, only *lexical gap, discourse marker, repetition* and *other*

Table 5.9 Functions of all intrasentential codeswitches (single lexemes and islands)

Language of inserted item	Lexical gap	Other	Discourse markers	Word focus	Fixed vocabulary	Transla-tions	Repeti-tion
English $n = 105$	33	35	13	0	7	7	10
Spanish $n = 23$	0	3	0	12	6	2	0
Total $n = 128$	33	38	13	12	13	9	10

are similar to those found in naturalistic child codeswitching corpora (McClure, 1981; Zentella, 1997). These four categories accounted for 75% (94) of the intrasentential turns. The other 25% of intrasentential turns, those coded as *word focus*, *fixed vocabulary* and *translations*, appear to be unique to this classroom environment (perhaps other classrooms as well) and not to naturalistic exchanges.

Intersentential codeswitches

Finally, I will examine the intrasentential codeswitches.[27] Table 5.10 displays the functions of the 47 turns that contained intersentential codeswitches. These formed 27% of the entire codeswitching corpus.

As was the case for lexical insertions and for island insertions, the largest proportion of intersentential codeswitches (36%, or 17) constituted a

Table 5.10 Functions of intersentential codeswitches

Direction of switch	Other	Repeti-tion	Fixed vocabulary	Discourse markers	Lexical gap	Transla-tions	Word focus
English → Spanish $n = 16$	3	8	4	1	0	0	0
Spanish → English $n = 21$	14	4	2	1	0	0	0
Total $n = 47$	17	12	6	2	0	0	0

variety of functions subsumed under the category 'other'. Matt, Melissa and Otto produced between three and seven of these turns each, while Carolina produced only one. Examples 23–26 contain one example per student, to exemplify the similarity of these switches among first-language and heritage students.

Intersentential 'other'

(23)

Teacher: ¿Se te olvidó? [Did you forget?]
Carolina: No, no me lo olvidó [sic]. *I had, I had to go to soccer practice.*
                 [No, I didn't forgets (sic)]

(24) [*In groups, students are reading and evaluating each other's written para-graphs*]

Juan: Amen to that. Amen.
Matt: Sí, porque ella incluyó todo como, muchas palabras. *It doesn't make sense.*
              [Yes, because she included all like, a lot of words.]

(25)

Melissa: ¡Ay, no se ve! *Oh well. OK, I'm gonna take a chance.*
                 [Oh, you can't see it!]

(26)

Otto: Ms Torres, en el, um, libro de *Cahokia,* puedo ver, um, donde los, um diferentes tribus viven. *At the end of it.*
Teacher: ¿Sí? En el final del libro de *Cahokia Mounds*? ¿En este?
Otto: Ms Torres, in the, um, Cahokia book, I can see, um, where the, um, different tribes live. At the end of it.
Teacher: Yes? At the end of the book Cahokia Mounds? In this one?

The second most common type of intersentential codeswitching, pre-sented in Examples 27–30, involved a repetition. In most cases, as was seen with island repetitions, these were cases of repair in which the student said something in English but then repeated it in Spanish, most probably in order to conform to the language expectations of the teacher (Examples 27 and 28). However, in some cases students repeated or rephrased in English something they had just said in Spanish (Examples 29 and 30), perhaps for emphasis or clarification.

Intersentential repetitions

(27)

Otto: *We're readin' that one.* Estás leyendo esto. [Spanish L2 boy]

(28)

Teacher: Lo mejor sería hacer el resumen sobre las tribus. [The best would be to do a summary abou the tribes]

Carolina: *Yaay, I did it!* ¡Yo hice de tribus! [Spanish L1 girl] [I did it about the tribes]

(29)

Teacher: ¿Dónde trabaja ella?   [Where does she work?]

Carolina: No sé. I'm not sure.   [I don't know]

(30) [*Discussing which type of markers to use on a plastic transparency*]

Joaquín: It'll come off of here.

Melissa: ¿Se quita de aquí? Like does it come off if you touch it? [It comes off here?]

Most important to note about the intersentential codeswitches is that there were no patterns according to student type; heritage speakers and second-language students produced relatively equal numbers of these types of codeswitching, except for one student, Carolina, which may be a case of individual variation.

Discussion and Conclusions

This study compared the forms and the functions of 175 codeswitches produced by heritage and second-language dual immersion students. The majority of codeswitches (73%) were intrasentential, while only 27% were intersentential. Given that intrasentential codeswitching is thought to be more complex than intersentential codeswitching, this finding may reflect a relatively strong degree of Spanish proficiency by both groups of students. There were no differences found between the two types of students in either the number or the functions of single lexeme insertions in either language. Where the two groups differed was on the embedded language island insertions. Heritage speakers produced almost twice as many embedded language English islands in Spanish discourse. According to Zentella (1997) and Poplack (1980), intrasentential codeswitches beyond the lexical level are more difficult because they require greater grammatical knowledge in order to avoid violating the rules of either language.

The explanation offered here for this finding is that the heritage speakers are in fact more proficient in Spanish than the second-language learners, and therefore engage in more structurally complex codeswitching (Zentella, 1997). This is similar to past findings including Montrul (2005) on syntax and Au *et al.* (2002) in phonology. In Montrul (2005), intermediate and advanced second-language learners and heritage speakers who were matched for proficiency on a DELE[28]-based measure displayed comparably similar knowledge of the syntax and semantics of unaccusativity, which the author attributed to convergence. However, the heritage speakers displayed a significant linguistic advantage over the second-language learners. Au *et al.* (2002) tested phonological and morphosyntactic abilities of second-language Spanish learners and heritage speakers, showing that heritage speakers performed significantly better on phonology and pronunciation tests. The authors concluded that even interrupted acquisition during childhood can lead to advantages in some linguistic areas.

Turning to the second-language learners, if codeswitching is in fact developmental (Reyes, 2004; Zentella, 1997), it may be the case that second-language students develop codeswitching skills more slowly than do bilinguals. This would be due to the fact their Spanish input is limited to the school context, while heritage speakers have early and continued exposure in the home. Longitudinal work would be required to ascertain whether second-language speakers' codeswitching develops and matches that of the heritage speakers over time.

Another important factor is the amount of exposure to codeswitching. Heritage speaker children are more likely exposed to a greater amount of naturalistic bilingual codeswitching in their homes and neighborhoods than are second-language children, and this exposure to community norms of codeswitching may also influence children's exhibition of codeswitching patterns.

It must be noted that the codeswitching in this study was produced under a non-naturalistic sociolinguistic condition: Spanish was the official language of the classes, and students were sanctioned for using English. Previous work in this classroom (Potowski, 2007a) showed that Spanish was rarely (only 18% of the time) used for social, off-task turns. Thus, the students much preferred to use English, and had it been allowed, I am convinced that they would have done so exclusively. Therefore, without the threat of sanctions, little to no Spanish would be used by either heritage speakers or second-language learners, which would undermine the entire purpose of the program. This is a vastly different context from

McClure (1981), Zentella (1997) and Reyes (2004), where during free social talk the children chose to use some Spanish. In a dual immersion school where the minority language was used freely and spontaneously by the students, without threat of sanctions, different codeswitching patterns might be obtained. This leads me to offer a final word about the role of codeswitching in a dual immersion setting. It has been suggested that classroom codeswitching to clarify meaning through translation is learned at a young age and can support learning (McClure, 1981; Reyes, 2004), and some of the codeswitching examples presented in this chapter suggest that use of English does in fact support learning in this classroom. However, commenting on codeswitching in dual immersion contexts, Cloud *et al.* (2000) separate problems with lexical retrieval, which they ascribe to lack of linguistic knowledge, from codeswitching, which occurs when the two languages are mixed for pragmatic and social reasons. They acknowledge that borrowing a word or phrase from English is a creative strategy for keeping communication flowing, yet argue that codeswitching in general should be avoided in dual immersion classrooms because:

> First, it will be easier for students in the long term if the two languages they are learning are kept as separate as possible so that they have clear expectations of when and where the use of each language is appropriate. Second, since students' languages are still developing, it is likely that they are code switching because it is easier and not because they are controlling the two languages for social reasons and in a skilled way. [...] Until proficiency levels in their two languages are balanced, students should be encouraged to hold a conversation in one language only, at least in instructional settings.

When claiming that codeswitching is 'easier' for students, these authors may be referring to lexical gaps, yet lexical gaps constituted only 25% ($n = 33$) of my corpus. Therefore, the majority of students' codeswitching fulfilled other functions. Cloud *et al.* (2000) recommend that teachers can encourage monolingual production without shaming students by repeating what a student says in the single target language and expanding on it. However, in my observations, this practice does not push students to generate a greater amount of output (nor more accurate output) in Spanish. Nor does it seem beneficial to require students to repeat themselves in monolingual Spanish. As pointed out in an earlier section, immersion classroom teachers find it extremely difficult to sacrifice the content of the lesson by requesting that students repeat themselves in Spanish.

Nichols and Colon (2000) present evidence that allowing students to speak and write in codeswitched language leads to greater academic quality. The teacher in that study used Spanish almost exclusively, codeswitching himself only rarely to capture students' attention or clarify an especially difficult point. However, Nichols and Colon (2000) worked with high school heritage speakers, not second-language learners, and not with children. In dual immersion contexts, it seems to me that the best approach is for the teacher to use the minority language exclusively and to insist that students do the same, yet allow the types of codeswitching that move the lesson forward – including the functions presented here – and also those that promote learning.

Chapter 6

How Bilingual Children Talk: Strategic Codeswitching Among Children in Dual Language Programs

JANET M. FULLER

Introduction

This chapter, like others in this volume, focuses on use of the Target Language in the language classroom and takes the position that there are times and places where the target language need not be the sole language used in classroom interactions. However, unlike other chapters in this volume, this chapter looks at learners in dual language programs, not foreign or second language classrooms. Classrooms in this model of bilingual education are made up of both majority and minority language speakers who are learning each others' languages (in these data, German is the majority language and English the minority language). The goal of these programs is the lifetime maintenance of bilingual skills. The learners in dual language programs begin their experience with bilingualism at a young age – usually by the age of five – and learn the language in a natural setting, although they also receive grammatical instruction. Although the competencies of the children of course vary, as they do in foreign or second language classrooms, some of the children in this study are the closest thing to the ideal of the 'balanced bilingual' that we can find.

This research contributes to the discussion of first language use in a classroom where it is not the TL by showing that the bilingual children in these programs, regardless of proficiency levels in their two languages, all use codeswitching in many of the same ways. These data support the argument that foreign-language or second-language learners should also be allowed to 'talk like bilinguals,' and this means using both (or all) of the languages in their repertoires, that is, codeswitching. I use codeswitching as an umbrella term, encompassing all uses of two languages within a single conversation: the insertion of single lexical items from one language into an utterance in another language, switching at phrasal or clausal boundaries, or differing languages choices across speakers or turns.

The analysis here integrates perspectives from two different areas of research: the sequential approach and a social constructionist perspective on language use. The first approach is used to show how codeswitching employs strategic, and not random, use of two languages; the second addresses the issue of social identity construction through codeswitching.

The sequential approach

Work on codeswitching in the Conversation Analysis framework (Auer, 1988, 1995; Li, 1988) is often called the sequential approach, as it looks at the sequential structure of codeswitching. The sequential approach distinguishes between participant-related codeswitching, in which speakers make code choices related to the preferences and proficiencies of their interlocutors, and discourse-related codeswitching, in which contrasts in language choice contribute to the structural organization of interactions. In this view, language choice is viewed as a contextualization cue, and it shares many of the same functions as changes in volume or pitch, pauses, and other aspects of spoken language which carry pragmatic or procedural meaning. That is, the switch in code provides information about how to process the content of the utterance, for example, marking it as a dispreferred response or a change in conversational focus. Macro-social values are not attributed to codes unless they are 'demonstratively relevant' to the participants (Li, 1988: 163); therefore, without direct evidence from the conversation that the code choice is tied to social identity, this link is not part of the analysis in this approach.

Codeswitching as construction of social identity

Although we can see clear patterns in how language choice structures discourse, it would still be possible to fulfill these conversational functions without the use of codeswitching – as monolinguals do regularly in their interactions. Especially when mixing two languages is stigmatized or even forbidden (as is the case in many classrooms, including some of those in this study), why do speakers persist in using codeswitching? I suggest that the motivation for its use is linked to social identity.

Within a social constructionist approach, identities are said to be discursively brought into being (Kroskrity, 2000). Although social identity categories do exist in the minds of people, often linked to particular ways of speaking, speakers use language in creative ways to both associate themselves with pre-existent categories and to create new social identities for themselves (Mendoza-Denton, 2002). However, it is important to remember that these social identities are not fixed but are fluid, and speakers may construct different identities across social situations. There is also no one-to-one correspondence between language and identity; instead, speakers use their languages differently across social contexts to construct social identities which fit the immediate situational demands (Bailey, 2001; Blackledge & Pavlenko, 2001).

In this study, I show how these pre-teen bilinguals use their two languages to construct their social identities as bilinguals, as legitimate speakers of particular languages, and as members of multiple communities. These are aspects of their identities which are clearly linked to the languages they use, and are directly parallel to the identities of language learners in other contexts, that is, in foreign or second language classrooms. I build on other work which argues that codeswitching practices are common in the bilingual world and thus should be allowed into the classroom (Edmondson, 2004; Liebscher & Dailey-O'Cain, 2004). I suggest that outlawing use of languages other than the TL denies language students the opportunity to construct themselves as bilinguals. If the goal of language learning is bilingualism, this restriction on bilingual practices is counter-productive to the ultimate goals of language instruction.

Data and Methodology

The data here come from 4th and 5th Grade classrooms in German-English bilingual programs in Berlin, Germany; the children in these classrooms are pre-teens, 9–11 years old. All children in these programs are categorized as either English Mother Tongue or German Mother Tongue, and the other language is considered their Partner Tongue. Students of both Mother Tongues are together in the classroom except for English and German instruction, for which they are separated according to their Mother/Partner Tongue designations.

The data presented here were collected through fieldwork done in English classrooms (both Mother Tongue and Partner Tongue). From October 2005 to June, 2007, I was present in three different classrooms in two German-English bilingual schools in Berlin, Germany, the John F. Kennedy School and the Charles Dickens School. In all of these classes, I functioned as a classroom aide, a role which gave me legitimacy in the eyes of the children as well as access to their natural conversations. Because I was working in English classrooms, and the teachers generally wanted the children to speak English (either primarily or exclusively), I decided I would not speak German with the children, although I speak it fluently (albeit as a second language). Although I did sometimes translate words for the children or indicate comprehension of German, they children generally did not initiate German conversations with me. On the whole, they treated me the way they treated their English teachers – as an adult with whom it was most appropriate to speak English.

The activities I took part in within these classrooms varied from day to day. I would sometimes just observe whole class instruction, but more often the children would be working in pairs or small groups and I would either work with one particular group or float around the classroom to help the children with their assignments as needed. If the children were working on collaborative assignments, I recorded small-group conversations or children working in pairs; I did not record whole-class interactions. Over the course of the academic year I made 60 recordings (approximately 100 hours) including 65 children; the excerpts here are representative examples from this data set.

The nature of the students and their language backgrounds are highly relevant to this analysis. Although in principle it would seem that the English Mother Tongue classrooms would contain only speakers whose dominant language was English, and the English Partner Tongue classroom would be made up of students who are learning English as a Foreign language, in practice this is not at all the case. Each classroom contains students with a wide range of abilities in English, and the groups form an overlapping continuum of abilities.

Students are classified as English Mother Tongue for a variety of reasons, the most common being that they have one or more English-speaking parent and have learned English in the home from infancy on. While this may seem straightforward, it is not. Many of these children have grown up in Berlin and therefore have also learned German from early childhood on, and tend to speak German with their peers. Also, the home domain is rarely a purely English one; many of the children also have a German- (or some other language) speaking parent at home, and many of the Anglophone parents are also long-term residents of Germany who speak fluent German. A survey of the children (see Fuller, 2006) shows that *all* of the children use some form of codeswitching at home.

Either they report mixing English and German (or English and some other language, instead of or in addition to German) with their family members, or they report that they sometimes speak English and sometimes German (or another language) with certain family members. Thus these children are rarely immersed in an English context in their homes, even if this is the source of their competence in English.

The second most common reason for children being classified as English Mother Tongue is that they have lived abroad and their early schooling was in English. Some of these children have lived in Anglophone countries and were English monolinguals upon arrival in Berlin; others have attended international schools while living abroad and their home language is German, and/or another language. These varied experiences often lead to disparate levels of English proficiency.

The German Mother Tongue (or English Partner Tongue) children were also a diverse group in terms of their language backgrounds. Only about half (14/29) of these German Mother Tongue children had two parents who spoke German as their first language. Six of the children had one parent who spoke English as his/her first language Some of the children had also lived in countries where English was the dominant language, or at least a common lingua franca. Thus although the strongest language of the German Mother Tongue children was German, in many cases their experience with English was much greater than the average child who learns English as a foreign language.

In addition to these differences in background and experience external to their schooling, the children's experiences since coming to the bilingual school were quite varied. Although more German than English was heard in peer interactions, there were some friendship groups in which more English was used, a factor which also influenced the children's proficiency in English.

This overview of the participants in this research serves primarily to highlight the variation in proficiency among these bilinguals. However, I suggest that this is not as drastically different from Foreign Language classrooms as one might assume. I have myself sat in college-level German and Spanish language classrooms with other students who have traveled to or even lived in German or Spanish-speaking countries, who had parents who spoke those languages as their first language and who had themselves learned the languages as children. But in many ways, these potential similarities or differences between the population studied in my research and students in Foreign or Second Language classrooms are beside the point. Unless the goal of language instruction is to replace the first language, all language learners, regardless of their experience with the language they are learning, are budding bilinguals. If we accept this, then we must ask the question, how do bilinguals talk?

Codeswitching as a Structuring Device

The data from both Mother Tongue and Partner Tongue English classrooms show that these children use their two languages to structure conversation. One pattern of conversational codeswitching which can readily be seen in these data is the use of English for task-related discussion, and German for conversation that is not related to their academic assignments. Example (1) illustrates this. This excerpt is taken from a recording between two English Mother Tongue girls, Elena and Nora (all names have been changed), who are also fluent German speakers. The two girls being recorded are working on a worksheet about the book they are reading, *Stuart Little*. Up to this point, their conversation has been strictly on-task and completely in English. As this example begins, about five minutes into the recording, the researcher is asking them about the differences between the book and the movie.

Note that at the point where the conversation is no longer directed at the researcher (whom they consistently address in English), and veers off the topic of their assignment and into peer talk, they switch to German. After this excerpt, there is a silence of about 15 seconds (presumably as the girls write down answers on their worksheets) and when they resume talk about their assignment they once again speak entirely in English. When they are done with the assignment they begin reading further in *Stuart Little*, and the tape is turned off, so this is the only German excerpt in the 17 minute recording. German is used for a topic that is clearly (a) peer-related and (b) not directly related to the topic of their assignment, and in that way is serves as a contextualization cue to signal these two features of talk.

(1)[29]

JMF: So I suppose you guys have seen the movie?
N: /Yeah/
D: /Yeah/, I did, in an airplane
JMF: Is the book better than the movie or is the movie better?
D: Well,
M: Book
D: In the movie Stuart Little has this really round face, he looks like really xxx, and he doesn't look very thin.
JMF: You think the book's better?
D: Yeah

JMF: Usually the book is better, but this book is really
old-fashioned, so I wasn't sure if

D: Yeah, I can't, I can never read the chapter numbers,
so I have to ask my mother [Note: the chapter numbers
are in Roman numerals]

M: **(Sie sind) voll einfach.** ('They are totally easy')

JMF: {Chuckles}

M: **Hier is (der) fünf, und dann plus die zwei. Da is ja sieben**
('Here is five, and then add two. That's seven.')

D: Mmhmm

M: **Und die nächsten, fünf plus die drei, xxxxxx {sound of pages
turning} hier, fünf und drei, acht. Okay. (Das war's.) Das is
eigentlich ganz leicht. Ab neun wird's dann schwierig, weil dann**
('And the next, five plus three xxxxx {sound of pages turning}
here, five and three, eight. Okay. (That's it) That's really pretty
easy. Starting with nine it gets harder, because then')

D: **Ja xxx und bei zehn hat man Vee-Vee** ('Yes xxxx and for ten you
have VV)

M: **Ja, ich glaub schon.** ('Yeah, I think so.') (4MTKS1g:76–101)

Further evidence for this distribution of labor across languages can be found in groups of children who are not as diligent about sticking to their assignment as these two girls. Data from a group of boys in a fifth grade classroom show frequent use of German in the same way, that is, to signal peer-directed and off-task utterances. Example (2) shows a particularly salient example. Here, the researcher is discussing the themes of the book the children have read. In lines 7 and 9, Markus is teasing Nico (he seems to be talking about Nico sucking on the end of his pen), a conversation which is clearly off-task and is marked as such by occurring in German. It is interesting to note that Nico does not follow this code choice; instead, part of his resistance to Markus's teasing is to respond in English, refusing to be drawn into Markus's conversation. Contrast this with the mutual switch to German in (3), where both Thomas and Markus switch to German to have a conversation that is unrelated to their classroom assignment.

(2)

1 JMF: What is another theme, besides you know, being
independent

2 T: The town Redding

3 JMF: That's not a theme, that's a place

4 M: New York!

5	**JMF:**	Not a place, a theme. What's going, what is a lot of the conflict about xxx
6	**T:**	About the three pence taxing for the Boston tea party
7	**M:**	**Ich denk du willst den ablutschen** ('I think you want to suck on that')
8	**JMF:**	Okay, a conflict between
9	**M:**	**Doch, du nimmst den so zum lutschen** ('yeah, you use it to suck on')
10	**N:**	Stop it!
11	**JMF:**	The conflict between/
12	**M:**	/xxxx/
13	**N:**	Ha ha
14	**JMF:**	The Patriots and the Americans, or at least some of the Americans and the Patriots. So, the war! (5MTKS 3b:220–224)

(3)

T: May I please have a piece of paper, man this is getting a bit disturbing, where am I supposed to write with this thing, what the heck are you. (2) **Auch nur achtzig Blatt, ich hab' hundert Blatt, Junge.** ('Just eighty pages too, I have a hundred pages.')

M: **Ee, Junge, (komm), ich habe echt nicht so viel.** ('Hey, come on, man, I really don't have that much.')
        (5MTKS3b:288–291)

In (3), Thomas's turn begins with a legitimate topic for the classroom, the request for a piece of paper. This segues into a complaint (related to the fact that the desk is crowded with books and papers, and he is struggling to find space for the binder he is writing in). Finally, he moves clearly out of the sphere of anything task-related by teasing Markus about having a mere 80 pages in his notebook, while claiming that he himself has 100 pages in his. This move away from on-task discussion is marked by a switch to German. Markus follows suit in terms of code choice to continue on this topic, but in their subsequent turns in the class discussion, they again speak English.

Lest the reader be given the impression that the only function of German in these English classrooms is to discuss off-task topics, the next example will dispel this notion. This excerpt is taken from a recording of three fourth grade boys who are working on a poster about foxes. *All* of the talk in this approximately 20-minute recording is about the project that are working on, so there is no codeswitching according to on-task versus off-task topics, but there is still use of codeswitching to structure their discourse. In particular, German is used to discuss the process of making the poster, while English is used primarily to discuss the content material. As can be seen in Example 4, much of the English is verbatim suggestions for what should be written on the poster. They discuss the meaning of the English phrases and offer agreements and evaluations in German.

(4)

Q: **Sie sind also**, they are not very organized, **also, damit meine ich sie machen ganz wie,** ('They are then, they are not very organized, so, by that I mean they just do like')
O: You can't train them
Q: **(Gezüchtet)**, right ('(bred), right')
O: You can't train them very good
G: You can't tame them.
Q: You can't train them and they're not organized, **damit meine ich dass** ('... by that I mean that')
G: They're not **stubenrein** ('They're not housetrained')
Q: **Ja, ganz genau, ganz genau.** ('Yes, exactly, exactly')
G: They're not tameable, **ich glaube xx xxx, (sie sind nicht zahm)** ('They're not tameable, I think xxx they're not tame')
Q: **Ja, xxx ist auch gut. Ja,** they're not tame, **habe ich auch gesagt.** (Yes, xxx is good too. Yes, they're not tame, that's what I said too.')
O: Foxes ... {speaking as he writes}
G: **Ja, das haben wir eigentlich richtig /xxx/** ('Yeah, actually we have that right') (4PTKS2b:55–67)

The pattern seen in (4) is different from the previous examples in one significant aspect: it comes from an English *Partner* Tongue group. Clearly, the children's higher proficiency in German contributes to their pattern of code choice. However, it would be false to say that it was based on a lack of proficiency in English. The following examples, all from English Mother Tongue classrooms, show that English Mother Tongue children who have high German proficiency use this same pattern in their interactions. In (5), the children are creating a dialogue; Ben says something and then writes it down, then passes the paper to Elena, who says something and writes that down, and so on. Because of the considerable pauses between turns, Ben apparently has lost track of what his question was, and in line 3 initially accuses Elena of providing a response that did not fit his last utterance. This part of his turn, which is not part of the dialogue they are creating, is in German. He uses English only to provide the verbatim answer and original question. In (6), the children are doing a vocabulary exercise, and

Nathan asks for the meaning of an English word (*loathe*) in German; the answer Quentin gives is in German with an English equivalent for *loathe*, 'hating', which shows an interesting adherence to English for the content of the assignment. In (7), the children recite their answers in English, but they are framed in German (*Ich hab' geschrieben* 'I wrote ...').

(5)

B: Are you good in math? {lengthy pause while he writes this down}
E: Yes, I think so.
B: 'I think so' **kannst du auch gar nicht xxxx oh, oh,** 'are you good in math' **Ich dachte ...** ('You can't say "I think so"...oh, oh, "are you good in math". I thought ...') (4MTKS2x:112–117)

(6)

N: **Was bedeutet** loathe? **Wie heisst** loathe? ('What does loathe mean? What's loathe?')
Q: Loa:::the.
N: **Was ist denn** loathe ('What is loathe anyway?')
Q: **Es bedeutet** ha::ting. ('It means ha:ting') (4MTKS2b:69–70)

(7)

N: Ok. {Reading answer} Minute men were soldiers that were on the patriots' side.
T: **Ich hab' geschrieben,** ('I wrote'), Minute Men are special soldiers. (5MTKS5b: 569–570)

These data have shown how codeswitching can be used to structure conversation, but there are other perspectives on codeswitching which examine the social reasons that motivate speakers to use two languages in their conversation. In the next section one of these approaches, which presents language as a means to construct social identity, will be presented as it applies to these data.

Codeswitching to Construct Identity

Previous research on speakers in bilingual education programs has shown how speakers use their two languages to construct themselves, and others, as bilingual – or as dominant in a particular language (Fitts, 2006; Fuller, 2007; Potowski, 2007a). This same trend can be seen in these data. The children would often switch languages based on their construction of themselves and others as monolingual or bilingual. For instance, a German Mother Tongue boy, Oliver, usually spoke German with his friends, but used English with one particular boy, Daniel. Daniel had lived in Germany for several years, but did not like to speak German and constructed himself in peer interactions as an English monolingual. Oliver's choices went along with that construction of Daniel, as well as constructing himself as a bilingual.

One particularly interesting example is that of Jamie Lee, a 5th Grade girl at the Dickens School. She was originally from Australia and had lived in Germany for about two years at the time I began my research. Since all of the other children in the classroom had spoken German since early childhood, the pressure to speak German was fairly great; but the potential loss of face if she made mistakes was also great. In one recording during English instruction, she repeatedly uses codeswitching in interactions with her friend Magda and a boy, Karl, who is sitting next to them. Examples 8–10 exemplify this. These examples show how she uses more German than her peers in these exchanges. Jamie Lee's use of German, I suggest, has much to do with her own construction of herself as bilingual. In (8), she uses the German exclamation of disgust, *iii* (equivalent to the English 'ick' or 'ugh'), and the words *knabber* 'nibble, chew' and *ekelig* 'disgusting' in an otherwise English conversation. Note that Magda does not use German in her response. In (9), Jamie Lee opens up a new topic in German by asking Karl how much he has left to do on the project they are working on, but Magda and Karl continue the conversation in English, indicating that either they are not cooperating with Jamie Lee's construction of herself as a German speaker, or that they are constructing the situation as an English one. Finally, in (10) Jamie Lee and Magda have abandoned all pretenses about doing work and Jamie Lee is trying to teach Magda a game where they clap their hands and slap each other's palms in a particular rhythm (to the syllables Pi-ka-chu). Jamie Lee includes some German in her instructions, most notably the German discourse marker *also* (glossed as 'well'), but also the phrases *ich weiss nicht* 'I don't know' and *noch mal* 'once more'.

(8)

JL:	**Iii,** you **knabber** on your finger ('ick, you chew on your finger')
M:	No I don't, this one is broke off
JL:	**Ekelig** ('Gross')
K:	What, it broke off
JL:	**Iii,** ('ick') it's all white and dirty. Uh: (5MTDS3g:170–174)

(9)

JL:	**Wieviele Seiten musst du noch machen?** {to K} ('How many pages do you still have to do?')

M:　　Uno. One? I don't believe you. And?

K:　　And what

JL:　　And where's the other papers?

K:　　In my xxx

M:　　I don't think xxx I don't believe that's all of it.

K:　　But xxxx (5MTDS3g:290–296)

(10)

JL:　　**Ich weiss nicht** ('I don't know'), just do what I do. No, move your hand. **Also** ('so') {Girls begin doing some sort of clapping game}

JL:　　Pi, ka, chu, Pikachu up, Pikachu down, Pikachu, like, **also**, ('okay') look, you go like this. Pi-ka-chu. Pikachu up {clap} Pikachu down, {clap) Pikachu punch, Pikachu elbow {M laughs} Now you have to do right, this way, Pi: ka: chu.

M:　　Oh, got it

JL and M:　Pi:ka:chu

JL:　　Xxx jetzt hast du xxx noch

M:　　Yeah? What

JL:　　You have to hold (my ear) And then, **noch mal** ('again')

JL and M:　Pi: Ka: chu Pi: ka: chu. Pi: ka: chu Pi: ka: chu. Pi: ka: chu. (5MT DS3g:254–267)

At both of the schools, there was a strong tendency for German to be used to index peer relationships. Many children who learned German in their pre-teen years, like Jamie Lee, used German with their peers who had grown up with the language. I suggest that German use must be seen not merely as constructing oneself as bilingual, but also as constructing oneself as mainstream, part of the larger youth culture which is carried out in German.

In addition to the use of German by Anglophone children, however, we also see lots of use of English by German-dominant speakers; this construction of self revolves around bilingualism. These children have a vested interest in being seen as proficient in English; they have, after all, spent all or most of their school careers to date in programs that are focused on gaining and maintaining English proficiency. Much of the English use in all Partner-Tongue groups of children is in intrasentential codeswitching, as shown in (11) and (12). Note that in (11), although the use of the word 'family' by Oliver in the first line is a suggestion of what to write, Quentin's use of 'families' in the second line is part of an argument why not to follow Oliver's suggestion. In (12), the conversation is mostly in English because it was initiated by the researcher; but in line 7 Q switches to German, a indication that this utterance is aimed at his peers, but nonetheless he carries over the English noun 'information' and the prepositional phrase 'from me' from his utterance in line 3.

(11)

O: **Oder wir könnten ja einfach schreiben,** family, **dann können wir sagen, wieviele** ('Or we can just write family, we can say how many')

Q: **Aber aber, wir haben doch gar keine Idee von** Families. **Wir wissen nicht wie, wieviel' bei einem Geburt geboren (wurden) oder so was.** ('But, but we don't know anything about families. We don't know how, how many are born in a litter or anything like that.') (4PTKS2b:223–225)

(12)

JMF: This is really good you guys

O: I wrote all this and xxx Patrick made the sled, and I made / the xxx /

Q: / Ja::::: / and most of this information we got from me. {thumping on something} {small laughs from others}

JMF: Okay.

G: Xxx got all the information from

Q: **Ja, ja, da wir alle haben** information from me. ('yeah, yeah, there we got all the information from me.') (4PTKS2b:299–307)

In these examples, language choice does not serve to prove proficiency; but as I have argued, even when proficiency is an issue, code choice is doing more than constructing the speaker as proficient in a given language. Membership in a linguistic group is only one of many aspects of identity which are constructed through language choice. When the choice is made is to use codeswitching, a dual or hybrid identity may be constructed (Auer, 2005; Bailey, 2001; Elías-Olivares, 1976; Nayar, 2002). Many of the children in this study, who have parents from different countries and have themselves lived in various places, do not perceive themselves as one nationality or as belonging to only one group. Of the 27 children who answered a question on the survey they were given about self identity, 10 said that they felt they were German. Sixteen of the remaining 17 claimed some sort of multiple or hybrid identity, for example, saying they felt English and German, Greek and American, and so on. One child wrote, *Ich bin überall zu Hause. Ich fühle mich als Weltmensch.* ('I am at home everywhere. I am a citizen of the world'). Given these self identities, codeswitching is an unsurprising linguistic outcome of proficiency in two languages; it is a means of expressing the dual, hybrid or even international nature of a speaker's identity.

Perhaps the best evidence for 'how bilinguals talk' comes from conversations across the Mother Tongue–Partner Tongue boundary. The following excerpts from a recording of two 4th Grade girls, one English Mother Tongue (Fran) and the other German Mother Tongue (Bettina), show how they move back and forth between the two languages. In the following examples, the girls are working together to create flashcards for multiplication problems they have difficulty with; Fran does not initially understand what they have been asked to do. In (16), we see how Bettina begins her explanation of their task in German, but goes on to use mostly German, while Fran uses mostly English. But this pattern of nonconverging discourse is not consistently held; in (17), we can see that English is used for several turns, then both girls switch to German, then both switch back to English.

(16)

F: I have/problems with ele-, oh no, seven times, no, seventy-seven times ninety-nine.

B: **Ja, guck doch mal**! ('Yeah, look at this!')

F: Ninety-nine seventy-seven, **also**, xxxx ('So, xxx')

B: **Nein, guck mal, hier, xxx hier**, (No, lookit, here, xxx here') eleven times five. Or five times eleven.

F: {making odd noises}

B: Fifty-five!

F: {making odd squeaking noises}

B: **Wir können auch so ein Ding holen, na?** ('We could also get a think like that, huh?') [she means a calculator, which the boys in the group in front of them have]

F: I don't get it.

B: Look, Fran, you see this, (no) those numbers. **Oder mit irgendwas in den Kästchen hast du ja Schwierigkeiten, na? Ja, und dann** ('Or you have problems with something in the box, right? Yeah, and then') (4ATKS2g:49–61)

(17)

B: So, you see a number here? A number here. You take **zum Beispiel** ('for example'), ten, not a good example, nine, say, and let's take,

F: (xxx)

B: And then you go down and that's
F: Fifty-four.
B: Six
F: Let's do that one.
B: **Nee** ('No')
F: **Nein, warte ich check(e) einmal durch, ja?** ('No, wait, I'll check through it, okay?')
B: It's something with ni:ne. **Ja, (warte) hier,** (Yeah, wait, here') nine xxx **sechs.**
F: Nine times six is four, fifty-four. Good jo:b. (4ATKS2g:177–188)

These children, like language learners in a foreign or second language classroom, are not without their linguistic weaknesses and insecurities. Bettina, the German Mother Tongue girl, speaks English without any apparent inhibitions, but had interference in her English from German on both the morphosyntactic and phonological levels. Fran, the English Mother Tongue girl, spoke English (and Polish) at home; although she has lived in Berlin since birth and learned German in early childhood, she claimed not to like to speak German. These very different language preferences and competencies were not detrimental to the girls' close alignment in the classroom; they often sat together and chose to work together on assignments. To construct their friendship, as well as to carry out the practical matters of communication and class work, both girls use both languages. This is a choice; they have other options. Each could speak her own dominant language, for instance, which they know the other understands (as they do for a few turns in Example 16, but not consistently). They choose to use the strategy of switching back and forth between languages. Space does not allow a discussion of why these children switch at the points they do in these interactions; the point here is that these children use all their linguistic resources to get the task of communication done, which encompasses communication of their own social identities as bilinguals.

Conclusion

This chapter has shown that bilingual children – both those who have learned both languages from early childhood on, as well as those who have learned their second language in school – use codeswitching to both structure conversation and construct social identities. While language dominance or preference does play a role in how these children speak, the overall patterns of codeswitching remain the same regardless of proficiency levels in the two languages. Certain codes are often associated with specific tasks or interlocutors, and switching in these languages serve to mark changes in topic or addressee. In the English classes in which these data were recorded, English was generally used to discuss the content of lessons, while German was used for discussion of how to do an assignment, evaluation of performance, and so on, or conversations that were not related to academic tasks. English was also used almost categorically to address English teachers (and the researcher, in her guise as a classroom aide).

In addition to providing such contextualization cues, language choice is an important aspect of the construction of social identity by these speakers. Social identity is viewed in this research as something which is discursively brought into being, and as such is fluid and situational. Switching languages allows these speakers to alternate between aspects of their identity, such as being a dutiful student of English or a part of the local (German-speaking) peer network, and also allows them to create a dual identity. In this way, they create new categories for social identity – not merely (for example) German or American, but an identity which allows them to be both at the same time.

Students of foreign or second language should also, ideally, seek to construct identities which encompass identification with the languages they are learning, but they should not be forced to abandon their first-language identities to do so. I argue that foreign and second-language learners should be allowed to use their two languages in the ways of other bilinguals – and most bilinguals engage in codeswitching. The use of strategic codeswitching should be seen as part of language acquisition, not a distraction from it.

Chapter 7

Teacher and Student Use of the First Language in Foreign Language Classroom Interaction: Functions and Applications

JENNIFER DAILEY-O'CAIN and GRIT LIEBSCHER

First Language Use in the Language Classroom: The Great Debate

In contrast to earlier references to the prohibition of all first language use in the foreign language classroom, many scholars are now arguing that the first language can be beneficial as a cognitive tool that aids in second language learning (Antón & DiCamilla, 1998; Blyth, 1995; Brooks & Donato, 1994; Cook, 2001; Swain & Lapkin, 2000), and these claims have prompted them to argue in favour of some sort of principled alternation between first and second language use in the foreign language classroom. But allowing such an alternation requires a reconceptualization of the foreign language classroom as a bilingual environment and language learners as aspiring bilinguals. This, in turn, means that research on bilingualism and bilingual interaction outside the classroom has become relevant for similar kinds of research in the classroom. After all, it is bilingual speakers in general which our learners aspire to emulate. Further, it also means that classroom policies must take into account patterns of language alternation found in non-classroom bilingual communities.

One extremely common feature of bilingual speech is codeswitching, which we define here as the systematic, alternating use of two languages or language varieties within a single conversation or utterance. From several decades of research on bilingual interaction, it is clear that codeswitching is a characteristic feature of bilinguals' talk rather than a sign of deficiency in one language or the other (Li, 2000: 17). In the context of a communicative approach to language learning, then, both teacher and students need to be aware that codeswitching is a normal part of bilingual linguistic behaviour. However, in order to suggest policies for the classroom, there is a need for more empirical research on classroom codeswitching (*cf.* Liebscher & Dailey-O'Cain, 2004: 502–504), a gap that this chapter tries to fill. While we agree that codeswitching serves strategic and cognitive purposes in the language acquisition process, we also argue that it has other functions that are related to language learning as a process of becoming a bilingual speaker.

In acknowledging that systematic codeswitching can be beneficial to learners, many scholars have supported some sort of teacher-driven modeling of the desired bilingual behaviour. Castellotti and Moore (1997), for example, argue that teacher codeswitching must be deliberate if it is to increase learner proficiency, and that teachers should decide in advance of a given lesson whether they are going to use the first language or not. Macaro (2001: 545), in focusing on vocabulary learning, insists that applied linguists should be working toward 'a theory of optimality for the use of codeswitching by the teacher', in other words, that we 'need to provide, especially for less experienced teachers, a framework that identifies when reference to the first language can be a valuable tool and when it is simply used as an easy option'. Levine (2003: 355) argues that instructors should 'seek to formalize the relationship between the L1 and the target language, in order to create, in essence, bilingual norms that tend to develop organically in multilingual environments outside the classroom'. All of these arguments, however, focus on making the case for *whether* the first language should be used in the classroom, as well as *to what extent*. By contrast, we find in this chapter that when teachers make policies for first language use in their classrooms, a third factor needs to be considered as well, namely *who* is using the first language – that is, whether it is the teacher or the students.

Sociocultural Theory, Conversation Analysis and Codeswitching: Theory and Method

Our methodology derives primarily from Auer's (1998) conversation-analysis-based framework for the analysis of codeswitching in naturally occurring, noninstitutional bilingual interaction. Using this kind of interactional framework in the traditions of Sacks *et al.* (1974) and

Gumperz (1982) allows us to focus on details of the interaction such as hesitations, cut-offs and reformulations as meaningful in the interaction. It also stresses the importance of the sequential nature of the interaction, in that certain kinds of conversational moves – such as the choice of the first or the second language in a given situation – can in turn provoke certain responses in other participants. As in our earlier work,[30] we will apply this conversation analysis-based framework and Auer's (1998) theory on conversational functions of codeswitching in comparing codeswitching in the classroom data with similar occurrences outside the classroom. In addition, we will further support this analysis with observations from the point of view of Vygotskian sociocultural theory (Lantolf & Thorne, 2006).

In recent years, many researchers have grown dissatisfied with the neglect of the social dimension of second language acquisition born of the emphasis on individual cognition in second language acquisition research (Block, 2003), and have instead begun viewing their work through the lens of sociocultural theory. Because of this dual emphasis on cognition and human interaction, sociocultural theory is a useful framework within which researchers can investigate first language use in second and foreign language classrooms. It is also a natural partner for the kinds of methodological tools found in conversation analysis (Lazaraton & Ishihara, 2005; Mondada & Pekarek Doehler, 2004; Young & Miller, 2004), because it links communicative processes with the accomplishment of social relationships, cognition and human learning (Lantolf, 2004). In the context of first language use in the second or foreign language classroom, an analysis inspired by this link can reveal correspondences between particular interactional or cognitive functions on the one hand, and different types of codeswitching on the other.

From the perspective of sociocultural theory, it is important to consider not just whether and to what extent the first language should be used, but by whom it should be used. This is because conversational moves in the first language can serve different functions – or have different meanings – depending on whether the person using them is a student or the teacher. Meaning in this sense is 'not of the referential sort (signifier-signified) described by Saussure; rather, it is comprised of conceptual meanings created by communities of speakers as they carry out goal-directed activity mediated through language' (Lantolf & Thorne, 2006: 5). If we were to acknowledge that students create their own meanings out of the signs available to them – which are different from the meanings created by the teacher, even though the same signs are used – we would then admit that teacher modeling has its limitations. The implication of this is that policies for classroom use of the first and the second language may in fact need to be different for the students and for the teacher, something that this chapter seeks to show.

Data

The data on which our analysis is based comes from two German language classrooms at a western Canadian university. The first, referred to here as the content-based classroom, is a third-year seminar on applied linguistics taught in German with second language female students. Eleven class sessions were recorded, including eight regular sessions consisting of discussions of readings and three sessions where students gave oral presentations which were then followed by class discussion. The course syllabus explicitly states that the students are permitted to speak the first language (English) during class discussions, but both students and teachers spoke German most of the time – presumably because learning and using German was a major goal of the class.

The second classroom is a more conventional second-year university German class, referred to here as the intermediate language class. Eighteen students comprised this group, with slightly more women than men, and the data were collected between September and December of 2003.[31] In these sessions, students were split into small groups and asked to discuss questions or prepare a role-play that had to do with the day's lesson. Although the syllabus for this class did not forbid the use of English, neither did it give explicit permission for that use.[32] Nonetheless, codeswitching did occur in the intermediate classroom as well and was tolerated by teacher and students alike.

In the analysis that follows, we will closely examine data segments from these two classrooms in which codeswitching occurred. In our discussion of these findings, then, we will return to our initial concerns of (1) the importance of the distinction between teacher and student codeswitching; (2) whether or not the teacher needs to model 'natural' codeswitching as it occurs among bilinguals outside the classroom; and (3) the search for principled guidance for both teachers and students concerning first language use.

Analysis

The first part of the analysis will centre around a use of codeswitching in the two classrooms that has only rarely been mentioned in the classroom literature on L1 use,[33] even though it is typical for bilingual discourse.

What we mean are those functions of codeswitching which Auer (1998) has termed *discourse-related*. Such switches serve to structure and organize conversation by flagging particular conversational items as functionally different from the parts of conversation that preceded them. These kinds of codeswitches have been widely discussed in research on non-classroom bilingual interaction, such as in their functions as setting off an aside (Alfonzetti, 1995: 188–190; Zentella, 1997: 94) or marking a shift in the different roles a given speaker can take up over the course of a conversation (Álvarez-Cáccamo, 1996). Both the teachers and students use the L1 in these discourse-related ways, and in both the content-based classroom and in the intermediate language classroom.

An example of the teacher employing a discourse-related switch can be found in the following segment 1 from the content-based classroom, in which the class tries to find a definition for the term 'Gemeinsprache' (everyday language), a term used in the applied linguistics article the class had read for the day's lesson:

Segment 1:[34]

1	**BQ:**	denn (.) **it can have** (.) **like** wenn ich sage eine gemeinsprache ist kann
		because (.) when i say it's a general language can
2		es (.) äh (..) kann es teil einer fachsprache (.) sein? oder man kann
		it (.) uh (..) can it be a part of the technical language? (.) or you
3		fachsprache äh (.) wörter benutzen in einem- gemein- in einer
		can use the uh (.) vocabulary from the technical language in a- general-
4		gemeinsprache vielleicht?
		in a general language maybe?
5	**TR:**	**okay (..) you're ge- you're getting ahead of me here**
6		ähm um (.) um fachsprache zu definieren (.) müssen wir zuerst (.)
		um in (.) in order to define technical language (.) we first have to (.)
7		gemeinschafts- äh gemeinsprache (.) definieren
		define community- uh general (.) language

After an exchange in which the students discuss the concept of everyday language largely in German, the teacher uses a discourse-related switch into English to mark a bit of metatalk (line 5), which is literally a plea to halt the conversation and bring it back to the original question. While English is used for this plea, the teacher switches right back into German, and continues working on the definition of the term. It is therefore clear that the teacher in segment 1 uses English to mark the contrast between language used to give an explanation and language used to bring students back to the topic. When carried out by students, uses of English like this in a classroom setting are often assumed to be evidence of a lack in proficiency, but we are less likely to interpret the switch that way when carried out by a teacher who has both the authority of an instructor of German and the recognizable ability to speak the language well. In the classroom, these kinds of codeswitches can serve important functions in the acquisition process in that they mediate language learning and mark different aspects of meaning-making in this classroom.

Given the fact that the students in this classroom are treated as aspiring bilinguals, it is perhaps not surprising that these kinds of discourse-related switches are not restricted to teacher use, but are also done by students.[35] This is true in the intermediate language classroom as well, as the following segment 2 shows. The excerpt is from a student–student interaction in the context of group work. The student, CW, uses codeswitching to provide contrast between what he plans to say in an upcoming roleplay (in German) and the talk that sets up the roleplay (in English).

Segment 2:

1	CW:	like- like i'll ask (.) wo waren sie (.) like i'll do the intro and then
		where were you
2		like {singing} dadadadada (.) and then like (.) i'll intro us (.) and
3		then i'll be like (.) jetzt die frage (.) wo waren sie (.) an diese (.)
		now the question (.) where were you (.) on this
4		wichtige (.) ähm tag
		important (.) um day

All of the paraphrased utterances that the student will be saying in front of the class are in German, which are framed by English utterances for organizing this future talk. While the obvious pauses might have been sufficient to contextualize these differences – these pauses are in fact how monolingual speakers tend to structure discourse in these ways – the codeswitch gives him an additional tool for demarcating the two types of talk. This kind of alternating use of first and second languages has also been observed by Swain and Lapkin (2000: 257) who determine that it functions to grapple with and move the task along and to sequence the talk. From the perspective of sociocultural theory, we can further say that this use of the first language helps the interacting students establish intersubjectivity, or a shared perspective on the task at hand, which is an important element of language learning within a task-based situation (Antón & DiCamilla, 1998: 319).

The following segment 3, from the teacher–student interaction in the advanced content-based classroom, also contains a discourse-related switch performed by the student (lines 3–4) during a discussion of an article the students had read. This segment involves several different uses of the first language, whose functions we discuss further below.

Segment 3:

1	**TR:**	und beim zweiten satz (.) ist das eine aussage (.) **statement** (.) und der
		and in the second sentence (.) it's a statement and the
2		illokutionäre akt ist (.) behaupten (.) **state something**
		illocutionary act is (.) stating
3	**BU:**	**uh sorry can you repeat the- the- the meaning of** (.) predikation **in**
4		**german?**
5	**TR:**	äh
		uh
6	**BU:**	**the explanation of-**
7	**TR:**	von predikation?
		of predication?
8	**BU:**	ja
		yes
9	**TR:**	okay? (.) also wir- wir beziehen uns auf gegenstände (.) das ist also
		okay? (.) okay we- we refer to objects (.) so that's
10		die referenz
		the reference

The teacher's turn (lines 1–2) is predominantly in German, ignoring for now the two brief English insertions. Line 3, however, contrasts with the teacher's turn in that the student uses English. This switch has a discourse-related function, in that it lets the student indicate a halt to the current discussion and flag a problem with a term discussed previously. As in the two examples above, the use of English here directs the conversation with the goal of demarcating different kinds of speech activities.

Segment 3 also contains switches that carry *participant-related* functions (Auer, 1998). These are switches that correspond to the preferences of either the person performing the switch or his or her fellow conversation participants, such as momentarily forgetting a word or phrase and 'falling back' on the word from the other language, or switching to the language one thinks one's conversation partner might prefer (whether for comprehension- or identity-related reasons). All of these happen in bilingual speech both inside and outside the classroom, but as we will argue below, their functions and meanings within the classroom vary depending on whether the teacher or the student performs the switch.

The participant-related switches in segment 3 happen when the teacher gives the English translations for the German terms 'aussage' and 'behaupten', since she can be interpreted as accommodating to the students preferred language for understanding: English. From the perspective of sociocultural theory, this can also be viewed as the teacher anticipating difficulties that the students are likely to have with these terms and using the switch into English as a scaffold, that is, a device that allows the teacher to take control of those portions of a task that are beyond the learners' current level of competence and allow them to focus on the elements within his or her ability (Wood *et al.*, 1976: 90).[36] As such, the switches help students acquire the German terms as well as assist in transporting meaning. Because they construct the interaction as a learning incident, these kinds of switches are typically associated with a learning situation. In fact, they frequently occur in caregiver-child bilingual interaction (García, 1983: 155) as well, in which the child is provided with scaffolded help during the process of bilingual language acquisition.

It is important to note that these kinds of 'translation' switches take on different functions when students or children,[37] rather than teachers or caregivers, perform them. In a previous paper (Liebscher & Dailey-O'Cain, 2005: 237), for example, we find that when a student provides a translation from German into English, just as the teacher does in our segment 3 above, this is not interpreted as the student providing a scaffold for the other students who are present. While the function of this switch may in fact be intended to accommodate the other students, it also carries a participant-related function with regard to the learner herself. By providing the English reformulation, the learner transmits insecurity about the use of the German term. This is a learner-specific interpretation, since a teacher's or caregiver's codeswitch is not likely to be interpreted as indicating insecurity in this sort of situation unless it is clearly marked with rising or 'question' intonation.

A different function for both teacher and student is associated with the switch in the other direction, the translation of a term from English to German. Antón and DiCamilla (1998) discuss such cases in the classroom in which English serves as a cognitive trigger, that is, a stepping stone to help learners to come up with the German word during their own talk. In a classroom where the use of German is a primary goal, this can serve as a device that helps learners get back onto that path. An example from our data in which a student performs this kind of switch is discussed in Liebscher and Dailey-O'Cain (2005: 238). These cases can also be referred to as *self-scaffolding* (Behrend *et al.*, 1992), since the speakers are providing the scaffold for themselves rather than for other participants.[38] There are also cases in our data where the students switch into English for a term or phrase but do not follow that up with the German (e.g. Liebscher &

Dailey-O'Cain, 2005: 240). Lüdi (2003: 176) suggests that these kinds of codeswitches into the first language are used to avoid communication breakdown and to allow the student to continue holding the floor.

The function of holding the floor and avoiding communication breakdown may also be realized by a switch in the other direction: from English into German. An example can be found in segment 3 above, when the student, in line 3, inserts a German term into her otherwise English utterance. This time, however, neither she nor the teacher later on provide a translation for the term in English. This makes sense since the German term is an English cognate, which means that the translation is not necessary for determining meaning. Another function of using the German term in this example may be in establishing textual coherence through applied linguistics jargon, something that is frequently done in this classroom. Such usage corresponds to a practice Auer (1998: 7) has noted among bilinguals who insert terms from the other language in order to establish textual coherence. This codeswitch usage is then discourse-related rather than participant-related, especially if the terms are used consistently and inserted without hesitations. BU's use of term in segment 3 is preceded by a brief pause, however, indicating that there may still be a participant-related aspect in addition to the discourse-related function. One explanation for this, given that this is the content-based course, in which most of the students have been given permission to use both languages in alternation, is that the student may still be getting used to being allowed to codeswitch. In fact, in non-classroom bilingual communities, seamless language mixing unmarked by pauses and hesitations is only typical for the most comfortable codeswitchers, and it is found in contexts in which the mixing of multiple languages is not marked and is the preferred way of talking (Poplack, 1985).

In language classrooms, however, learning and practicing the second language is and needs to be the primary goal. The question then becomes how teachers can promote this goal without prohibiting first language use and thereby sacrificing the kinds of classroom practices of first language use that serve important communicative and cognitive purposes for bilingual language users and learners that we have shown in our analysis so far. Also related to this question is a second question, namely whether there is anything the teacher can do to direct the students' use of the first and second languages through strategic language choice in the interaction. We will address these two questions in the last part of this chapter.

By analysing teacher and student practices in the language classroom, we can observe their perceptions about classroom language use. In fact, even in the content-based classroom, where the use of English is specifically allowed, the teacher's use of English overall is much less than her use of German. If we count all words used by the teacher in three randomly chosen class periods – one toward the beginning of the semester, one in the middle, and one closer to the end – we find that she in fact uses German more than 90% of the time. This would suggest that the teacher believes in German as valuable input, something that we can also observe through her language choices in the segments we have already analysed. In segment 3, for example, the teacher uses German throughout, despite the fact that the student asks the question in English. The fact that she uses German, and does not interpret the student's English question as a preference for English, indicates the teacher's perception of this classroom as an environment in which German is understood and that a question in English is not necessarily linked to the fact that the student is still learning the language. In addition, the preference for the teacher to speak German indicates to the students that this class is about speaking German as much as it is about understanding the content. The student, in turn, seems to pick up on the teacher's preference for German, answering in German ('ja') in line 8 instead of English as before. The message received by the students as a result of the teacher's resistance to codeswitch herself seems not to be 'do not codeswitch', but 'speaking German is important and valued'.

In the analysis of the next two segments, we also focus on the language choice of teacher and students, discussing one type of conversational move used by the teacher that helps answer the question about strategies teachers can employ that facilitate L2 use by students.

Segment 4:

1	**TR:**	ich befehle dir herzukommen (.)
		i command you to come here (.)
2		unter welchen umständen würde man das sagen
		in which circumstances would somebody say that
3	**NI:**	**a mum (.) a mother to the child**
4	**TR:**	äh- nicht meine mutter [{laughter}
		uh- not my mother [
		[
5	**CL:**	[{laughter}
6	**NI:**	**she might not (.) i was just giving an example**
		(2 sec)
7	**OQ:**	**army**
8	**TR:**	wie bitte?
		excuse me?

9   **OQ:**   **the army**
10   **TR:**   ja vielleicht beim militär
     yes maybe in the military

Despite the fact that both NI and OQ speak exclusively English in this segment, the teacher consistently responds in the target language. While this sort of behaviour is extremely atypical for non-classroom environments, where speakers tend to respond to their co-conversationalists' code choices,[39] it is quite typical for this particular classroom. Conversely, it is interesting to note that the teacher does not enforce the use of German when students speak English. This can be seen quite clearly in the fact that the student in line 9 responds in English to the teacher's request to repeat (*wie bitte?*),[40] indicating that she does not understand the teacher's question as demanding a switch into German but rather as a simple request to repeat. The alternative for the student would be to be motivated by the teacher's use of German and switch to German herself – something that students may not be able to do without scaffolding (Lyster & Mori, 2006: 273). The teacher provides this scaffold by reformulating some or all of the students' English utterances into German (lines 4 and 10).

The last segment shows that when the teacher uses German in her reformulations of students utterances, students may, in fact, be encouraged to continue in German themselves.

Segment 5:

1   **TR:**   so in welche dieser zwei teile gehört die linguistik- die fachsprache
              so to which of these two parts does linguistics- the technical language
2   der linguistik hinein (..) **trick question**
              of linguistics belong
3   (4 sec)
4   **OQ:**   **i think in the middle**
5   **TR:**   in der mitte? (.) in wie fern
              in the middle? (.) how do you mean that
6   **OQ:**   weil es ein bisschen praktische? (.) und ein bißchen (.) theoretisch
              because it's a bit practical? (.) and a bit (.) theoretical
7   **TR:**   okay (.) es kann ein bisschen (.) praktisch sein und ein bisschen
              okay (.) it can be a bit (.) practical and a bit
8   theoretisch
              theoretical

The codeswitch in line 2 relates to our discussion earlier in that through this switch, the teacher provides an example of the functions code-switches can serve in bilingual communities. The 'trick question' tagged on to the rest of the utterance in German, again has the discourse-related function of setting a metacomment off from the rest of the talk. By contrast, the student's use of English in line 4 does not have that function. The student simply provides an answer to the teacher's question of lines 1–2, and there is no particular reason why this answer is in English other than the student's own personal preference, possibly due to the cognitive complexity of the discussion. The teacher responds to this by reformulating the student's utterance in line 5 ('in der mitte') in German, and follows this up in the same turn with a request for more information, also in German. In contrast to her previous utterance in English in line 4, the student now continues in German in line 6. This student's use of German seems to be instigated by the fact that the teacher uses German rather than English in her request for more information. The student seems to perceive this as a request not only to provide more information, but to use German as language in which to express that information, in order to practice the language they are all learning. This reaction to the teacher's German reformulation is a strong statement that she perceives the teacher's reformulation as a subtle encouragement to continue in the second language,[41] especially since OQ is a student who frequently struggles when speaking German and may therefore often choose to speak English for comfort reasons. As this example indicates, a code-switch by the teacher as part of a translation of the student's first-language utterance, may instigate the use of the second language by students.

Classroom Applications and Directions for Further Research

Our findings here support the work by previous scholars who have suggested that allowing both student and teacher codeswitching in the classroom can support learning through scaffolding or the promotion of intersubjectivity. These are functions of codeswitching that are found in non-classroom learning situations as well, such as caregiver–child interaction. They serve important purposes both inside and outside the classroom. However, while the focus in the classroom literature thus far has often been on these learning-specific participant-related switches, we also find discourse-related switches to be just as important in these classrooms, where they serve identical discourse-structuring functions to those found in non-classroom bilingual communities, both for students and for the teacher. Just as learning-specific switches can help students in the acquisition of the second or foreign language, learning how to use codeswitching to structure discourse also strongly promotes the goal in language learning of aspiring to bilingualism in that it allows learners to interact as fluent bilingual speakers do.

The analysis of our data suggests that it is important to distinguish between student and teacher codeswitching. Although the teacher in the content-based classroom[42] favours the second language even when the students are speaking the first language, the students nonetheless use codeswitching in ways that are not modelled by the teacher. These findings lead us to conclude that envisioning the foreign language classroom as a bilingual community does not entail saddling the instructor with the task of formally training learners to behave as bilinguals, or even modeling the conventional codeswitching norms found in non-classroom bilingual communities. In fact, burdening the teacher with the task of explicitly teaching codeswitching has limitations, since some of the codeswitches take on different meanings depending on whether the students or the teacher perform them – something that we not only found in our data, but which is also supported by sociocultural theory. When teachers give students permission to use both languages during classroom interaction, they tend to use them in ways that promote both second-language learning and bilingual language behaviour. At the times when students do switch to the first language for simple comfort reasons, the teacher can make use of conversational moves such as second-language translations of a student's first-language utterance that can scaffold the student's use of the second language and encourage the student to use the second language for practice purposes. Teachers are thus free to promote the target language by maximizing their own target-language use in the classroom, while at the same time making space for a bilingual community of practice – and the resulting naturalistic norms of codeswitching – to develop among learners.

In this chapter and in our previous work, we have provided data from both advanced and intermediate classrooms that suggest that learners use codeswitching in all of the ways bilinguals do, with both participant-related and discourse-related functions. Since it is clear that they are not doing this simply in response to teacher modeling, it seems likely based on these findings that even beginning language learners may well be using their first language in these same ways as they begin practicing their increasing linguistic repertoire. Further research will need to be done to confirm this hypothesis, but if it is confirmed, we will have a much better idea of how the norms of codeswitching are acquired. In addition, while we have shown that the teacher does not seem to have to model codeswitching behaviour in order for students to use it naturally in the classroom, based on the framework of language awareness, it is still possible that alerting students to the existence of codeswitching and its usefulness may have an impact on fostering codeswitching in the classroom (Liebscher *et al.*, 2007). Further empirically-based research such as the work presented in this chapter and in the other chapters in this volume may contribute not only to devising policies for classroom first and second language use, but also to drawing attention to the social in second language acquisition theory.

Chapter 8

Building Meaning Through Code Choice in Second Language Learner Interaction: A D/discourse Analysis and Proposals for Curriculum Design and Teaching

GLENN S. LEVINE

> *The authentic environment of an utterance, the environment in which it lives and takes shape, is dialogized heteroglossia, anonymous and social as language, but simultaneously concrete, filled with specific content and accented as an individual utterance.* (Bakhtin, 1981: 272)

Goals and Structure of the Chapter

The purpose of the analysis presented in this chapter is to explore some of the discursive functions of first language use in second-language interaction, as well as to expand the collection of conceptual and pedagogical tools available to the language teacher, curriculum developer, and language student to make principled use of the first language in second-language learning contexts.[43] *Principled use* is understood to mean that the speaker gains awareness of the functions of first language use as an integral part of second-language interaction and learning. In the first part of the chapter I locate first language use in second language learning within an ecological and sociocultural-theory framework (Lantolf, 2000; Vygotsky, 1978). Next I link this to what I believe is an appropriate set of analytical tools for thinking about and understanding some aspects of first language use in second-language learner interaction, namely an adaptation of Gee's

(2005) approach to discourse analysis. This approach distinguishes between 'little "d"' discourse, or language-in-use, and 'big "D"' Discourses, or the enactment of specific identities and activities. Thereafter an analysis is presented of a second-language learner conversation, focusing in particular on the ways the two learners enact Discourses as they make creative use of the first language in a second-language German conversation. Thereafter, a working definition of 'awareness' is established, for here it is important to connect the analysis with what we wish to do with it, namely use it to approach classroom first language use in a principled way. Finally, I close the chapter with several guidelines and proposals for raising learner awareness of first language use in second language learning.

An Ecological Perspective, D/discourse Analysis and First Language Use

The discussion and analysis in this chapter are based on the tenets of sociocultural theory and an ecological perspective of language and learning. An ecological perspective of language learning was developed by van Lier in his 2004 book, *The Ecology and Semiotics of Language Learning: A Sociocultural Perspective*. The book presents a sophisticated synthesis of multiple, convergent trends in philosophy, psychology, anthropology, linguistics and other fields with the goal of providing a theoretical framework for approaching *meaning, context, activity* and *learning and development*. In an ecological framework, *meaning* is always socially constructed in context and dialogic in nature; it does not enjoy an objective existence, rather it exists only for the speaker and hearer in interaction and particular contexts. At the same time, situations in which speakers interact are infused with layers of meaning that determine the ways that meaning-making in the moment can happen. This is *context*, which includes all aspects of the physical, social and symbolic worlds. Further, language is *activity*, not an object, and as such is in the world and not in the head (van Lier, 2004: 19). With regard to *learning and development*, these occur through situated activity and interaction, and through affordances for learning created by mediated activity, perception and interpretation. Learning is emergent and dynamic and cannot be accounted for in simple cause-effect chains.

An ecological perspective thus requires us to view language as situated activity in context. The way to analyze any (use of) language is to consider the 'layers' of meaning, from the situated talk-in-interaction to the sociohistorical aspects of context (van Lier, 2004: 20). Examining these layers of meaning helps us understand what people do in interaction, and how learning can or does happen. In this framework, there is no such thing as either an aberrant use of the first language by second language learners, nor a meaningless one.[44] Just as language is but one semiotic tool available for making meaning in an ecological and sociocultural-theory framework, so too is the first language but one linguistic-semiotic tool.

One method of analyzing language use from this ecological perspective is Gee's (2005) discourse analysis.[45] Gee describes language-in-use in terms of discourse with a 'little d', language that is used to enact activities and identities 'on site' (7). It's about 'getting the words right' to accomplish something with language or be a certain person using language (7). In line with van Lier's notion of layers of meaning, Gee makes the crucial observation that activities and identities are rarely enacted through language alone: 'When "little d" discourse (language-in-use) is melded integrally with non-language "stuff" to enact specific identities and activities, then ... "big D" Discourses are involved' (7). Any instance of language-in-use is *never* simply an instance of language-in-use: it is always connected to other spheres of meaning, other Discourses that both influence language-in-use in complex ways, and necessarily, language-in-use can and does affect the recreation or change of Discourses.

The Workshop Project

In this chapter I delve into numerous aspects of one half-hour conversation. The purpose of the analysis is two-fold. First, my aim is to look at numerous facets of meaning building through the first language at the intersection of multiple Discourses. Second, I intend to use the analysis itself as the jumping-off point for curriculum design and providing affordances for learning through the principled use of the learners' first language in second language learning.

The interaction analyzed here was recorded as part of an action-research project conducted in my home department in the spring of 2006, with the intention to integrate several workshops or instructional units on bilingualism and codeswitching into the language curriculum. Students were asked to attend a set of workshops on issues of bilingualism and codeswitching in the German-speaking world.[46] Eight students attended the workshops. Subsequent to the workshops, two of the students met with me outside class time for an hour-long interview and performed a few text-based tasks similar to those in their language classes. The conversation analyzed here was recorded during one of these extra-curricular meetings.

The first student, Elena, was an 18-year-old first-year university student.[47] She was born in the United States and grew up in a monolingual English environment in southern California. She took four years of German in high school. She was undecided about her major but was sure it would be in the humanities. The other student, Sybil, was a 23-year-old senior, double-majoring in Biological Sciences and European Studies. Sybil was born and lived in Nicaragua for the first 14 years of her life and was thus a first-language speaker of Spanish. She began learning English only upon arrival in California, primarily through her school's English as a Second Language program. Impressively, she joined the non-English as a Second Language class after one year in the United States.[48] Sybil did not study a foreign-language in high school and began studying German as a junior at UC Irvine. So effectively, except for her English as a Second Language classes in middle school, her first conventional classroom second-language learning experience was at the university. At the time of the study, neither participant had been to a German-speaking country.

The Data

This conversation analyzed here is typical of the sort of task both students routinely carried out during the academic term in their German classes, in this case a task based on 'discussion questions' about a short literary text. The two met in a room next door to my office. The instructions asked them to read and discuss a one-page short story by Wolfgang Borchert entitled, 'Das Brot'.[49] The entire conversation totaled just over 30 minutes, including the time they needed to read the story aloud. In line with the purpose and content of the workshops I had held, they were asked to begin the session by deciding how they wanted to deal with using the first language. They decided to use German as much as possible, and to use English only if they did not know or could not remember the meaning of a German word or phrase. They had two dictionaries with them, a German-language dictionary and German-English dictionary. Elena served throughout as the keeper of the dictionaries, looking up words for the task. The task involved four questions, one of which contained vocabulary with which the students were likely unfamiliar.

The 30-minute conversation was transcribed. There were 71 discrete uses of English in the conversation, excluding the actual reading of English words from the dictionary. Of these, 41 were produced by Sybil and 30 were produced by Elena. Of the 71 instances of the first language use, 22 involved insertion of an English word or discourse marker (such as 'well' or 'y'know'). Fourteen of the instances of first language use were self-translations or brief glosses. Further, there were just five clear instances in which the speaker abandoned German, switching entirely to English for that moment. In short, the instances of codeswitching were typical of second language learner codeswitching as attested by numerous studies (e.g. Antón & DiCamilla, 1998; Duff & Polio, 1990; Liebscher & Dailey-O'Cain, 2004; Swain & Lapkin, 2000).

Gee's Building Tasks

The purpose of the following analysis is to shed light on the ways the first language serves to help enact multiple Discourses beyond the vicissitudes of the conversation. Claims made about the ways their first language use indexes these Discourses ultimately are the basis for 'hypotheses', with further revision and refinement of the statements possible or likely. According to Gee's method, 'when we speak or write, we always and simultaneously construct or build seven things or seven areas of "reality"' (11). Gee calls these the 'building tasks' of language, of which four are applicable to analyzing the conversations between Elena and Sybil.[50] These are: building identities; building relationships; building connections (intertextualities); and building sign systems and knowledge. A discourse analysis 'involves asking questions about how language, at a given time and place, is used to construe the aspects of the situation network as realized at that time and place and how aspects of the situation network simultaneously give meaning to that language' (110). In this analysis, then, I seek to illuminate how the L1 is used at this time and place to construe aspects of context, and how context may determine aspects of L1 use.

Building identities

In order to arrive at viable hypotheses about the ways Sybil and Elena build identities through this conversation, and about the roles played by the first language in the interaction, we should consider a few of the Discourses that intersect with it. First, the occurrence of a German-language conversation between two speakers of English is itself entirely due to the educational and/or research environment in which Sybil and Elena participate. Second, there are two women 'doing being' German students carrying out a text-based language task. These first two points may seem like stating overly obvious givens, but in fact this is not an entirely inevitable state of affairs. Consider how the conversation might have proceeded if both women had been unwilling to participate in the task but were somehow forced to do so in order to receive a grade, or if they had chosen to disregard the German-language component of the task and discussed the short story in English. Either of these scenarios would likely have led to very different conversations, in structure, content and of course code choice. The point is that even the most obvious discursive practice should not be taken for granted, it always occurs with or for particular individuals in particular contexts. This conversation thus occurs in the context of a Discourse known to both of these women, one we could call 'doing being German language students who share the same first language discussing a literary text'.

As Gee puts it, discourse analysis is about making mountains out of molehills. So let us zero in on some examples of how one particular identity beyond 'doing being a German language student' is enacted by Sybil and Elena in demonstrable ways, particularly in terms of the part first language appears to play. Consider the following exchange:

Excerpt 1

1	S:	ok .. (reading instructions) zuerst sollten sie sich entscheiden ob sie codeswitching
		ok .. first you should decide whether you would like
2		machen möchten oder nicht .. ..
		engage in codeswitching or not
3	E:	ja .. ja .. ich glaube codeswitching ist ok (laugh)
		yes .. yes .. I believe codeswitching is ok
4	S:	mm hm ..ok .. (laugh) (reading instructions) falls sie englisch erlauben wann und wie
		mm hm .. ok .. in the case you allow english when and how
5		darf man englisch benutzen .. hmm .. wenn wir .. wissen nicht wie ein wort zu
		may one use english .. hmm .. if we .. don't know how a word is said
6		sagen vielleicht wir können englisch benutzen? .. .. (elena flipping spages)
		perhaps we could use english? .. ..
7		ele::na:: (tone of voice to bring elena back on task) .. was denkst du?
		ele::na:: .. what do you think?
8	E:	xxx
9	S:	alles ok? .. .. kann man einfach sprechen wie man will? .. ja ..
		is that ok? .. .. can one just speak however one wants? .. yes ..
		(S continues to read directions for task to the end)
10	S:	(flipping pages) wir müssen das text lesen ..
		we have to read the text
11	E:	laut
		aloud
12	S:	laut ..
		aloud
13	E:	ok ja
		ok yes
14	S:	vielleicht können wir um das ersten paragraph und dann .. nur das ersten
		perhaps we can um the first paragraph and then .. just the first
15		paragraph der nächsten zweite und so weiter
		paragraph the next the second and so forth
16	E:	ok
17	S:	ok .. hier xxx .. so .. **begin?**
		ok .. here xxx .. so .. begin?
18	E:	Ja ..
		yes ..

Excerpt 1 is the beginning of the conversation, starting after I, the teacher/ researcher, left the room. Sybil begins by reading the first part of the first item in the instructions (lines 1–2), which elicits an affirmative response from Elena (line 3). Here we can say that in the teacher's absence Sybil positions herself as the German Teacher (Davies & Harré, 1990; van Langenhove & Harré, 1999).[51] She then reads the second portion of the first item in the instructions (in line 4) and follows it (in lines 5 and 6) with a question characterized by marked, or clearly noticeable, rising intonation: 'wenn wir .. wissen nicht wie ein wort zu sagen vielleicht wir können englisch benutzen?' This suggests a hedge on the part of Sybil, a willingness at this early point in the conversation to yield the position of German Teacher. But here Elena is flipping through one of the dictionaries and not attending to what Sybil has said. This prompts Sybil (line 7), after a pause, to seek Elena's attention in what could be labeled a 'teacherly' tone, as Sybil lengthens the vowel, apparently to bring Elena back on task: 'ele::na:: .. was denkst du?' The way that she calls her name, with the noticeably sustained vowel, suggests that she is positioning herself in this conversation as the German Teacher. By then receiving from Elena simple, acquiescent responses, Sybil continues throughout most of remaining 30-minute conversation to enact this subject position or identity.[52] This may be related in part to Sybil's stronger German language abilities, or to some other factors; in this analysis it is actually unimportant why Sybil chooses to adopt this function in the conversation, simply that she chose to do so.

With regard to first language use, the first instance occurs in line 17 of Excerpt 1, when Sybil switches to English to command/request that they begin reading the text. The German verb *beginnen* is cognate with its English counterpart, but the recording indicates this to be a clear switch, in part because of the lack of German inflection or use of German morphosyntax (*sollen wir beginnen* 'should we begin' or *beginnen wir* 'let's begin'). This codeswitch appears to underscore Sybil's positioning as Teacher in the conversation, as marking her leadership of the conversation thus far.

In the next excerpt below, we see Sybil continuing to position herself as the Teacher, but of course she could not function as such if Elena did not position herself as the Student (imagine two people trying to lead a ballroom dance):

Excerpt 2

98	**S:**	(reading from sheet) warum lügt der mann warum konfrontiert ihn die frau nicht, wenn
99		sie erkennt, dass er lügt

100	E:	um hm .. **well** er möchte dass die .. er essen xxx er essen hatte .. und so er lüge
101	S:	aber was ist was ist die lüge?
102	E:	die lüge?
103	S:	wo ist die lüge
104	E:	er sagt um .. wann sie fand er in die küche er sagt oh ich habe die wind gehört
105		**I dunno that** .. ich
106	S:	o ja (quoting story) ich dachte es wäre in der küche es war wohl die dachrinne

Sybil reads the questions from the sheet (lines 98–99), guides Elena through the responses (lines 101 and 103), and pursues further clarification until she receives what appears to be a satisfactory response (line 105). Of interest here is the way that Elena, working in what we could call the Discourse of Student, employs English. In line 104 she begins to answer the question in the way she apparently believes Sybil to want it but then encounters what is likely a vocabulary gap. In line 105 she chooses to step outside of her answer, and outside of German, to request assistance: 'I dunno that.' Sybil recognizes this appeal for assistance and then quotes the appropriate line from the story. Here we see Elena accommodating to Sybil's enactment of the Teacher's position. Put another way, it is not just about Sybil positioning herself as the Teacher, rather also about Elena positioning herself as Student to Sybil's Teacher.

And yet, Teacher is not a consistent position adopted by Sybil, and the first language appears to mark the shift. Jumping ahead to late in the conversation, Sybil positions herself as what we could call Fellow Student with an unprompted switch to English.

Excerpt 3

234	S:	aber die seele **maybe we can** um wir können um Glenn fragen *yeah maybe we can um we can um ask Glenn*
235	E:	xxx
236	S:	**so I say it means where does the smallness of the man lie**
237	E:	xxx (laugh)
238	S:	**and the generosity of the** frau **of the woman** .. should we ask
239	E:	sure
240	S:	**because if we don't even understand the question what's the point in**
241		**answering a question**
242	E:	mm

Due to apparent frustration they are having working out the meaning of one of the questions, in line 234 we see Sybil's thoughts turning to seeking the teacher's assistance, marked by a switch to English within the utterance. Elena's response was not comprehensible in the transcription process (line 235), but Sybil makes the switch to English to consider the meaning of the question, which in line 239 Elena joins with 'sure'. In lines 240–241, Sybil remains in English to express her frustration about the question to Elena. It is interesting to add is that in coming next door to consult with me about the question, both students used only German, and I responded in the same language.

Building relationships

The exchange in Excerpt 3 is also evidence of the fostering of intersubjectivity (Antón & DiCamilla, 1998), or the marking of the relationship between the two students, in some ways in opposition now to the teacher or the task itself. Excerpt 1, line 7, in which Sybil gets Elena's attention using a noticeably 'teacherly' tone, is also an example of relationship marking. Gee (2005: 12) writes that we 'use language to signal what sort of relationship we have, want to have, or are trying to have with our listener(s), reader(s), or other people, groups, or institutions about whom we are communicating; that is, we use language to build social relationships' (see also Davies & Harré, 1990). Another example of relationship building in which first language use plays a part can be seen in Elena's use of language in Excerpt 4.

Excerpt 4

255   E: .. sie war sch .. seine die frau ok ein moment ein moment ich kann das sagen ..
256   ok .. die seele von der von der frau war starker als die seele von der dem mann
257   S: mm hm
258   E: ok?
259   S: ok
260   E: sie war die große **cavrone** und sie hat die die erliebnis in die welt .. **like**
261   **experience in the world? yeah she experienced the world better like she**
262   **handled it better**
263   S: oh:

264	E:	und er hat der mann war gebrochen und die war .. **his last pillar of .. the plank**
265		**holding the ..**
266	S:	ja
267	E:	ja

In lines 255–256 Elena works hard at expressing herself in German on what has proven to be a difficult question, both lexically and conceptually. But despite encouragement from Sybil (lines 257 and 259), Elena abandons German in favor of making her point in English (lines 261–263). This is a common code-choice practice among language learners, but in this instance it appears also to serve the purpose of marking the solidarity between these two students working out a difficult task. Elena shows that she can express herself in German with 'erlebnis in die welt' (line 260) but then translates her own statement immediately, 'experience in the world'. Such an action with language, in this case self-translation, is, in my view, not just about ensuring comprehensibility, though this is one outcome, rather also about fostering a connection to another person; at this moment it appears to be very important to Elena that Sybil understand her point, which she then elaborates on in lines 262–263, remaining in English: 'yeah she experienced the world better like she handled it better'. She switches back to German briefly (line 264), stating that the man was broken (spiritually), but then uses English (lines 264–265), albeit haltingly, to emphasize the strength of the wife in the story.

Building connections (intertextualities)

The question here is, What sorts of connections are made within and across utterances to previous or future interactions, to other people, ideas, texts, things, institutions, and Discourses outside the current situation (Gee, 2005: 111)? Of course, the entire discussion of the short story could be considered intertextual, but here we are interested in the ways the first language is used to create intertextualities, and what role intertextualities related to the first language (language/culture) appear to serve in the conversation overall. Consider two overt intertextual examples involving English uttered by Elena:

Excerpt 5

61	E:	um ich .. ich denke .. der .. ich find die eine mutter **always thinks the worst**
		um I I think the I believe the a mother always thinks the worst
62	S:	oh oh
63	E:	**a mother** und so sie woch sie wache halb drei (exclaims by inhaling sharply)
		a mother and so she week she wakes two thirty

64		und denke mein gott! das ist ein .. **robber** mit eine .. um .. **gun** ein **gun**
		and think my god! that is a robber with a um gun a gun
65		oder ein messer ein
		or a knife a
66	S:	ein ..
67	E:	**Lizzie Borden!** (makes shooting sound)
68	S:	**yeah** .. um vielleicht um wenn um ich dachte dass um der mann verrückt war

Excerpt 6

283	E:	wir haben das in die deutschkurse sagen haben gesagt in (.) zweitausendsechs
		we have that in the German course say have have said in two-thousand six
284		.. du bist hungrig?
		you're hungry?
285	S:	mm hm
286	E:	**go to jack-in-the-box! it's open 24 hours!**
287	S:	**I know!** (laugh)

In Excerpt 5 Elena struggles to make her point, indicated by the many pauses and restatements (lines 61–66). Rather than continue trying to express herself in this way, though, in line 67 she exclaims 'Lizzie Borden!' and assumes her point to be made, that at this point in the story she expected the mother to be a vicious murderer. Note that this line (67) cannot be called codeswitching per se, or even lexical borrowing, rather a sort of 'culture switching' or cultural 'crossing' (Rampton, 1995). While it is not clear whether Sybil understood Elena's intertextual reference (recall that Sybil spent her childhood in Nicaragua, not the United States), of note is that Elena invokes the story that is arguably a part of United States popular lore, in place of expanding her point in full, exactly because she can in this context.

In Excerpt 6, Elena invokes yet another US cultural icon. When the two discuss the question of whether the story is dated or timely, and whether today's generation can understand the hunger of the time and place described in the story, in lines 284 and 286 Elena says 'du bist hungrig? go to jack-in-the-box! it's open 24 hours!' As with her Lizzie Borden exclamation, this also references a specific US-cultural artifact, contrasting it with the rationing and shortages of the post-War period in Germany. In addition, in stating that the observation came from her German class she also is referencing that other 'text'. Note also that Sybil responds to Elena's 'culture switch' in English before the conversation goes back to German; this too serves as relationship-marking or building in Gee's terms.

Building sign systems and knowledge

The question Gee asks with regard to building sign systems and knowledge is, What sign systems, ways of knowing, languages or social languages are relevant or irrelevant, and how are they made relevant/ irrelevant (113)? In terms of first language use, the question is how first language use itself is made relevant, and how in this case the relevance of English is enacted in the conversation. Consider the following example:

Excerpt 7

186	S:	yeah .. ok (reading) worin aüßert sich die kleinheit des mannes
187	E:	ok
188	S:	was bedeutet aüßert?
189	E:	ein moment (looks up word in dictionary) und kleinheit
190	S:	kleinheit bedeutet etwas wie **kinda small .. the smallness of the man**?
191	E:	(long silence looking in dictionary) ich habe das nicht gefunden .. nicht hier
192	S:	(reading) aüßert sich die kleinheit des mannes .. **I guess it's asking where does**
193		**the smallness of the man lie**
194	E:	**the weakness?**
195	S:	**the smallness**
196	E:	**the smallness doesn't make sense .. what do you mean smallness**
197	S:	kleinheit

This passage is the beginning of a segment of the conversation that does not resolve or move to the next topic until line 272. In line 188 we see the attempt to answer the question held up by the need to establish the meaning of the word *äußert* 'expresses'. Immediately Elena asks Sybil about the meaning of a further word, *kleinheit* 'smallness'. Sybil switches to English to explain the meaning of the word in line 190. In line 191 Elena announces she cannot find *äußert* 'expresses' in the dictionary. Thus Sybil rereads the question and switches to English as she guesses at the meaning of the question. Note how Sybil continues to position herself as the Teacher, as described earlier, supported by Elena in line 196 as the original question is no longer Glenn's as the teacher, but Sybil's, marked by Elena's 'what do you mean smallness'. At this point we see English taking on a relevance that goes beyond the lexical insertions and self-translations characteristic of most of the codeswitching in this conversation. The switch in lines 192–193 appears to convey that English holds a privileged position when frustration enters the scene, which it clearly has with Elena's failure to find the meaning of the word *äußert* in the dictionary.

The hypothesis at this point is that English has now moved into a more significant position until the problem with this discussion can be worked out. Let us move on to determine whether this continues to hold:

Excerpt 8

218	S:	ich bin sehr .. **graceful** .. seelen, seelen ist seele **is is soul** .. **soul is the**
		I am every graceful spiritual spiritual **is soul is is soul soul is the**
219		**bigness of the soul? I think it's generosity right**
220	E:	xxx
221	S:	xxx ja vielleicht .. kleinheit **was smallness**
222	E:	**so maybe it's got like uh a bigger connotation like .. his smallness**
		o' heart
223		**like his evilness or something** (flipping through dictionary)
224	S:	**yeah maybe he's evilness ..**
225	E:	(flipping) seelen was ..
		soul what?
226	S:	seelengröße
		spiritual greatness
227	E:	(giving up search in dictionary) **yeah we're gonna go with bigness of soul** (laugh)

Up to this point the students have made a strong effort to remain in German for the discussion, but they become increasingly frustrated, culminating later on, in line 240 (see Excerpt 3 above) in Sybil's statement, 'because if we don't even understand the question what's the point in answering a question'. In Excerpt 8 here, however, we see English retaining it's privileged function, expressed in line 227: 'yeah we're gonna go with bigness of soul'. To understand what is meant by 'privileging' English here we need only consider ways Elena might have otherwise expressed herself here. Clearly the entire conversation shows that both women are able to switch at will between German and English; Elena could have said simply '*wir akzeptieren* bigness of soul' or similar, but using 'we're gonna go with' underscores that this is a task to be performed, a set of decisions to make to satisfy its demands, in this case the very meaning of the question; for this, English itself is given relevance and significance as a discursive tool.

Building Meaning Through Code Choice and Awareness

In the preceding sections, I have analyzed several examples of learner use of the first language in a second-language task and hypothesized how the first language appears to be used to enact particular identities, build relationships, mark intertextualities (which themselves serve to enact identities and foster intersubjectivity) and enact or mark sign systems and knowledge, which in this case means privileging or making relevant the first language *over* the second language. My chief concern is for the ways in which instances of first language use serve to enact Discourses beyond the moment and place these speakers in this conversation within historical bodies or trajectories. What I have highlighted is thus the *what* of awareness-raising with regard to code choice.

In the interaction between Sybil and Elena it is quite clear that neither student was 'aware', in the sense of consciously attending to, their use of the first language as they used it, despite the fact that they began the conversation with the official sanction to codeswitch if need be. In this regard, codeswitching in learner conversation indeed just 'happens' in many of the same ways it happens in bilingual conversation in societal (i.e. non-language classroom) bilingual or multilingual situations (Chavez, 2003; Dailey-O'Cain & Liebscher, this volume). At issue is not whether learners engage in codeswitching in 'unconscious' (i.e. in not-attended-to ways), for clearly they do. Rather we are concerned about whether teachers and learners can make principled pedagogical use of this fundamental aspect of learner interaction.

But here the term 'awareness' should be clarified. This term is both ambiguous and variously defined and described in the literature, often with apparent circular definitions, such as 'consciousness is awareness of ...'. There also appears to be quite a bit of overlap in definitions and usage of the terms awareness, attention, consciousness, noticing, and so on. van Lier (1996) sees awareness as one of a trio of key factors involved in second language learning, together with autonomy and authenticity. Based on Schmidt (1995), van Lier distinguishes between consciousness and awareness, with consciousness implying the intentional focus of attention. So when we say the learner is 'aware' of some aspect of language or social activity using language, we do not always mean that the speaker *consciously attends* to details during talk-in-interaction. Yet a speaker in interaction is 'aware' of myriad aspects of both the discourses (getting the words right) and the Discourses enacted through the conversation, as evidenced not so much by what the speaker says or does at any given moment, rather by what she or he *does not say or do*. Consider the simple fact that Elena and Sybil 'agreed' to allow codeswitching prior to beginning the task. They both knew, or were aware of, what codeswitching is by virtue of the workshops I had held. They also were aware of the fact that they were German language students, and of course that they were both speakers of English. To illustrate the role of awareness of all these factors facilitating the ways the first language was used in the conversation, we need only suppose how the conversation might have gone had one of the interlocutors been a monolingual, native-speaker of German. Here awareness of this fact would be important; the second language learner would know that the first language use would not be available as a tool. Or consider how the conversation might have gone had I 'forbidden' first language use. We know from numerous studies that English still would have played a role in the conversation, yet that role would likely have manifested itself differently from how it did in this conversation.

Hence, awareness and consciousness are different. Consciousness is characterized by attention and intentional control; awareness is knowledge of the very sorts of Discourses we have been looking at in the conversation between Elena and Sybil. This conversation, in the exact form it took, was possible only and entirely because the two students were *aware* of the many Discourses being enacted and of the discourses (getting the words right) available to them in this situation.

This brings us now to the question of the curriculum design and teaching, of ways we can make use of these insights about first language use to provide affordances for learning. If we seek to raise learner awareness of the roles of the first language in second language communication and learning, what are the parameters of this awareness? I propose the following:

- awareness of codeswitching as normal verbal behavior for bilinguals (destigmatize codeswitching);
- awareness of (some) purposes of codeswitching in conversation;
- awareness and destigmatization of and identification with bilingual speakers in the target culture.

Seen in this way, awareness as the foundation of a principled approach to code choice is *not* then about consciously controlling the codeswitching during talk-in-interaction, though this may happen, rather it is about raising learner awareness of some of the Discourses and discourses speakers may enact.

With regard to awareness of first language use as part of the language curriculum, few language professionals would argue against the assertion that students in the classroom should use the second language as often and as richly as they are able for their language level. At the same time, teachers' experiences and the now numerous studies of first language use in second language learning show that regardless of whether the teacher uses the second language most or all of the time, and whether or not the teacher 'forbids' the use of the first language, students in fact use their first language in myriad ways when they communicate in the classroom. Yet simply 'allowing' the first language in classroom communication is neither sufficient nor pedagogically sound, any more than simply 'allowing' any other approach, method, or technique to be adopted in an unprincipled manner. Though we may be living in a postmodern era of eclectic choice in all spheres of life, pedagogical practice need not devolve into an anything-goes, meaningless relativism; to create affordances for learning in a classroom setting, the teacher or curriculum designer should have a sense of the range of choices and relative truths that can prevail and serve students in context.

There are two things I have tried to show through the analysis of the conversation between Sybil and Elena that relates to curriculum and teaching. First, nearly every use of first language in talk-in-interaction serves discourse-related functions, but it also enacts Discourses beyond the moment. Context is created by first language use but also knowledge of context serves to enrich our understanding of what these learners are doing with language. Second, Sybil and Elena's 'awareness' serves to build meaning in interaction, and it allows them to carry out the task using the first language and the second language in creative and dynamic ways. I suggest that raising learner awareness of these very patterns can enrich communication and learning in ways that should create affordances for sophisticated communication and learning, and at the very least, contribute to destigmatizing the use of the first language in the language classroom.

Proposals and Guidelines for Curriculum Design and Classroom Affordances

In this last section I offer several proposals and guidelines for applying the ideas thematized in this chapter to curriculum design and classroom practice. This list is of course not comprehensive, rather a starting point intended to be expanded, revised and adapted through further empirical work as well as teaching and learning practice.

Teach students the terminology and concepts to discuss bilingualism and codeswitching

Too often teachers keep many of the 'secrets' of linguistics, applied linguistics and language pedagogy out of classroom. It is not important whether this is because we believe the ideas of these fields are too difficult for students to understand, or whether one thinks we should maintain some magician-like ethos in the profession. Whatever the root of current practice, I propose that we allot time in our curricula for explicit attention to some of the concepts we use to think about language, language learning and teaching and relationships between language, culture (in its many definitions), history, politics, and so on.

Develop instructional units dealing with bi- or multilingual individuals or communities in the L2 culture

Broadening the scope of letting students in on what we do, I also propose, as I have presented elsewhere (Levine, 2005) that students study and learn about bilingual/multilingual situations in the target culture. This need not be only in the form of tangential or 'extra-curricular' learning, rather it can be integrated into the fabric of activities that make of the 'normal' business of the language classroom. For example, students can learn about and discuss texts, video, audio or other materials about bilingual individuals (such as authors or entertainers) or communities, either from the perspective of the ways they use language, or from other perspectives (social, historical).

Perform 'discourse analyses' of bilingual/multilingual speech with students

Either as part of the preceding proposal or independently of it, teachers can engage with their students in various sorts of 'analysis' of conversations or texts. While some teachers may scoff at this as a mode of language classroom activity, one need only consider what sorts of critical thinking activities are going on in any number of other courses at the university, activities that conventional communicative language teaching has tended to keep out of the largely 'skills-based' language classroom. These classroom analyses can be based on transcripts and/or recordings of actual bilingual conversations, which are available from a number of sources, including the applied linguistics literature, recorded by students themselves, or taken from commercial or Internet audio or video recordings. Students can perform lay analyses of these texts in order to gain insights into how the languages of the speakers in the texts are used in 'real life' situations. In addition, this sort of close examination of bilingual language use can serve to validate learners' own language as emerging bilinguals themselves.

Develop explicit, collaborative classroom norms for first language use

As outlined in Levine (2005), teachers and students can use class time to analyze and discuss the roles the first language can or should play in their own classrooms, specific to the place, time and goals of the particular learning environment. They can then 'agree' on acceptable norms for different sorts of situations. Whether these 'rules' end of being followed or flouted is of course of consequence, and should be examined and reflected upon (see last item below), but of undeniable value is the way this sort of discourse in the classroom serves to draw learners' attention to numerous important aspects of little-d discourses at work in classroom interaction as well as of these ways these might be related to some big-D Discourses.

Develop classroom surveys or use recordings to assess and evaluate the role of the first language and code choice practices overall

At intervals it could be useful for teachers and students to take a measure, in the form of surveys or audio or video recordings, of how language is being used in the classroom, and in particular on the roles and functions the first language appears to serve. 'Othering' the entire class's own discursive practices in this way need not be time consuming, but it could be invaluable in giving learners insights into, and in granting them a stake in, how their language learning proceeds and how they develop as users of both their new second language and their first language.

Chapter 9

The Impact of Pedagogical Materials on Critical Language Awareness: Assessing Student Attention to Patterns of Language Use

CARL S. BLYTH

Introduction

This chapter reports on an exploratory, qualitative study based on a foreign language program that developed an online curriculum featuring linguistic hybridity and bilingualism. In addition to bilingual speakers, the new materials also included a much wider range of proficiencies than what is typically found in commercially-produced materials: from fluent bilinguals to so-called 'incipient' bilinguals (i.e. second language learners). The materials explicitly contrasted two groups of bilingual speakers in a series of videos: native European French speakers living in the United States and American students just beginning to learn French. All native French speakers had lived in the United States for many years, were married to an Anglophone spouse, and had achieved a superior level of proficiency in English. In contrast, the American students possessed variable levels of French proficiency – from novice to intermediate. Their frequent grammatical mistakes and communicative difficulties were captured on the videos and became part of the input for learners.

Consciously designed to increase learner awareness of authentic language use and of the language learning process itself, these videos were intended to help learners project themselves onto the virtual identities of the non-native speakers who were beginning foreign language students themselves. Previous formative evaluation of the materials had been limited to usability studies and surveys of student satisfaction (Blyth & Davis, 2007). As such, little was known about whether the videos achieved the goals intended by the developers – to raise student consciousness about the nature of bilingualism and second language learning. This chapter reports on a qualitative study designed to answer four research questions:

(1) Do beginning Anglophone students notice the use of English in videos of spontaneous French discourse?
(2) Does the proficiency of the speaker in the video affect whether students notice the use of English?
(3) If students do notice the use of English in the videos, how do they interpret such behavior?
(4) How do students feel about the inclusion of non-native speakers in pedagogical materials?

Re-examining the Ban on First Language Use: From Classrooms to Textbooks

Throughout the 1990s, scholars reexamined the consequences of the 'myth' of the idealized educated native speaker for applied linguistic research, not only challenging the *identity* but also the *authority* of the native speaker (Blyth, 1995; Byram, 1998; Cook, 1992, 1999; Davies, 1991; Koike & Liskin-Gasparro, 1999; Kramsch, 1997; Ortega, 1999a, 1999b; Rampton, 1990, 1995). These articles prompted subsequent research concerning the proper use of the L1 in foreign and second language classrooms (Chavez, 2003; Cook, 2001; Levine, 2003, 2005; Liebscher & Dailey-O'Cain, 2004; Macaro, 2001; Turnbull, 2001; Turnbull & Arnett, 2002). This line of research analyzed student–student and student–teacher interaction in an effort to discern the cognitive and affective benefits of the L1 (e.g. increased learner efficiency and attention, improved interpersonal interaction, more positive attitudes toward language learning, etc.).

Despite interest in classroom language, the language used in pedagogical materials received much less attention. This is not to say that the reexamination of the native speaker construct and the ideology of monolingualism had no consequences for textbooks. In fact, throughout the 1990s, scholars criticized textbooks for presenting idealized versions of the foreign language and culture that unwittingly reinforced stereotypes (Heilenman, 1993). These studies typically showed that textbooks over-represented certain social groups, namely educated speakers of the prestige dialect, for example, bourgeois Parisians and wealthy Madrileños (Ramirez & Hall, 1990; Wieczorek, 1991, 1994). According to Blyth (1995: 169), language educators who bemoaned the lack of sociolinguistic diversity in pedagogical materials, rarely seemed to notice the lack of multilingual speakers:

> While there are encouraging signs of a multicultural trend in textbook publication, most foreign language textbooks depict foreign personages – real or imagined – as bearing a striking resemblance to Chomsky's *ideal speaker-listener*; they inhabit a homogeneous speech community and they know the language perfectly. In other words, the people populating textbooks are almost always monolingual native speakers.

Exhorting teachers to reimagine the foreign language classroom as a multilingual speech community where students were best seen as 'incipient bilinguals' rather than 'aspiring monolinguals', Blyth (1995: 169) noted the irony of using monolingual speakers as role models for learners striving to overcome their own monolingualism. In addition to calling for multilingual speakers as role models, Blyth (1995: 170) argued for the inclusion of non-native speakers in pedagogical materials.

Français Interactif: From Monolingual to Multilingual Role Models

In 2004, the Lower Division French program at the University of Texas at Austin, launched a curriculum that sought to reframe the first year French course in terms of bilingualism. The new online curriculum, entitled *Français interactif* (Kelton *et al.*, 2004) focused on the subjective language learning experiences of a group of actual students enrolled at the University of Texas during their study abroad program in Lyon, France. In essence, these real-life study abroad students serve as virtual tour guides assisting students 'back home' who watch the videos in their classrooms and homes. In the videos, the study abroad students speak in a mixture of French and English, communicating as best they can.

In addition to the videos of American students living in France, the program also includes videos of native French speakers living in America. By juxtaposing videos of incipient and fluent bilinguals, the developers hoped to raise learners' awareness about the nature of bilingualism and second language learning. The pedagogical agenda of *Français interactif* was inspired, in part, by recent work in the field of Critical Language

Awareness. According to Fairclough (1992), language awareness in most classrooms is uncritical and prescriptive, leading students to become aware of language production only in terms of how it deviates from the native standard. Train (2003: 16) describes Critical Language Awareness as an attempt to problematize the notions of accuracy and appropriateness based on native-speaker norms that reflect the language practices of a dominant group in society. Train (2003: 16) maintains that the overarching goal of Critical Language Awareness is 'more inclusive conceptions and practices of language and culture'.

Affordance and projective identities

While the pedagogical materials contain no mention of codeswitching, lexical borrowing and grammatical transfer, such bilingual phenomena are present throughout the videos for students to notice and analyze. But this raises two questions: Do students even notice such language behavior? And, if so, does this affect whether they identify with some speakers and not others?

Central to these questions are three psychological constructs – affordance, virtual identity and projective identity. The term affordance originates with the psychologist Gibson (1979: 127) who defined it as 'what the environment offers the animal, what it provides or furnishes, either for good or ill'. Simply put, an affordance is an opportunity for learning that exists in a given environment. In this sense, the videos in *Français interactif* are affordances waiting to be noticed and interpreted. van Lier (1996, 2004) argues for replacing the mechanistic term *input* with the semiotic-ecological term *affordance* because it highlights the dynamic triadic relationship between the learner, the object perceived by the learner and the learner's interpretation of the object.

The notion of videos as affordances is also related to the concepts of virtual and projective identities (Gee, 2003). Recall that the developers of *Français interactif* intended for classroom learners to identify with the study abroad students caught on video, the so-called virtual tour guides who explore the foreign language and culture *for the students back home.* In fact, one of the most often expressed goals for the materials was to motivate beginning language students to follow in the footsteps of their virtual role models and choose to study abroad. It was hoped that learners would initially identify with the study abroad students but then eventually go beyond these role models and project new identities for themselves based on their own values and goals for language learning. The transformation intended by the developers reflects Gee's (2003: 208)

Identity Principle, a formal statement of classroom learning as a process of identity construction entailing three separate, yet related identities: the learner's real-life identity, the virtual identity (as represented by the teacher or more advanced peer) and the projective identity (the learner's new, imagined identity).

Identity principle

Learning involves taking on and playing with identities in such a way that the learner has real choices (in developing the virtual identity) and ample opportunity to meditate on the relationship between new identities and old ones. There is a tripartite play of identities as learners relate, and reflect on, their multiple real-world identities, a virtual identity, and a projective identity. (Gee, 2003: 208)

Overview of *Français interactif*

Français interactif is built around various communicative tasks that language teachers commonly want their students to perform (e.g. identifying the members of one's family, etc.). The developers videotaped native and non-native speakers performing these tasks and inventoried the vocabulary and grammar used to perform the task. These inventories became the basis for 13 chapters with different themes. For instance, chapter nine focuses on current events in the context of French media–newspapers, radio, internet, television, cinema, and so on.

Each chapter contains three different kinds of videos that feature the voices of native and non-native French speakers:

(1) *Introductory video.* Each chapter begins with a short video of a student in France who presents the chapter's thematic and grammatical material.
(2) *Vocabulary presentation videos.* These videos present vocabulary items in an authentic cultural context. To make these contexts more accessible for beginners, the videos aim at maximizing the redundancy between the visual image and the spoken language.
(3) *Video interviews.* Four native French speakers and three non-native French speakers (American students) were interviewed discussing the themes of each chapter. In these unscripted interviews, speakers respond to questions that require them to employ the grammar and vocabulary featured in the chapter. These videos are accompanied by an online transcript of the French and an English translation.

Language Awareness Research

Recent studies in second language acquisition have increasingly suggested that some degree of learner awareness or attention is a necessary but not a sufficient condition for adult language learning (Leow, 1997, 1998; Schmidt, 1993, 2001; Tomlin & Villa, 1994). At the heart of these studies is the so-called Noticing Hypothesis: 'Second language acquisition is largely driven by what learners pay attention to and notice in target language input and what they understand the significance of noticed input to be' (Schmidt, 2001: 3–4). The growing interest in the attentional processes of learners has in turn given rise to focus-on-form studies that manipulate target language input in an effort to render pre-selected linguistic forms more cognitively salient to the learner (Bardovi-Harlig & Reynolds, 1995; Doughty & Williams, 1998; Jourdenais *et al.*, 1995; Leeman, 2003; Leeman *et al.*, 1995).

While these psycholinguistic studies differ in significant ways, their point of departure is the same – the controlled manipulation of the input itself. Moreover, these studies are also similar in their focus on grammar (typically morphosyntax) as opposed to discursive or interactional patterns. Nevertheless, it seems highly plausible that characteristics of the speaker (e.g. sex, age, occupation, etc.) might render patterns in the input more or less salient for learners. Thus, the basic premise motivating the present study is a well-accepted sociolinguistic fact: utterances are interpreted for social information (information referring to the social context) in addition to the so-called propositional content. In more simple terms, utterances are attended to and interpreted in terms of who is speaking. Therefore, it is likely that learner awareness of grammatical or discursive form is affected by social and affective factors (e.g. whether one identifies with the speaker).

The study of metalinguistic awareness, the awareness of language as a formal object to be controlled and manipulated, has generally been considered the purview of psycholinguistics (Birdsong, 1989; although see Preston, 2004 for a sociolinguistic approach). For example, there have been many empirical studies concerned with the relationship between language learners' metalinguistic knowledge and their second language proficiency. These studies typically employ test-based instruments. According to Roehr (2006: 180), the 'tests of metalinguistic knowledge employed in such research usually require participants to judge the grammaticality of L2 sentences, to identify and correct errors, and to state the violated grammar rules'. Roehr (2006: 180) summarizes the three major findings of such research: (1) learners do not always learn the rules they are taught; (2)

some grammar rules and categories are acquired more successfully than others; and (3) moderate positive relationships between level of second-language proficiency and levels of metalinguistic knowledge have generally been identified. Based on her review of the research, Roehr (2006: 182) calls for more qualitative research, especially fine-grained analyses of small data sets: '... a qualitative perspective seems to be just what is needed to shed more light on the construct of metalinguistic knowledge and its possible role in instructed L2 learning'.

Research Method

The methodology for this study consisted of an immediate recall protocol followed by a guided interview to investigate learner awareness of code mixing while performing a typical pedagogical task that required students to fill out a form with the correct information. The protocols were tape recorded for later transcription and analysis. Eleven students who were all enrolled in different sections of the same second semester beginning French course watched short video clips of native and non-native speakers of French on a computer screen. The speakers in the videos all answered the same series of questions. The videos appeared alongside several online tools meant to aid comprehension (e.g. clickable transcripts of the interviews as well as English translations). After viewing each video, the participants were required to perform an immediate verbal recall (Egi, 2004; Philip, 2003).

The 11 participating students were asked the same question after watching each of the seven interview videos appearing in Chapter 9: 'What were you thinking while watching this video?' The students watched the videos in the order that they appear on the website, beginning with the four French native speakers (Franck, Virginie, Jean-Charles and Stéphanie), and then followed by the three American students (Laila, Blake and Karen). The two groups of speakers who appear in the interviews are clearly indicated on the website: *Les Français à Austin* (The French in Austin) and *Les étudiants – UT-Austin* (The students – UT-Austin).

After watching the videos, the participants were asked to recall in as much detail as possible what they had been thinking during the task. Because it is quite possible to perform the task without noticing the targeted phenomena, a summative interview followed the recall protocols in order to establish whether the targeted phenomena had been noticed. Equally important, the summative interviews indicated the participants' evaluation of the targeted language behavior and produced a large data set of folk metalanguage, that is, descriptions of bilingual behavior by nonlinguists (Preston, 2004).

Results of Immediate Recall Protocols

Thoughts about comprehensibility

While two participants made no metalinguistic comments at all during their recall protocols, the other nine participants made frequent metalinguistic comments that focused on two major topics: the comprehensibility of the speakers' discourse and the speakers' linguistic proficiencies. Given that the protocols were based on a comprehension task, it is understandable that comprehensibility turned out to be a frequent topic. Participants noted that comprehensibility was affected by the rate of speech, the familiarity of the referent (e.g. American vs. foreign referents), the accent (American vs. French), the size and complexity of the vocabulary, the length of the answer the directness of the answer and various structural properties of the answer (e.g. whether the answer echoed the syntactic frame of the question). These linguistic properties and their effect on comprehensibility are mentioned in (1) and (2).

(1)

(Jean-Charles – native speaker)[53]
He is really hard to understand. He talks really fast. Have to pay attention or you'll miss it ...

(Laila – non-native speaker)
It is easier to understand her because she talks slower. Things that she says are Americanized. It was very easy to understand what her TV series was ...

(Blake – non-native speaker)
Blake is very simple in his answers and I understand him perfectly. I know exactly what he is saying.

[participant 2]

(2)

(Virginie – native speaker)
I could understand. Yeah ... her answers were pretty short.

(Jean-Charles – native speaker)
He speaks really, really fast. And his answers are really long. And ... I dunno. He generally doesn't answer direct.

(Stéphanie – native speaker)
Ahmmm ... that was good! She was pretty easy to understand. She ... I dunno. Stéphanie is my favorite.

[participant 6]

Thoughts about linguistic proficiency

The next most prevalent metalinguistic topic discussed in the protocols was the proficiency of the non-native speakers. Note that while participants frequently compared the comprehensibility of both native and non-native speakers as seen in (1) and (2), they only compared non-native speakers in terms of their proficiencies. In (3), evaluations of the non-native speakers' accents are embedded in what is otherwise a rambling recall of a wide variety of thoughts and associations. Note that the participant closely identifies with Blake's lack of proficiency and infers that Blake must feel anxiety because of his inadequate skills.

(3)

(Laila – non-native speaker)
Ah, I was thinking that she had a pretty good accent. Uhmmm .. and that I hate the Simpsons. She's from Dallas. I wonder what high school she went to. I looked at her shirt – pretty color. Pretty typical American teen from her answers.

(Blake – non-native speaker)
I think he is a sweet guy. He tries. I like how … I can tell that he tries really hard. And more … his accent is definitely a work in progress and that is something that I can relate to. That's something that he struggles with. He looks like a student. Yeah, I can relate to that, being on the spot kind of thing. He appears to be uptight. He's holding his breath which is exactly what I do when trying to speak French.

(Karen – non-native speaker)
Karen, uhm, well she looks tired too. I guess I always expect funny answers from her. She is kinda out there. And … I think she has a good accent.
[participant 4]

Participants not only compared the non-natives to each other as in (3), but they also tended to compare the non-natives to themselves. According to Gee's Identity Principle, the learner's new, projective identity is based on 'relevant' virtual identities. In other words, students saw themselves in the virtual identities of the less proficient speakers but were unable to see themselves in native speakers whose linguistic identities proved less relevant. In (4), while the participant evaluates Laila as being more fluent than the other students ('no painful, awkward pauses'), she identifies more with Blake because of his lack of proficiency.

(4)

(Laila – non-native speaker)
I think that Laila is probably the ... one of the students with a higher level of French in the whole project. Her answers are always a little better developed. I guess better, more fluid French. I guess she demonstrates better what they are trying to get you to learn in this chapter specifically cause her video is a little better.

(Blake – non-native speaker)
I think his answers are – a little more pauses, I guess. He's more, more around my level of French. He's probably just starting out.

[participant 5]

Thoughts about the use of English

In contrast to the frequent remarks about comprehensibility and proficiency, only two protocols out of a total of 77 contained comments about the use of English. In both cases, the remarks were triggered by Karen's video as noted in (5) and (6). In both instances, the use of English was judged negatively and in (6) was attributed to Karen's lack of vocabulary.

(5)

(Karen – non-native speaker)
It's always hard to understand her because she mixes a lot of English with her answers. She tries to make an English word sound French, y'know.

[participant 1]

(6)

(Karen – non-native speaker)
She's like Stephanie. It is hard for her to answer the question straight. She expands on it more than necessary. It is very contradictory. She likes to talk. She doesn't get a lot of things right. She doesn't know a lot of the vocabulary so she'll say it in English which makes it easy for us but defeats the purpose of the exercise cause it's not suppose to be in English.

[participant 2]

While these were the only two participants to mention Karen's use of English during the recall protocols, all eleven participants noted Karen's frequent use of English during the summative interview.

Thoughts about the task

In general, it appears that most participants were preoccupied with managing the task. In (7), the participant recalls thinking about how much information is appropriate as well as where to write the information on the page.

(7)

(Virginie – native speaker)
The first thing I started thinking about ... uhm ... she mentioned that she watched children's videos and I wasn't sure for a minute where to put that – under films or TV. And then I decided to put it into TV because it wasn't her favorite film.

(Jean-Charles – native speaker)
I was thinking about what he said, what was worth writing down and what wasn't worth writing. Because he said a lot of different things for each section ... 'Cause with shorter sentences it's OK to write down the whole thing and in class you can read it.

[participant 8]

Some participants recalled thinking about the most efficient way to find the right answer – by watching and listening to the video or by going straight to the transcripts and translations. In (8) the participant recalls 'cheating', that is, relying on the written texts instead of listening.

(8)

(Franck – native speaker)
I was focused on getting the right information. Trying to understand what he was saying, gonna say. And I cheated and looked at the English vocabulary ... I would read through the French conversation and then I would kinda half listen but I would mainly read. And then I would look at the English translation if I am not sure of something.

[participant 5]

In (9) and (10), the strategy of reading rather than listening is revealed to be the typical way that some students perform this task as part of their homework routine.

(9)

(Franck – native speaker)
Well, I think overall, it is really easy to understand what he was saying but you can't help but look right there (points to transcript on screen).

So, I'm not really listening that much. Honestly, a lot of times I wouldn't listen, I would just read it.

[participant 6]

(10)

(Franck – native speaker)
... And when I do my homework, I almost never listen to the talking and then go back.

[participant 8]

Thoughts about personality and affect of interviewees

Many participants recalled thinking about the personalities and attributes of the interviewees. These thoughts were often triggered by the interviewee's responses to the questions, but participants' thoughts were also the result of the interviewee's appearance or affect as in examples (11), (12) and (13).

(11)

(Jean-Charles – native speaker)
He always looks uptight ... His body language seems very stern, straightforward, poker face. Seems like he's not really into it.

(Stéphanie – native speaker)
My initial reaction to her was that she looks tired...

[participant 4]

(12)

(Karen – non-native speaker)
This is gonna sound horrible but I was wondering if, like ... is she high when she's doing this or something?!

[participant 5]

(13)

(Jean-Charles – native speaker)
I was thinking that he doesn't look French and ... ah ... He looks like he is from California or something.

[participant 7]

Results of Summative Interviews

The overall goal of the summative interviews was to ascertain whether participants had noticed the use of English in the videos even if they had not mentioned such usage during recall protocols. In addition, the summative interviews attempted to gauge reactions to the range of bilingual proficiencies as represented in the pedagogical materials. And finally, participants were asked to speculate about the reasons for including non-native speakers in a beginning French course.

The use of English

In contrast to the results of the recall protocols where few participants noted the use of English, all 11 participants readily acknowledged that they had noticed the use of English by the students during the interviews. Participants interpreted this behavior as the students' efforts to compensate for a lack of linguistic knowledge. While such behavior drew sympathy, it also drew universal criticism. In contrast, the participants rarely mentioned the use of English by native French speakers. In addition, participants were either neutral about the practice or slightly positive. Two participants claimed to have noticed no instances of English by the native French speakers.

In (14), after some questioning, the participant (P) acknowledges to the investigator of the study (I) that she is aware that the French speakers sometimes use English. She attributes this awareness to her instructor who had recently brought to the students' attention the French speakers' errors. According to her instructor, these errors were the likely result of prolonged English influence.

(14)

I: Does anybody use English?
P: Yep. They (= students) use English words when they don't know what the French translation is and the interviewer sometimes translates it or sometimes just leaves it as English.
I: You're speaking of the students?
P: Uh huh, the American students.
I: Did the French ever do that?
P: The French? Uhmmm ... I don't think so. I think sometimes they use different forms that we haven't used yet but I can still understand what they are saying. So, it is just a different way of saying things. But, I can still understand.
I: So, you've never noticed that they have ever used English?
P: Uhmm, actually... I think they have. And I think my French teacher has said that because they've been living here for a few years that sometimes they make a few errors too.

[participant 11]

In (15), the investigator notes that the participant makes no mention of the English used by the native French speakers. When the investigator asks the participant why she does not seem to be as aware of the use of English by the native French speakers, the participant rationalizes her lack of awareness as a reflection of her lack of knowledge of native French speakers in general.

(15)

I: Have you noticed the French speakers when they use English?
P: No. But now that you say it, it is obvious that they do.
I: You commented on Karen's use of English but not on Jean-Charles'. He uses English too.
P: Yeah, he does.
I: So, you agree with me then.
P: Yes, I just never noticed that before. I guess it's because I just think they're French. That is their first language.
I: What does that mean that you didn't notice it?
P: Well, I didn't think, oh, that's American. Or I've never spoken to a native French person, so I don't know what it is like for a native French speaker.

[participant 4]

While participants viewed the use of English by the American students as a clear sign of linguistic deficiency (e.g. 'cheating'), most participants did not evaluate the use of English by the French speakers. A few participants went so far as to interpret such behavior as evidence for balanced bilingualism. For example, in (16), a participant expresses a very positive reaction to English used by French natives.

(16)

I: Did you notice they (= French native speakers) use English?
P: Uh hmm, they did a little bit. I thought that was cool! Like even though they were native, they jumped right into English and their English wasn't like a French accent or anything.
I: Yeah, so what does that tell you?
P: That they most likely speak English most of the time.

[participant 3]

In (17), the participant claims that the use of English by the two groups differs in terms of the categories of words (proper nouns vs. 'regular words'). Note that the Americans' use is criticized but not the native French speakers' use.

(17)

I: Do the so-called Native Speakers ever do that (= use English)?
P: They do, but they do it with proper nouns so it's not as bad.
I: Whereas the Americans do it with...
P: ... with regular French words or like, words they don't know.

[participant 7]

Reactions to non-native speakers in pedagogical materials

Despite their mild critiques of the use of English by the American students, all participants expressed overwhelming support for the inclusion of non-native speakers in the materials. In fact, the same participants who criticized the American students for using English during the interviews often praised the videos for including samples of authentic language. It would appear that the learner's evaluation of the use of English depended largely on how the question was framed.

Many participants praised the videos because they presented learners in real-life situations. In (18), the participant mentions that the videos present useful communicative strategies such as circumlocution. To demonstrate the utility of circumlocation, the participant recounts a personal anecdote of trying to communicate with Spanish speakers in Peru.

(18)

Do you like having non-native speakers?

Yea, I do. I think it's instructive.... They speak slower. And they get it right. And it also shows ... cause they are on the hot seat with the video camera so they have to negotiate around words they don't know. So it is kinda like techniques that I may have to use or can learn from if I'm put in a similar situation. So even though she had to compensate by using 'check', or she didn't know the word *vérifier*, she still was able to continue.... I think that it is important to point out to students where the mistake comes from or tell students this is how you would answer that question or that situation. But I also think that it is instructive to see how they move in and out of the language. Like, I remember when I was in Peru learning Spanish and I would have to find ways to speak Spanish when I didn't know – communicate something with the words that I didn't have ... so that was always instructive to know how to do that.

[participant 1]

In a similar fashion, participants appreciated the video's realistic portrayal of the non-natives' linguistic proficiencies. According to the participants, the range of proficiencies represented in the videos helped learners to determine more realistic goals for their achievement. In (19), the participant mentions that the materials create a greater awareness of linguistic proficiency by facilitating the comparison of native and non-native speakers.

(19)

I think it's a good balance. I think you get the whole spectrum – what the different sounds are, the different speeds, ah, levels. I think its good cause then you kinda have what, you know, an example of what- where you're at or maybe gonna be.

[participant 4]

In (20) and (21), participants claimed that watching non-native speakers often boosted their confidence, especially when the non-native made mistakes or had to resort to English.

(20)

Whenever there was a mistake, I was like 'oh I knew that'. Or whenever they throw in an English word cause they don't know the French I was like 'Oh I knew that word.'

[participant 6]

(21)

... if you're listening to native speakers, they're going to be able to elaborate and say things. But I think that it gives me confidence that I'm going to be able to be ... speak like the students do when listening to them. Cause they don't use vocabulary that is out of my range. They don't use sentence structure or grammar that's something I don't know. So, it gives me more confidence. I really like it.

[participant 5]

When asked directly what they thought the value of having non-native speakers in language materials might be, some participants overtly mentioned the process of identification. For example, several participants spoke about sympathizing with the non-native speakers, 'relating to them', and having a 'close connection' with them. In (22), the participant imagines that the goal of the developers was to forge a connection between the learner and the non-native speaker.

(22)

So what's the value of having a non-native speaker?

I think it is probably to ... they feel like it would make the students associate themselves better with, like identify themselves with the students better, cause they are where, in the same level where we are at, just beginning learning French.

[participant 9]

In general, participants did not seemed at all worried that they were being exposed to defective input. On the contrary, non-native mistakes not only served to boost the participants' confidence, but also proved invaluable for learning. For example, participants routinely noted that errors, when explicitly corrected, became highly salient and reinforced learning. In (23), the participant underscores the importance of making sure that the non-native error is explicitly corrected in the transcript.

(23)

When I see them make mistakes, it helps to teach me that these are mistakes that I could make and to correct them. But it doesn't bother me.

[participant 7]

Later, during the interview, the same participant makes clear that mistakes are actually relatively rare in the materials and in the course as a whole. In (24), the participant points out that the instructor's oral input and the text's written input are largely error-free. The implication is clear: when the majority of the input is native-like and grammatical, a few non-native errors is nothing to worry about.

(24)

I don't feel like the instruction is, uhm ... because these (= these videos) are kind of like supplemental, cause my professors are very much in command of what they are teaching us, and so it didn't bother me that you could hear English and mistakes. It's not the only thing.

[participant 7]

Discussion

The first research question about whether beginning French students notice the use of English in pedagogical materials is partially confirmed by the results. Only two recall protocols out of a total of 77 contained evidence of noticing. The immediate recall protocols are meant to give a picture of the students' cognitive processes while watching the videos. It appears that the use of English in spontaneous French discourse was not particularly salient to the participants during the comprehension task. This lack of noticing may have been an artifact of the task that focused participants' attention entirely on their (in)ability to comprehend. In general, the use of English made the discourse easier to comprehend and therefore less noticeable to the participants. Of the two participants who did mention the use of English, only one commented that this practice 'broke the flow' and resulted in comprehension problems. To summarize, the participants seemed to notice phenomena that inhibited their comprehension and their efforts at completing the task. The use of English was not particularly salient in this regard.

Despite the lack of direct evidence in the immediate recall protocols for noticing the use of English, the summative interviews demonstrated a general awareness of the phenomenon. Even though all participants revealed an awareness of the use of English, that awareness was closely related to the speaker's proficiency. In other words, questions about the use of English triggered comments about the non-native speakers. Many participants did profess some awareness of the use of English by the native French speakers, but only after considerable prodding. In fact, some participants initially denied that the French natives ever used English at all. In addition, participants appeared to be very conscious of the non-natives' compensatory motives for using English, often relating such behavior to their own difficulties with communicating in the second language. However, the same was not true when it came to explaining the use of English by the native French speakers. For the most part, the participants could offer little explanation as to why the native French speakers would occasionally use English when speaking French.

In general, the participants seemed to be more aware of the non-natives' discourse than the native French speakers' discourse. This was especially apparent in the way the participants compared the non-natives in terms of their proficiency. On occasion, the participants compared the native speakers, but such comparisons were framed in terms of how easy or difficult the natives were to understand. In essence, the participants scrutinized the non-natives for instances of communicative success or failure but did not do the same for the native speakers. Based on their evaluative comments, the participants appeared more invested in the non-native speakers, whose performances were taken as a reflection of their own abilities. Conversely, the native speakers' performances were less symbolically charged for the participants, and as a result, less compelling and less relevant for the construction of projective identities. Such a finding is understandable in the context of instructional materials where the native speaker is commonly accepted as the unmarked category, the pedagogical given. In such a context, non-native speakers constitute the marked category, attracting attention and requiring explanation.

The final research question concerning the participants' opinions and feelings about the value of non-native speakers in pedagogical materials was conclusively answered. All the participants strongly agreed that videos of non-native speakers proved highly instructive. The most common benefits cited were a greater awareness of communication strategies such as circumlocution and a greater awareness of common learner errors. Participants also mentioned that the videos gave them a more realistic picture of second language acquisition and helped them gauge their own language development.

Conclusion

It is often claimed that qualitative research identifies consequential variables for later hypothesis testing as part of a more controlled study. As a result, qualitative research is often viewed as a preliminary step in exploring phenomena about which little is known. The use of non-native speakers and the representation of code choice in pedagogical materials is certainly a research domain that has yet to be explored by applied linguists. Based on a relatively small, self-selecting sample, the generalizability of this study is admittedly somewhat problematic. It is hoped that future studies will be based on larger, more representative samples and will examine the relevant linguistic phenomena more rigorously (e.g. intersentential codeswitching, intrasentential codeswitching, cultural borrowings, phonologically integrated loan words, etc.). Despite the limitations of the present study, the results suggest that beginning learners readily agree on the value of including multilingual speakers in second language materials. In turn, this finding suggests a provocative new hypothesis for future research: The virtual identities of non-native speakers as represented in pedagogical materials may prove more relevant for the construction of a learner's projective identity than those of native speakers.

Chapter 10

Concluding Reflections: Moving Forward

MILES TURNBULL and JENNIFER DAILEY-O'CAIN

This collection of studies raises as many questions as it answers, and serves as a jumping-off point for reflection, debate, and further research related to the following three questions, at least: (1) What is the optimal level of first language use?; (2) How might the optimal level of use vary across different kinds of second and foreign language contexts; and (3) What kinds of uses of the first language are positive and effective in different contexts?

It is not the intention of this volume to provide a definitive statement on the use of the first language in second and foreign language classrooms, as there is still so much to learn about this complex issue. Nevertheless, the volume's authors have convincingly demonstrated that an inflexible and extreme virtual position that excludes the learner's first language in communicative and immersion second or foreign language classrooms is untenable. In addition, the volume includes many examples of first language use that appears to contribute to linguistic and identity development in the target language. On the other hand, no single chapter clearly defines how optimal first language use can be conceived by a teacher within a classroom, something which is also reflected in different authors' stances on 'optimal first language use' as a concept, and the chapters demonstrate significant variability in the amount and reasons for first-language use across different teaching and learning contexts. Many of the questions around these issues therefore remain open.

As a way of synthesizing what this collected volume of studies brings to the field, we propose the following definition for optimal first language use:

Optimal first language use in communicative and immersion second and foreign language classrooms recognizes the benefits of the leaner's first language as a cognitive and meta-cognitive tool, as a strategic organizer, and as a scaffold for language development. In addition, the first language helps learners navigate a bilingual identity and thereby learn to function as a bilingual. Neither the classroom teacher nor the second or foreign language learner becomes so dependent on the first language that neither can function without the first language. Optimal codeswitching practices will ultimately lead to enhanced language learning and the development of bilingual communicative practices.

Implications for Policy, Practice and Teacher Development

In the introduction to this volume, we anticipated controversy because we are quite aware that this definition of optimal first language use will cause concern for many second and foreign language educators. For example, it has long been unacceptable to even utter the C-word (codeswitching) in Canadian French Immersion contexts, and many non-immersion communicative language programs are not much different. Furthermore, in dual language programs, teachers rarely discuss codeswitching and go to great lengths to keep both languages separate. Moreover, many university language programs in both North America and Europe also have an official policy to ban first language use in second and foreign language programs, even if these policies are not always necessarily enacted in individual classrooms.

As the chapters in this volume have shown, avoiding examination or conversation about the role of the learners' first language can only be counterproductive to the ultimate goals of communicative second and foreign language programs. Moreover, sweeping this complex topic under the carpet, so to speak, can lead to teacher and student guilt and anxiety. There is ample evidence from this volume and in previous research that teachers and students, alike, codeswitch even when rules or policy ban them from doing so, and we have shown here that far from being necessarily due to laziness or inattention to detail, there are sound pedagogical reasons for this. Moreover, learners' codeswitching resembles that of advanced bilinguals, which suggests that the use of the first language in classroom discourse in fact is an essential step toward bilingualism, the ultimate goal in language learning. We therefore argue that an open discussion of codeswitching in policy and in teacher education – pre-service and in-service – will lead to more emancipated, reflexive and enlightened language professionals. Open dialogue can lead to greater understanding of what optimal first language use looks like in a variety of classroom contexts. McMillan and Turnbull (this volume) go further than this by advocating an action research approach to further investigation into maximizing student comprehension and the use of the first and target languages through reflective activities. Along similar lines, Levine (this volume) argues that teachers can engage in a rudimentary discourse analysis of conversations or texts with learners, and use that kind of goal-oriented investigation to increase learner awareness of the functions of the first and second languages in bilingual talk. These kinds of suggestions not only serve to demystify the tools of linguistic and pedagogical research, but also provide a level playing field upon which both linguists and educators can build a larger base of knowledge about the use of the first language in second and foreign language classrooms.

These policy considerations are essential, because in the absence of them, teachers are making their own, often arbitrary rules. The contributions by Levine (this volume) and Dailey-O'Cain and Liebscher (this volume) both suggest that classroom teachers create guidelines around what is optimal, or for that matter acceptable, first language use in their classrooms. These authors propose discussing codeswitching with learners, its pitfalls, why and how it is useful for language and identity development, and what it means to be a true bilingual. Levine (this volume) even takes this one step further, suggesting teaching students the terminology and concepts to discuss bilingualism and codeswitching. He argues that rules or norms for classroom language use must be reflective of bilingual language practices, which include codeswitching as natural and common phenomena. Although, of course, these reflections need to be geared toward each group of students' developmental needs, we urge readers to reflect on the implications of these suggestions for policy, classroom practice and materials development. Blyth (this volume) provides some excellent examples for how to do this by showing that classroom materials that present non-native speakers, who codeswitch naturally, 'may prove more relevant for the construction of a learner's projective identity than those of native speakers'. But could classroom materials also include explicit consideration of optimal first language use along the lines suggested by Levine and Dailey-O'Cain, and Liebscher? Judging from the available evidence, that would seem to prove beneficial.

Future Research

The authors in this volume also offer many suggestions for future research. Evans, for example, confronts scholars and educators with the question of how teachers can make better use of the overlap between language learning and naturalistic communication that computer-mediated communication offers. As one of the few studies that has examined first language use and codeswitching in a virtual environment, it seems clear that more research would help understand the uniqueness of this environment and the resemblance or difference between spoken-language codeswitching. Nagy and Robertson suggest that the use of the first language by foreign language teachers, especially those who work with beginner level learners in non-intensive programs, is strongly influenced by the teacher's assessment of the cognitive and linguistic processing demands made on the learners by the texts and activities used in the classroom. Further research might usefully consider the features of classroom activities and materials that promote optimal codeswitching so that the first language does not become a crutch for both teachers and students which leads to decelerated language development. Both of these questions carry real-world implications for classroom teachers, for learners, and perhaps most significantly for curriculum developers.

On the sociolinguistic side, the chapters by Potowski, Dailey-O'Cain and Liebscher, and Fuller point toward the importance of further investigation into the acquisition of codeswitching among second language learners. Potowski's work suggests that second language learners may develop codeswitching skills more slowly than heritage language speakers, who may have learned to codeswitch outside of the classroom first, but it remains an open question as to whether this is a broad generalization that can be made, and future research will need to address this. Dailey-O'Cain and Liebscher's work, on the other hand, suggests that even early intermediate language learners may well be using their first language to structure talk rather than simply to fill gaps in knowledge of their second language, but additional research conducted with early beginners, including younger learners, could provide more information about the ways in which these skills develop. Fuller shows that bilingual children – both those who have learned both languages from early childhood on and those who have learned their second language in school – use codeswitching to structure conversation and to construct social identities. Fuller's data also suggest that overall patterns of codeswitching remain the same regardless of proficiency levels in the two languages. All of these findings have potential implications for both educators and educational policy-makers, but further work on the ways in which different kinds of learners codeswitch, and at which levels of their own language acquisition, is necessary to determine which kinds of bilingual language use can be expected by teachers at which stages of acquisition.

Finally, additional studies that further investigate the relationship between student learning and teacher and student codeswitching (or lack thereof), will go a long way to convince scholars and educators who seek 'proof' that codeswitching helps or hinders student learning of the target language. Macaro, for example, has summarized in this volume two quantitative, quasi-experimental studies that provide tentative evidence that codeswitching promotes student learning of the target language in terms of vocabulary acquisition. Future research that attempts to define optimal target and first language use might draw on mixed methods to help provide evidence for this assertion that goes beyond the level of vocabulary acquisition to look at language in interaction, and provide us with more in-depth understandings of questions that are clearly complex and impossible to control completely.

The most important contribution this volume can make, however, is less about specific classroom practices and more about classroom philosophy. Although researchers still disagree about how and whether optimal first language use can be defined, there is one point of agreement on which there remains no doubt: there is simply no evidence that a prescribed target-language only environment is beneficial to learners, and there is ample evidence that it may be detrimental. It is therefore essential for instructors and policy-makers to keep in mind that we need to begin envisioning learners not as ineffective and imperfect monolingual speakers of the target language, but as aspiring bilinguals. While on the surface of things this may seem like a radical departure from current thinking that holds unknown and potentially frightening consequences, it transforms the aim of both the learner and the educator into an attainable one. Learners can never become perfect monolingual speakers of the target language, and educators who take that as their goal cannot help but fail. But if both learners and their instructors come to think of learners as would-be bilinguals, the classroom can be transformed into an environment where this bilingualism is realized just as it is in non-classroom bilingual communities, and where the learning of both the structures of language and the functions of communication are far better served.

Notes

1. Macaro (2005) finds that the maximal position does not go far enough, and is too focused on quantity of target language use without discussing quality or optimal first-language use. The ultimate goal of this volume is to develop the concept of optimal first and target language use in second and foreign language teaching and learning in a variety of contexts.
2. All English words used in the lesson are italicized; other reported speech (non-italicized) given in English here was actually said in French by the teacher or by students.
3. The most common programs include Early Immersion, starting either at kindergarten or Grade 1, Late Immersion, starting generally at Grade 6 or 7, and Middle Immersion, starting at Grade 4. Over the course of these programs, the percentage of the curriculum delivered in French decreases from 80% to 100% at the beginning to when the students reach high school where they typically choose only a few subjects in French per year. By the end of grade eight a typical Early immersion program results in over 6000 hours total accumulated instruction in French. Students in Middle and Late immersion programs accumulate between 1200 and 2000 hours in French. In addition, these students are typically exposed to between 1000 and 1500 hours of high school courses taught in French.
4. Sanaoui (2005, 2007) is an extended analysis of Skerrit's Masters thesis work.
5. To help ensure anonymity of participants, pseudonyms are used throughout this chapter.
6. Prince Edward Island assesses teachers' French proficiency using the New Brunswick Oral Proficiency measure which was developed using the American Council on the Teaching of Foreign Languages proficiency scale (ACTFL, 1985). A superior level of proficiency is described by the Prince Edward Island Ministry of Education as 'Able to speak the language with great structural accuracy. Can participate in all formal and informal conversations on practical, social and professional topics. The speech has a natural flow and the vocabulary is broad enough to be used in all circumstances. Comprehension is accurate and complete in most situations. The speaker may still not comprehend all colloquial expressions and regionalisms.' Available on http://www.gov.pe.ca/languagetraining/index.php3?number=70666&lang=E.
7. In the interest of ethical concerns and because this study was considered controversial for many LFI educators, we stressed with participants that our goal was to understand this complex issue, not criticize their practice.

8. Stimulated recall has been widely used in second language research to 'explore participants' thought processes (or strategies) at the time of an activity' (Gass & Mackey, 2000: xi) and is intended to reduce recall error as much as possible.
9. See Calvé (1993), Wong-Fillmore (1985a) and Butzkamm (1998) for more on this.
10. All English words used in the lesson are italicized; other reported speech (non-italicized) given in English here was actually said in French by the teacher or by students.
11. Until recently, many French immersion teacher training programs only dealt with the topic of codeswitching in passing, if at all, usually dismissing it as being counterproductive to second-language learning; some programs now recognize that pedagogically principled first-language use can benefit second-language learning (e.g. the University of Prince Edward Island).
12. Frank never specifically mentioned the guidelines during the interviews, although he had a clear idea of what was officially expected and often made statements to the effect that immersion was supposed to be French-only. Pierre thought that the expectation was that teachers should *mainly* use French; he stated that learning outcomes (students' proficiency in the TL) was more important than the exact amount of English or French used by the teacher.
13. It is noteworthy that Pierre's first language use is within the 10–15% limit only after Christmas, since he does use 30–40% L1 in the first few months of the program to establish a critical base of vocabulary in French.
14. This is a weakness in French immersion learning outcomes, identified by Cummins.
15. The Effects of Codeswitching on Vocabulary Learning in the EFL Classroom. Unpublished Masters dissertation, 2005, University of Oxford, Department of Education.
16. A Case Study of Teachers' Codeswitching Behaviours in Mainland China's University EFL Classrooms and Students' Reactions to the Codeswitching. Unpublished Doctoral dissertation, 2007, University of Oxford Department of Education.
17. This distinction is related to whether the English lexical item has a direct concept equivalent in Chinese or has to be 'explained' by circumlocution.
18. In all textual quotations in this paper, pupil writing has been left uncorrected.
19. The comparison of the number of words in English and Hungarian text is not unproblematic. Hungarian is an agglutinative language, where bound morphemes perform the function which is performed by articles and prepositions in an isolating language like English, so a simple phrase in English such as 'with my dog' translates as one word 'kutyámmal' in Hungarian. This difference in the meaning of 'word' needs to be taken into account when comparing absolute word frequencies in the two languages, but it does not greatly affect the comparison of proportions of target language and mother tongue use in different individuals.
20. However, De Houwer (2009) insists that the term 'simultaneous' be reserved for children who began acquiring both languages since birth, and that situations of children with an age of onset of bilingualism later than the first six months of life employ the term 'Early Second Language Acquisition'.
21. Despite the presence of a lot of nouns in codeswitching, it is not correct to assume that children codeswitch because they do not know how to say the word in a given language. Zentella (1997) found evidence that the children in

her corpus in fact knew 75% of the lexical items they had switched. Similarly, Meisel (1994) found evidence of codeswitched words that had also been produced by the same speakers in the other language.

22. Since no evidence was presented that the children at three years eight months of age ceased using constructions that had previously been acquired, it is not clear whether their Chinese had undergone attrition or incomplete acquisition.

23. It is not possible to verify absolutely whether speakers are seeking to attract attention, set off a metalinguistic comment, or exercise agency with a particular codeswitch, or whether they simply had quicker access to English at that moment, which complicates the assigning of meanings and motivations for codeswitching both for L2 speakers (Liebscher & Dailey-O'Cain, 2004) and native bilinguals (Zentella, 1997).

24. The turn was used as the basic unit of analysis, defined as when a speaker stops talking or is interrupted by another speaker (Ellis, 1994). An analysis of a random sample of the 2050 turns in the corpus revealed that turns in each language were of similar average length.

25. The teacher was raised in Mexico until the age of 14 and was a very fluent bilingual. Research indicates that it is precisely high levels of proficiency in both Spanish and English that leads to the adoption of *so* and other English discourse markers into Spanish (Torres, 2002; Said Mohand, 2006; Torres & Potowski, 2008).

26. The turns immediately before and after these turns were in Spanish, so Spanish was determined to be the matrix language.

27. As mentioned earlier, there are no infallible criteria for determining when a restart in fact constitutes a new sentence. I relied on intonation and pauses.

28. The Diploma de Español como Lengua Extranjera (Diploma of Spanish as a Foreign Language), or DELE, is increasingly used as an independent measure of Spanish proficiency in empirical language acquisition research. However, the results presented here as well as those of Montrul (2005) require that we interpret such measures with caution.

29. Transcription key

,	short pause
(1), (2)...	pause of 1 second, 2 seconds, etc.
.	falling intonation
?	rising intonation
!	animated intonation
'I think so'	quoted speech
{laughs}	non-linguistic information inside curly brackets
('no')	translation into English
jo:b	elongated vowel
nein	German utterances in bold
(what)	unclear; this is the transcriber's best guess at what was said
xxx, **xxx**	unintelligible; if in bold, it is clear from the phonology that the word, although indiscernible, is German, if in regular type, it is clearly English; if in italics, the language of the word is not apparent

30. Our previous work on classroom discourse has dealt with repair phenomena (Liebscher & Dailey-O'Cain, 2003), Auer's (1998) codeswitching model as

applied to a content-based classroom (Liebscher & Dailey-O'Cain, 2005), code-mixing (Dailey-O'Cain & Liebscher, 2006), and a focus on the intercultural aspects of codeswitching in two different classrooms (Liebscher & Dailey-O'Cain, 2007).

31. The fieldworker in this classroom was Wendy Tiemer, and the data was collected in the context of her MA thesis (Tiemer, 2004).

32. This lack of an explicitly stated policy on L1 use, whether to permit or forbid it, is typical for German courses these students would have taken in this department.

33. See Gumperz and Cook-Gumperz (2005) and Liebscher and Dailey-O'Cain (2005) for two exceptions.

34. Transcription conventions are as follows: German utterances are in Roman type, while English utterances are in boldface type. English glosses of the German appear in italics beneath the German text. Conversational overlap is indicated with square brackets. Pauses lasting a beat (.) or two (. .) are indicated as shown; longer pauses are indicated in seconds. Students (BQ, CW, etc.) are labeled according to the initials of their pseudonyms; TR is the teacher, and CL is the whole class.

35. For more examples of codeswitching in this intermediate classroom, please see Tiemer (2004) and Liebscher and Dailey-O'Cain (forthcoming).

36. This kind of codeswitch is, however, only rarely used by the teacher in this classroom. One reason for this may be that, by doing these switches, the teacher clearly positions herself as somebody who sees the students as less capable, and as preferring English for understanding.

37. An example of this type of switch in caregiver-child interaction can be found in Köppe and Meisel (1995: 286).

38. In our data from this classroom, the teacher does not do these kinds of switches – perhaps because she is a very fluent speaker of German who does not often require English as a cognitive trigger for common German words.

39. In non-classroom bilingual communities, when people fail to accommodate the language preferences of a conversation partner, a tension may arise where the code choice becomes a marker for identity struggles (*cf.* Heller, 2005). However, the teacher continuing to speak the second language even when the students are speaking the first language is a technique that is promoted in certain kinds of classrooms where two languages are shared, such as immersion classrooms in Canada.

40. For a discussion of this part of the segment as a repair sequence, please see Liebscher and Dailey-O'Cain (2003: 376).

41. The teacher's translation of the student's words into the second language may look like a correction on the code (L2 instead of L1) that the student used. In that sense, the teacher's translation seems similar to a *recast* defined as 'the teacher implicitly reformulating all or part of the student's utterance' for corrective purposes (Lyster & Mori, 2006: 271). However, we want to argue that the translation here, in contrast to a recast, may well not have been *intended* by the teacher as a correction on the code used, even though the student may have *perceived* it as such.

42. Since we only have student-student interaction from the intermediate classroom, we cannot draw a similar conclusion for this classroom.

43. In the literature dealing with the US language classroom context, 'first language' usually means English. No assumption is made that it is the first language of the learners; in the United States increasingly this is not the case among students. More appropriate terms would be the 'socially dominant' or 'unmarked' language, but for the sake of stylistic simplicity, the term first language will be employed.

44. This does not mean that every instance of learner codeswitching must have an overt social motivation; many switches (or all for some scholars) can be traced to the local management of turns-at-talk. The issue I wish to highlight is that even those interactions in which the turns-at-talk are driven by the discursive (with a small 'd') needs of the moment, in fact the very occurrence of the talk in which the turns are taken are enabled by Discourses-with-a-big-D and themselves enact those Discourses.

45. There are numerous approaches to discourse analysis, all of which share the conviction that discourses are meaning-making tools and systems, and that some of these are linguistic. Often the goals of the analysis differ, as do the particular semiotic systems under investigation. For example, Fairclough's (1995, and elsewhere) critical discourse analysis seeks to affect social change. Scollon's (2001) and Scollon and Scollon's (2004) approach to mediated discourse and nexus analysis views language as just one sort of semiotic system. Gee's approach to discourse analysis does not go as far as Fairclough's in the social-change direction, and for him language use in interaction remains central. This makes it extremely adaptable for our investigation of second-language learner interaction.

46. The workshops that I held dealt with the following topics: An introduction to codeswitching and bilingualism; a study of the 'Russia Germans'; a study of *Türkenslang*, Turkish used by non-ethnic-Turkish youths in Germany (Dirim & Auer, 2004); and codeswitching norms for the language classroom.

47. The names of the two research subjects have been changed.

48. As a researcher accustomed to listening to and evaluating linguistic variation in German and English, I should state that had Sybil not informed me that she was not an first-language speaker of English, I would not have been able to discern this from her use of that language in our several conversations.

49. The one-page short story is about a married couple in post-World-War II Germany and is considered to be part of German *Trümmerliteratur* ('rubble literature'), which dealt for the most part with the hardships of civilians and returning soldiers during the post-War years. The couple lives on a small ration of bread. In the middle of the night the woman is awakened by a noise in the kitchen. She catches her husband having sliced an extra piece of bread for himself. He lies to her, telling her only that he had been awakened by a noise. She sees the breadcrumbs on the table but does not confront him. Later on, in bed, she hears him quietly chewing the bread he had taken. The next evening she insists he eat part of her ration, claiming that the bread did not agree with her.

50. The other three tasks relate to 'significance', 'activities' and 'politics'. Except for the issue of political contexts enacted through interaction, 'significance' and 'activities' appeared to show, at least in the analysis of this learner conversation, some overlap with the building tasks included in this discussion. In addition, Gee points out that not every use of language involves all seven building tasks.

51. Positioning theory, while not integrated by Gee in his approach to discourse analysis, in fact accords well with it. Harré and colleagues (Davies & Harré, 1990; van Langenhove & Harré, 1999, and elsewhere; see also Mirinova, 2004) frame what speakers do in interaction in terms of complex relationships among communication (both verbal and non-verbal), context, and intentions and motivations as *positioning* rather than the simple adoption of 'roles'. 'Role', they argue, is too static a term to account for the fluid, dynamic nature of the microinteractional and macrosocial aspects of human interaction.
52. This intersubjective phenomenon has been observed in sociocultural research of second-language learner interaction (e.g. Swain & Lapkin, 2000).
53. The names in parentheses refer to the speakers in the videos followed by their status as a native or non-native speaker. In example (1), the participant's immediate recall protocol is based on Jean-Charles' video. Jean-Charles is a native speaker. The participant is identified by a number at the end of each protocol in order to maintain anonymity as required by Institutional Review Board guidelines.

References

Ajzen, I. (1991) The theory of planned behavior. *Organizational Behavior and Human Decision Processes* 50, 179–211.

Alderson, C. and Szollás, K. (2000) The context: The current school-leaving examination. In C. Alderson, E. Nagy and E. Öveges (eds) *English Language Education in Hungary: Examining Hungarian Learners' Achievements in English* (pp. 9–21). Budapest: British Council.

Alfonzetti, G. (1995) Code switching e code mixing nell' Atlante Linguistico della Sicilia. In M.T. Romanello and I. Tempesta (eds) *Dialetti e lingue nazionali, Atti del XXVII Congresso della Società di Linguistica Italiana* (pp. 413–431). Rome: Bulzoni.

Alfonzetti, G. (1998) The conversational dimension in code-switching between Italian and dialect in Sicily. In P. Auer (ed.) *Code-Switching in Conversation: Language, Interaction, and Identity* (pp. 180–214). London: Routledge.

Álvarez-Cáccamo, C. (1996) The power of reflexive language(s): code displacement in reported speech. *Journal of Pragmatics* 25, 33–59.

American Council for the Teaching of Foreign Languages (1985) *ACTFL Proficiency Guidelines*. Hastings-on-Hudson, NY: ACTFL Materials Center.

Antón, M. and DiCamilla, F.J. (1998) Socio-cognitive functions of L1 collaborative interaction in the L2 classroom. *Canadian Modern Language Review* 54 (3), 314–342.

Arnett, K. (2001) The accommodation of grade 9 students with learning disabilities in the applied core French program. Unpublished master's thesis, The Ontario Institute for Studies in Education of the University of Toronto.

Arnfast, J.S. and Jørgenson, J.N. (2003) Code-switching as a communication, learning, and social negotiation strategy in first-year learners of Danish. *International Journal of Applied Linguistics* 13 (1), 23–53.

Atkinson, D. (1993) Teaching in the target language: a problem in the current orthodoxy. *Language Learning Journal* 8, 2–5.

Atkinson, D. (1995) English only in the classroom: Why do we do it? The Polish Teacher Trainer. On WWW at http://ettc.uwb.edu.pl/strony/ptt/feb95/8.html. Accessed 14.4.07.

Atlantic Provinces Education Foundation/La Fondation d'éducation des provinces de l'Atlantique (1997) Programme de français immersion tardive – 7e, 8e et 9e année (version provisoire). On WWW at http://www.ednet.ns.ca/pdfdocs/french-second-language/encadrement.pdf. Accessed 14.4.07.

Au, T., Knightly, L., Jun, S. and Oh, J. (2002) Overhearing a language during childhood. *Psychological Science* 13, 238–243.

Auer, P. (1984) *Bilingual Conversation*. Amsterdam/Philadelphia: Benjamins.

Auer, P. (1988) A conversation analytic approach to code-switching and transfer. In M. Heller (ed.) *Code-Switching: Anthropological and Sociolinguistic Perspectives* (pp. 183–114). Berlin: Mouton de Gruyter.

Auer, P. (1995) The pragmatics of code-switching. In L. Milroy and P. Muysken (eds) *One Speaker, Two Languages: Cross-disciplinary Perspectives on Code-switching* (pp. 115–135). Cambridge: Cambridge University Press.

Auer, P. (1998) Introduction. Bilingual conversation revisited. In P. Auer (ed.) *Code-Switching in Conversation: Language, Interaction and Identity* (pp. 1–25). London: Routledge.

Auer, P. (2005) A postscript: code-switching and social identity. *Journal of Pragmatics* 37, 403–410.

Bailey, B. (2001) The language of multiple identity among Dominican Americans. *Journal of Linguistic Anthropology* 10 (2), 190–223.

Bajard, T. (2004) L'immersion en français au Canada: Guide pratique d'enseignement. Ottawa: Association Canadienne des Professeurs d'Immersion.

Bakhtin, M.M. (1981) *The Dialogic Imagination. Four Essays.* (M. Holquist, ed.; C. Emerson and M. Holquist, trans.) Austin: University of Texas Press.

Bardovi-Harlig, K. and Reynolds, D. (1995) The role of lexical aspect in the acquisition of tense and aspect. *TESOL Quarterly* 29, 107–131.

Behan, L., Turnbull, M. and Spek, J. (1997) The proficiency gap in late French immersion: Language use in collaborative tasks. *Le Journal de l'Immersion* 20 (2), 41–44.

Behrend, D., Rosengren, K. and Perlmutter, M. (1992) Private speech: From social interaction to self-regulation. In R.M. Diaz and L.E. Berk (eds) *The Relation Between Private Speech and Parental Interactive Style* (pp. 85–100). Hillsdale, NJ: Lawrence Erlbaum Associates.

Belz, J. and Reinhardt, J. (2004) Aspects of advanced foreign language proficiency: Internet-mediated German language play. *International Journal of Applied Linguistics* 14 (3), 324–362.

Birdsong, D. (1989) *Metalinguistic Performance and Interlinguistic Competence.* Berlin/Heidelberg: Springer-Verlag.

Blackledge, A. and Pavlenko, A. (2001) Negotiation of identities in multilingual contexts. *International Journal of Bilingualism* 5 (3), 243–257.

Block, D. (2003) *The Social Turn in Second Language Acquisition.* Washington, DC: Georgetown University Press.

Blyth, C. (1995) Redefining the boundaries of language use: The foreign language classroom as a multilingual speech community. In C. Kramsch (ed.) *Redefining the Boundaries of Language Study* (pp. 145–183). Boston: Heinle.

Blyth, C. and Davis, J. (2007) Using formative evaluation in the development of learner-centered materials. *CALICO Journal* 25 (1), 1–21.

Breen, M.P. and Candlin, C.N. (1980) The essentials of a communicative curriculum in language teaching. *Applied Linguistics* 1, 98–112.

Broner, M. (2000) Impact of interlocutor and task on first and second language use in a Spanish immersion program. Unpublished doctoral dissertation, University of Minnesota.

Brooks, F. and Donato, R. (1994) Vygotskian approaches to understanding foreign language learner discourse during communicative tasks. *Hispania* 77, 262–274.

Brooks, F.B. Donato, R. and McGlone, J.V. (1997) When are they going to say "it" right? Understanding learner talk during pair-work activity. *Foreign Language Annals* 30 (4), 524–541.

Brown, P. and Levinson, S.C. (1987) *Politeness*. Cambridge: Cambridge University Press.

Burstall, C., Jamieson, M., Cohen, S. and Hargreaves, M. (1974) *Primary French in the Balance*. Slough, England: NFER Publishing Company.

Burt, S.M. (1992) Code-switching, convergence and compliance: The development of micro-community speech norms. In C. Eastman (ed.) *Code-Switching* (pp. 169–185). Clevedon: Multilingual Matters.

Butzkamm, W. (1998) Code-switching in a bilingual history lesson: The mother tongue as a conversational lubricant. *International Journal of Bilingual Education and Bilingualism* 1 (2), 81–99.

Byram, M. (1997) Cultural studies and foreign language teaching. In S. Bassnett (ed.) *Studying British Cultures. An Introduction* (pp. 53–65). London: Routledge.

Byram, M. (1998) Cultural identities in multilingual classrooms. In J. Cenoz and F. Genesee (eds) *Beyond Bilingualism: Multilingualism and Multilingual Education* (pp. 96–116). Clevedon: Multilingual Matters.

Calvé, P. (1993) Pour enseigner le français … en français. *Canadian Modern Language Review* 50 (1), 15–28.

Cameron, L. (2001) *Teaching Languages to Young Learners*. Cambridge: Cambridge University Press.

Canadian Parents for French (CPF) (2003) *The State of French Second Language Education in Canada*. Ottawa: Canadian Parents for French.

Canadian Parents for French (2006) *The State of French Second Language Education in Canada*. On WWW at http://www.cpf.ca/eng/pdf/resources/reports/fsl/2006/pdfs/CPFAnnualE.pdf.

Canale, M. and Swain, M. (1980) Theoretical bases of communicative approaches to second language teaching and testing. *Applied Linguistics* 1, 1–47.

Cantone, K. (2007) *Code-Switching in Bilingual Children: Studies in Theoretical Psycholinguistics*. New York: Springer.

Carless, D.R. (2004) A contextualised examination of target language use in the primary school foreign language classroom. *Australian Review of Applied Linguistics* 27, 104–119.

Carranza, I. (1995) Multilevel analysis of two-way immersion discourse. In J. Alatis, C. Straehle, B. Gallenberger and M. Ronkin (eds) *Georgetown University Round Table on Languages and Linguistics* (pp. 169–187). Washington, DC: Georgetown University Press.

Carroll, J.B. (1975) *The Teaching of French as a Foreign Language in Eight Countries*. New York: John Wiley and Sons.

Cashman, H. (2005) Identities at play: Language preference and group membership in bilingual talk in interaction. *Journal of Pragmatics* 37 (3), 301–315.

Castellotti, V. (1997) Langue étrangère et français en milieu scolaire: Didactiser l'alternance? *Etudes de Linguistique Appliquée* 108, 410.

Castellotti, V. and Moore, D. (1997) *Alternances des langes et apprentissages: Revue de dialectologie des langues-cultures*. Paris: Didier Erudition.

Chavez, M. (2003) The diglossic foreign language classroom: Learners' views on L1 and L2 Functions. In C. Blyth (ed.) *The Sociolinguistics of Foreign-language Classrooms* (pp. 163–208). Boston: Heinle.

Chambers, G. (1992) Teaching in the target language. *Language Learning Journal* 6, 66–67.

Chomsky, N. (1965) *Aspects of the Theory of Syntax*. Cambridge, MA: MIT Press.

Christian, D. (1996) Two-way immersion education: Students learning through two languages. *The Modern Language Journal* 80 (1), 66–76.

Clandinin, D.J. and Connelly, F.M. (2000) *Narrative Inquiry: Experience and Story in Qualitative Research.* San Francisco: Jossey-Bass.

Cloud, N., Genesee, F. and Hamayan, E. (2000) *Dual Language Instruction: A Handbook for Enriched Education.* London: Heinle & Heinle/Thompson Learning.

Cohen, A.D. and Macaro, E. (eds) (2007) *Language Learner Strategies: Thirty Years of Research and Practice.* Oxford: Oxford University Press.

Cook, G. (2000) *Language Play, Language Learning.* Oxford: Oxford University Press.

Cook, V. (1992) Evidence for multicompetence. *Language Learning* 42, 557–591.

Cook, V. (1999) Going beyond the native speaker in language teaching. *TESOL Quarterly* 33, 185–210.

Cook, V. (2001) Using the first language in the classroom. *Canadian Modern Language Review* 57, 402–423.

Cook, V. (2005) Basing teaching on the L2 user. In E. Llurda (ed.) *Non-Native Language Teachers: Perceptions, Challenges and Contributions to the Profession* (pp. 47–61). New York: Springer.

Crawford, J. (1995) *Bilingual Education: History, Politics, Theory and Practice* (3rd edn). Los Angeles, CA: Bilingual Educational Services.

Creswell, J.W. (2005) *Educational Research: Planning, Conducting, and Evaluating Quantitative and Qualitative Research* (2nd edn). Upper Saddle River, NJ: Pearson Education.

Cummins, J. (1996) *Negotiating Identities: Education for Empowerment in a Diverse Society.* Los Angeles: California Association for Bilingual Education.

Cummins, J. (2000) *Language, Power, and Pedagogy: Bilingual Children in the Crossfire.* Clevedon: Multilingual Matters.

Cummins, J. (2001) *Negotiating Identities: Education for Empowerment in a Diverse Society* (2nd edn). Los Angeles: California Association for Bilingual Education.

Dailey-O'Cain, J. and Liebscher, G. (2006) Language learners' use of discourse markers as evidence for a mixed code. *International Journal of Bilingualism* 10 (1), 89–109.

Davies, A. (1991) *The Native Speaker in Applied Linguistics.* Edinburgh: Edinburgh University Press.

Davies, B. and Harré, R. (1990) Positioning: The discursive production of selves. *Journal for the Theory of Social Behavior* 20 (1), 43–63.

DeFina, A. (2007) Code-switching and the construction of ethnic identity in a community of practice. *Language in Society* 36, 371–392.

De Houwer, A. (2009) *Bilingual First Language Acquisition.* Bristol: Multilingual Matters.

Dekeyser, R.M. (1993) The effect of error correction on L2 grammar knowledge and oral proficiency. *The Modern Language Journal*, 77, 501–514.

diSciullo, A., Muysken, P. and Singh, R. (1986) Government and code-mixing. *Journal of Linguistics* 22 (1), 1–24.

Doughty, C. and Williams, J. (eds) (1998) *Focus on Form in Classroom Second Language Acquisition.* Cambridge: Cambridge University Press.

Duff, P. and Polio, C. (1990) How much foreign language is there in the foreign language classroom? *Modern Language Journal* 74, 154–166.

Edmondson, W. (2004) Code-switching and world-switching in foreign language classroom discourse. In J. House and J. Rehbein (eds) *Multilingual*

Communication (pp. 155–178). Amsterdam/Philadelphia: John Benjamins Publishing Company.

Egi, T. (2004) Verbal reports, noticing and SLA research. *Language Awareness* 13 (4), 243–264.

Elías-Olivares, L.E. (1976) Ways of speaking in a Chicano community: A sociolinguistic approach. Unpublished PhD thesis, University of Texas at Austin.

Ellis, N. (2005) At the interface: Dynamic interactions of explicit and implicit language knowledge. *Studies in Second Language Acquisition* 27, 305–352.

Ellis, R. (1984) *Classroom Second Language Development*. Oxford: Pergamon.

Ellis, R. (1986) *Understanding Second Language Acquisition*. Oxford: Oxford University Press.

Ellis, R. (1994) *The Study of Second Language Acquisition*. Oxford: Oxford University Press.

Ellis, R. and He, X. (1999) The roles of modified input and output in the incidental acquisition of word meanings. *Studies in Second Language Acquisition* 21, 285–301.

Ellis, R., Tanaka, Y. and Yamazaki, A. (1994) Classroom interaction, comprehension and the acquisition of L2 word meanings. *Language Learning* 44, 449–491.

Evans, M. (2009) Using stimulated recall to investigate pupils' thinking about on-line bilingual communication: Codeswitching and pronominal address in L2 French. *British Educational Research Journal* 36 (3), 469–485.

Fairclough, N. (1992) The appropriacy of 'appropriateness'. In N. Fairclough (ed.) *Critical Language Awareness* (pp. 33–56). London and New York: Longman.

Fairclough, N. (1995) *Critical Discourse Analysis*. London: Longman.

Farrell, T. (1998) Reflective teaching: The principles and practices. *English Teaching Forum Online* 36, 4. On WWW at http://exchanges.state.gov/forum/vols/vol36/no4/p10.htm. Accessed 14.4.07.

Fitts, S. (2006) Reconstructing the status quo: Linguistic interaction in a dual-language school. *Bilingual Research Journal* 29 (2), 337–365.

Fortune, T. (2001) Understanding immersion students' oral language use as a mediator of social interaction in the classroom. Unpublished doctoral dissertation, University of Minnesota.

Fuller, J.M. (2006) Immigration into Germany: Language use and identity in a multilingual setting. Paper presented at The German Language and Immigration in International Perspective, Madison, WI, 28–29 September.

Fuller, J.M. (2007) Language choice as a means for shaping identity. *Journal of Linguistic Anthropology* 17 (1), 105–129.

Fuller, J., Elsman, M. and Self, K. (2007) Addressing peers in a Spanish-English bilingual classroom. In K. Potowski and R. Cameron (eds) *Spanish in Contact: Policy, Social, and Linguistic Inquiries* (pp. 135–151). Amsterdam: John Benjamins.

Gafaranga, J. and Torras, M.-C. (2002) Interactional otherness: Toward a redefinition of codeswitching. *International Journal of Bilingualism* 6 (1), 1–22.

García, E.E. (1983) *Early Childhood Bilingualism: With Special Reference to the Mexican-American Child*. Albuquerque: University of New Mexico Press.

Gass, S.M. and Mackey, A. (2000) *Stimulated Recall Methodology in Second Language Research*. Mahwah, NJ: Erlbaum.

Gee, J.P. (2003) *What Video Games Have to Teach Us About Learning and Literacy*. New York: Palgrave.

Gee, J.P. (2005) *An Introduction to Discourse Analysis: Theory and Method* (2nd edn). New York: Routledge.

Genesee, F. (1987) *Learning Through Two Languages: Studies of Immersion and Bilingual Education.* Cambridge, MA: Newbury House.

Genesee, F. (1994) Integrating language and content: Lessons from immersion. *Educational Practice Reports, 11.* National Center for Research on Cultural Diversity and Second Language Learning, Washington, DC: Center for Applied Linguistics.

Gibson, J.J. (1979) *The Ecological Approach to Visual Perception.* Hillsdale, NJ: Erlbaum.

Glaser, B.G. (1992) *Basics of Grounded Theory Analysis: Emergence vs Forcing.* Sociology Press: Mill Valley, CA.

Glaser, B.G. and Strauss, A.L. (1967) *The Discovery of Grounded Theory: Strategies for Qualitative Research.* New York: Aldine de Gruyter.

Gumperz, J.J. (1982) *Discourse Strategies.* Cambridge: Cambridge University Press.

Gumperz, J.J. and Cook-Gumperz, J. (2005) Making space for bilingual communicative practice. *Intercultural Pragmatics* 2 (1), 1–23.

Håkansson, G. and Lindberg, I. (1988) What's the question? Investigating questions in second language classrooms. *AILA Reviews* 5, 101–116.

Hatch, E. (1992) *Discourse and Language Education.* Cambridge: Cambridge University Press.

Heilenman, K. (1993) Of cultures and compromises: Publishers, textbooks, and the academy. *Publishing Research Quarterly* 9, 55–67.

Heller, M. (2005) Identities, ideologies, and the analysis of bilingual speech. In V. Hinnenkamp and K.Meng (eds) *Sprachgrenzen überspringen. Sprachliche Hybridität und polykulturelles Selbstverständnis* (pp. 267–288). Tübingen: Narr.

Holderness, J. (1990) *Chatterbox, Pupil's Book, Level 3.* Oxford: Oxford University Press.

Hulstijn, J.H. (2001) Intention and incidental second language vocabulary learning: A reappraisal of elaboration, rehearsal and automaticity. In P. Robinson (ed.) *Cognition and Second Language Instruction* (pp. 258–286). Cambridge: Cambridge University Press.

Jacobs, G.M., Dufon, P. and Fong, C.H. (1994) L1 and L2 vocabulary glosses in L2 reading passages: Their effectiveness for increasing comprehension and vocabulary knowledge. *Journal of Research in Reading* 17, 19–28.

Jin, L. and Cortazzi, M. (1998) The culture the learner brings: A bridge or a barrier? In M. Byram and M. Fleming (eds) *Language Learning in Intercultural Perspective* (pp. 98–118). Cambridge: Cambridge University Press.

Jourdenais, R., Ota, M., Stauffer, S., Boyson, B. and Doughty, C. (1995) Does textual enhancement promote noticing?: A think-aloud protocol analysis. In R. Schmidt (ed.) *Attention and Awareness in Foreign Language Learning* (pp. 183–216). University of Hawaii: Second Language Teaching and Curriculum Center.

Kelton, K., Blyth, C. and Guilloteau, N. (2004) Français interactif. An Online Introductory French Course. On WWW at http://www.laits.utexas.edu/fi. Accessed 30.10.07.

Kennedy, C. and Kennedy, J. (1996) Teacher attitudes and change implementation. *System* 24 (3), 351–360.

Kern, R.G. (1994) The role of mental translation in second language reading. *Studies in Second Language Acquisition* 16, 441–461.

Kharma, N.N. and Hajjaj, A.H. (1989) Use of the mother tongue in the ESL classroom. *International Review of Applied Linguistics* 27, 223–235.

Kim, Y. (2006) Effects of input elaboration on vocabulary acquisition through reading by Korean learners of English as a foreign language. *TESOL Quarterly* 40, 341–374.

Kobayashi, H. and Rinnert, C. (1992) Effects of first language on second language writing: translation versus direct composition. *Language Learning* 42 (2), 183–215.

Koike, D. and Liskin-Gasparro, J. (1999) What is a near-native speaker? Perspectives of job seekers and search committees in Spanish. *ADFL Bulletin* 30, 54–62.

Kötter, M. (2003) Negotiation of meaning and code-switching in online tandems. *Language Learning & Technology* 7 (2), 145–172.

Kramsch, C. (1993) *Context and Culture in Language Teaching.* Oxford: Oxford University Press.

Kramsch, C. (1997) The privilege of the non-native speaker. *Publications of the Modern Language Association* 112 (3), 359–369.

Krashen, S. (1981) *Second Language Acquisition and Second Language Learning.* New York: Pergamon.

Krashen, S. (1982) *Principles and Practice in Second Language Acquisition.* New York: Pergamon.

Krashen, S. (1984) *Writing: Research, Theory and Applications.* Torrance: Laredo.

Krashen, S.D. (1985) *The Input Hypothesis: Issues and Implications.* London: Longman.

Kroll, J. (1993) Assessing conceptual representations. In R. Schreuder and B. Weltens (eds) *The Bilingual Lexicon* (pp. 249–277). Amsterdam/Philadelphia: John Benjamins.

Kroskrity, P. (2000) Identity. *Journal of Linguistic Anthropology* 9 (1–2), 111–114.

Lai, M.L. (1996) Using the L1 sensibly in English language classrooms. *Journal of Primary Education* 6, 91–99.

Lantolf, J.P. (ed.) (2000) *Sociocultural Theory and Second Language Learning.* Oxford: Oxford University Press.

Lantolf, J. (2004) Sociocultural theory and second and foreign language learning: An overview of sociocultural theory. In K. van Esch and O. St. John (eds) *New Insights Into Foreign Language Learning and Teaching* (pp. 13–34). Frankfurt: Peter Lang Verlag.

Lantolf, J.P. and Thorne, S.L. (2006) *Sociocultural Theory and the Genesis of L2 Development.* Oxford: Oxford University Press.

Lapkin, S. and Swain, M. (1990) French immersion research agenda for the 90s. *The Canadian Modern Language Review* 46, 638–674.

Larsen-Freeman, D. (1985) State of the art on input in second language acquisition. In S.M. Gass and C.G. Madden (eds) *Input in Second Language Acquisition* (pp. 433–444). Rowley, MA: Newbury.

Laufer, B. (2005) Focus on form in second language vocabulary learning. *EUROSLA Yearbook* 5, 223–250.

Laufer, B. and Shmueli, K. (1997) Memorizing new words: Does teaching have anything to do with it? *RELC Journal* 28, 89–108.

Lawson, M.J. and Hogben, D. (1998) Learning and recall of foreign language vocabulary: Effects of a keyword strategy for immediate and delayed recall. *Learning and Instruction* 8, 179–194.

Lazaraton, A. and Ishihara, N. (2005) Understanding second language teacher practice using microanalysis and self-reflection: A collaborative case study. *Modern Language Journal* 89 (4), 529–542.

Leeman, J. (2003) Recasts and second language development: Beyond negative evidence. *Studies in Second Language Acquisition* 25, 37–63.

Leeman, J., Arteagoitia, I., Fridman, B. and Doughty, C. (1995) Integrating attention to form with meaning: Focus on form in content-based Spanish instruction. In R. Schmidt (ed.) *Attention and Awareness in Foreign Language Learning* (pp. 217–258). University of Hawaii: Second Language Teaching and Curriculum Center.

Leow, R. (1997) Attention, awareness, and foreign language behavior. *Language Learning* 47, 467–505.

Leow, R. (1998) Toward operationalizing the process of attention in SLA: Evidence for Tomlin and Villa's (1994) fine-grained analysis of attention. *Applied Psycholinguistics* 19, 133–159.

Levine, G.S. (2003) Student and instructor beliefs and attitudes about target language use, first language use, and anxiety: Report of a questionnaire study. *Modern Language Journal* 87 (iii), 343–364.

Levine, G. (2005) Co-construction and articulation of code-choice practices in foreign language classrooms. In C. Barrette and K. Paesani (eds) *Language Program Articulation: Developing a Theoretical Foundation* (pp. 110–130). Boston: Heinle.

Levinson, S. (1983) *Pragmatics*. Cambridge: Cambridge University Press.

Li, W. (1988) The 'why' and 'how' questions in the analysis of conversational code-switching. In P. Auer (ed.) *Codeswitching in Conversation: Language, Interaction and Identity* (pp. 156–179). London: Routledge.

Li, W. (2000) Dimensions of bilingualism. In W. Li (ed.) *The Bilingualism Reader* (pp. 3–25). London: Routledge.

Liang, X. (2006) Identity and language functions: high school Chinese immigrant students' code-switching dilemmas in ESL classes. *Journal of Language, Identity, and Education* 5 (2), 143–167.

Libben, G. (2000) Representation and processing in the second language lexicon: The homogeneity hypothesis. In J. Archibald (ed.) *Second Language Acquisition and Linguistic Theory* (pp. 228–248). Oxford: Blackwell.

Liebscher, G. and Dailey-O'Cain, J. (2003) Conversational repair as a role-defining mechanism in classroom interaction. *Modern Language Journal* 87, 375–390.

Liebscher, G. and Dailey-O'Cain, J. (2004) Learner code-switching in the content-based foreign language classroom. *Canadian Modern Language Review* 60 (4), 501–525.

Liebscher, G. and Dailey-O'Cain, J. (2005) Learner code-switching in the content-based foreign language classroom. *The Modern Language Journal* 89 (2), 234–247 [reprint].

Liebscher, G. and Dailey-O'Cain, J. (2007) Interculturality and code-switching in the German language classroom. In J. Plews, C. Lorey and C. Rieger (eds) *Intercultural Literacies and German in the Classroom. Interkulturelle Kompetenzen im Fremdsprachenunterricht, a Festschrift for Manfred Prokop* (pp. 49–67). Giessen: Gunter Narr Verlag (Giessener Beiträge zur Fremdsprachendidaktik).

Liebscher, G., Dailey-O'Cain, J. and Schmenk, B. (2007) The use of English in the German foreign language classroom. Paper presented at the Canadian Association for University Teachers of German annual meeting, Saskatoon, SK, Canada.

Lightbown, P. (1991) What do we have here? Some observations on the influence of instruction on L2 learning. In R. Philipson, L. Selinker, M. Sharwood Smith and M. Swain (eds) *Foreign/Second Language Pedagogy Research* (pp. 97–212). Clevedon, UK: Multilingual Matters.

Lindholm-Leary, K. (2001) *Dual Language Education*. Clevedon: Multilingual Matters.

Littlewood, W. (1981) *Communicative Language Teaching. An Introduction*. Cambridge: Cambridge University Press.

Liu, J. (2008) L1 use in L2 vocabulary learning: facilitator or barrier? *International Education Studies* 1 (2), 66–70.

Liu, D., Ahn, G., Beak, K. and Han, N. (2004) South Korean high school English teachers' code switching: Questions and challenges in the drive for maximal use of English in teaching. *TESOL Quarterly* 38, 605–638.

Long, M. (1981) Input, interaction and foreign language acquisition. In H. Winitz (ed.) *Native Language and Foreign Language Acquisition* (pp. 259–278). Annals of the New York Academy of Sciences 379.

Lortie, D.C. (1975) *Schoolteacher: A Sociological Study*. Chicago: University of Chicago Press.

Lüdi, G. (2003) Code-switching and unbalanced bilingualism. In J.M. Dewaele, A. Housen and W. Li (eds) *Bilingualism: Beyond Basic Principles* (pp. 174–188). Clevedon: Multilingual Matters.

Lugossy, R. (2003) Code-switching in the young learner classroom. In J. Andor, J. Horváth and M. Nikolov (eds) *Studies in English Theoretical and Applied Linguistics* (pp. 300–309). Pécs: Lingua Franca Csoport.

Lyster, R. and Mori, H. (2006) Interactional feedback and instructional counterbalance. *Studies in Second Language Acquisition* 28, 269–300.

Macaro, E. (1997) *Target Language, Collaborative Learning and Autonomy*. Clevedon: Multilingual Matters.

Macaro, E. (2000) Issues in target language teaching. In K. Field (ed.) *Issues in Modern Foreign Language Teaching* (pp. 171–189). London: Routledge.

Macaro, E. (2001) Analysing student teachers' codeswitching in foreign language classrooms: Theories and decision making. *The Modern Language Journal* 85 (4), 531–548.

Macaro, E. (2005) Codeswitching in the L2 classroom: A communication and learning strategy. In E. Llurda (ed.) *Non-Native Language Teachers: Perceptions, Challenges and Contributions to the Profession* (pp. 63–84). New York: Springer.

Macaro, E. (2006) Strategies for language learning and for language use: Revising the theoretical framework. *Modern Language Journal* 90 (3), 320–337.

Macaro, E. and Mutton, T. (2002) Developing language teachers through a co-researcher model. *Language Learning Journal* 25, 27–39.

MacDonald, C. (1993) *Using the Target Language*. Cheltenham: Mary Glasgow Publications.

McClure, E. (1981) Formal and functional aspects of code-switched discourse of bilingual children. In R. Duran (ed.) *Latino Language and Communicative Behavior* (pp. 69–94). Norwood, NJ: ABLEX.

Medgyes, P. (1994) *The Non-Native Teacher*. London: MacMillan.

Medgyes, P. and Miklósy, K. (2000) The language situation in Hungary. *Current Issues in Language Planning* 1, 148–242.

Mehan, H. (1979) *Learning Lessons: Social Organization in the Classroom*. Cambridge, MA: Harvard University Press.

Meisel, J. (1994) Getting FAT: Finiteness, agreement and tense in early grammars. In J. Meisel (ed.) *Bilingual First Language Acquisition. French and German Grammatical Development* (pp. 89–130). Amsterdam: John Benjamins.

Mendoza-Denton, N. (2002) Language and identity. In J.K. Chambers, P. Trudgill and N. Schilling-Estes (eds) *The Handbook of Language Variation and Change* (pp. 475–499). Oxford: Blackwell.

Mirinova, D. (2004) Two approaches to negotiating positions in interaction: Goffman's (1981) footing and Davies and Harré's (1999) *Positioning Theory. University of Pennsylvania Working Papers in Linguistics* 10 (1), 211–214.

Mondada, L. and Pekarek Dohler, S. (2004) Second language acquisition as situated practice: Task accomplishment in the French second language classroom. *The Modern Language Journal* 88 (iv), 501–518.

Montes-Alcalá, C. (2005) "Dear amigo": Exploring code-switching in personal letters. In L. Sayahi and M. Westmoreland (eds) *Selected Proceedings of the Second Workshop on Spanish Sociolinguistics* (pp. 102–108). Somerville, MA: Cascadilla Proceedings Project.

Montrul, S. (2002) Incomplete acquisition and attrition of Spanish tense/aspect distinctions in adult bilinguals. *Bilingualism: Language and Cognition* 5 (1), 39–68.

Montrul, S. (2005) Second language acquisition and first language loss in adult early bilinguals: Exploring some differences and similarities. *Second Language Research* 21 (3), 199–249.

Montrul, S. (2007) Interpreting mood distinctions in Spanish as a heritage language. In K. Potowski and R. Cameron (eds) *Spanish in Contact: Educational, Linguistic and Social Perspectives* (pp. 23–40). New York: John Benjamins.

Montrul, S. and Bowles, M. (2009) Is grammar instruction beneficial for heritage language learners? Dative case marking in Spanish. *Heritage Language Journal* 7, 9.

Muysken, P. (1995) Code-switching and grammatical theory. In L. Milroy and P. Muysken (eds) *One Speaker, Two Languages: Cross-Disciplinary Perspectives on Code-Switching* (pp. 177–198). Cambridge: Cambridge University Press.

Myers-Scotton, C. (1983) The negotiation of identities in conversation: A theory of markedness and code-choice. *International Journal of the Sociology of Language* 44, 115–136.

Myers-Scotton, C. (1993) *Dueling Languages: Grammatical Structure in Codeswitching.* Oxford: Clarendon.

Nagy, M. (2006) *A Katona József Általános Iskola Évkönyve, 2004–2005* (Yearbook of Katona József Általános Primary School, 2004–2005). Budapest: Katona Általános Iskola.

Nassaji, H. and Wells, G. (2000) What's the use of 'triadic dialogue'? An investigation of teacher-student interaction. *Applied Linguistics* 21 (3), 376–406.

Nation, I.S.P. (2001) *Learning Vocabulary in Another Language.* Cambridge: Cambridge University Press.

Nayar, B. (2002) Ideological binarism in the identities of native and non-native English speakers. In A. Duszak (ed.) *Us and Others: Social Identities Across Language, Discourses and Cultures* (pp. 464–479). Philadelphia: John Benjamins.

NCC. (2004) *National Core Curriculum of Hungary.* Budapest: Ministry of Education and Culture.

Nespor, J. (1987) The role of beliefs in the practice of teaching. *Journal of Curriculum Studies* 19 (4), 317–328.

Nichols, P. and Colon, M. (2000) Spanish literacy and the academic success of Latino high school students: Code-switching as a classroom resource. *Foreign Language Annals* 33, 498–511.

Nikolov, M. (1999) Classroom observation project. In É. Fekete, H. Major and M. Nikolov (eds) *English Language Education in Hungary* (pp. 221–246). Budapest: The British Council.

Nikolov, M. (2000) *Kódváltás pár-és csoportmunkában általános iskolai angolórákon.* (Code-switching in pair and group-work in the primary English lessons). *Magyar Pedagógia* 100, 401–422.

Nyikos, M. and Fan, M. (2007) A review of vocabulary learning strategies: Focus on language proficiency and learner voice. In A.D. Cohen and E. Macaro (eds) *Language Learner Strategies: Thirty Years of Research and Practice* (pp. 141–160). Oxford: Oxford University Press.

Obadia, A. (1996) French Immersion in Canada: Frequently asked questions. Canadian Parents for French. On WWW at http://www.cpf.ca/English/FAQ/Immersion.pdf. Accessed 14.4.08.

Ontario Ministry of Education and Training (1998) *The Ontario Curriculum – French as a Second Language: Core French, Grades 4–8.* Toronto: Queen's Printer for Ontario.

Ortega, L. (1999a) Rethinking foreign language education: Political dimensions of the profession. In K.A. Davis (ed.) *Foreign Language Teaching and Language Minority Education* (pp. 21–39). Honolulu: University of Hawaii, Second Language Teaching and Curriculum Center.

Ortega, L. (1999b) Language and equality: Ideological and structural constraints in foreign language education in the U.S. In T. Huebner and K.A. Davis (eds) *Sociopolitical Perspectives on Language Policy and Planning in the USA: Studies in Bilingualism* (pp. 243–266). Philadelphia: John Benjamins.

Pajares, M.F. (1992) Teachers' beliefs and educational research: Cleaning up a messy construct. *Review of Educational Research* 62 (3), 307–332.

Pennington, M.C. (1995) Pattern and variation in use of two languages in the Hong Kong secondary English class. *RELC Journal* 26, 80–105.

Petzöld, R. and Berns, M. (2000) Catching up with Europe: Speakers and functions of English in Hungary. *World Englishes* 19, 113–124.

Pfaff, C.W. (1979) Constraints on language mixing: Intrasentential code-switching and borrowing in Spanish/English. *Language* 55 (2), 291–318.

Philip, J. (2003) Constraints on 'noticing the gap': Non-native speakers' noticing of recasts in NS-NNS interaction. *Studies in Second Language Acquisition* 25, 99–126.

Phillipson, R. (1992) *Linguistic Imperialism.* Oxford: Oxford University Press.

Polio, C. and Duff, P. (1994) Teachers' language use in university foreign language classrooms: A qualitative analysis of English and target language alternation. *The Modern Language Journal* 78, 313–326.

Poplack, S. (1980) Sometimes I'll start a sentence in Spanish y termino en español: Toward a typology of code-switching. *Linguistics* 18, 581–618.

Poplack, S. (1985) Contrasting patterns of code-switching in two communities. In H.J. Warkentyne (ed.) *Methods V: Papers from the V International Conference on Methods in Dialectology* (pp. 363–385). Victoria, BC: University of Victoria.

Potowski, K. (2007a) *Language and Identity in a Dual Immersion School.* Clevedon: Multilingual Matters.

Potowski, K. (2007b) Some characteristics of the Spanish proficiency of dual immersion graduates. *Spanish in Context* 4 (2), 187–216.

Potowski, K. and Lee, M. (2009) Reactions to variable grammaticality in codeswitching: Heritage speakers vs. second language learners (submitted). Paper presented at Bilingual Forum, University of Illinois at Chicago (April).

Preston, D. (2004) Folk metalanguage. In A. Jaworski, N. Coupland and D. Galasinski (eds) *Metalanguage: Social and Ideological Perspectives* (pp. 75–101). Berlin/New York: Mouton de Gruyter.

Qi, D.S. (1998) An inquiry into language-switching in second language composing processes. *Canadian Modern Language Review* 54 (3), 413–435.

Ramirez, A. and Hall, J. (1990) Language and culture in secondary level Spanish textbooks. *The Modern Language Journal* 74, 48–65.

Rampton, B. (1990) Displacing the 'native speaker': Expertise, affiliation and inheritance. *ELT Journal* 44, 338–343.

Rampton, B. (1995) *Crossing: Language and Ethnicity Among Adolescents.* London/New York: Longman.

Reyes, I. (2004) Functions of code switching in schoolchildren's conversations. *Bilingual Research Journal* 28 (1), 77–98.

Richards, J.C. (1996) Teachers' maxims in language teaching. *TESOL Quarterly* 28 (1), 153–156.

Roehr, K. (2006) Metalinguistic knowledge in L2 task performance: A verbal protocol analysis. *Language Awareness* 15 (3), 180–198.

Rolin-Ianziti, J. and Brownlie, S. (2002) Teacher use of the learners' native language in the foreign language classroom. *Canadian Modern Language Review* 58, 402–426.

Rubinstein-Avila, E. (2002) Problematizing the 'dual' in a dual-immersion program: A portrait. *Linguistics and Education* 13 (1), 65–87.

Sacks, H., Schegloff, E.M. and Jefferson, G. (1974) A simplest systematics for the organization of turn-taking in conversation. *Language* 53, 361–382.

Said-Mohand, A. (2006) Estudio sociolingüístico de los marcadoes como, entonces, tú sabes en el habla de bMiligÜes estadounidenses. Unpublished PhD dissertation, University of Miami.

Sanaoui, R. (2005) English in the discourse of four French immersion teachers. Paper presented at the International Association of Applied Linguistics, Madison, WI (July).

Sanaoui, R. (2007) English in the discourse of four French immersion teachers. Paper presented at the annual conference of the American Association of Applied Linguistics, Costa Mesa, CA, April 2007.

Schmidt, R. (1993) Awareness and second language acquisition. *Annual Review of Applied Linguistics* 13, 206–226.

Schmidt, R. (1995) Consciousness and foreign language learning: A tutorial on the role of attention and awareness in learning. In R. Schmidt (ed.) *Attention and Awareness in Foreign Language Learning* (pp. 1–63). Manoa: Second Language Teaching and Curriculum Center.

Schmidt, R. (2001) Attention. In P. Robison (ed.) *Cognition and Second Language Instruction* (pp. 3–32). Cambridge: Cambridge University Press.

Scollon, R. (2001) *Mediated Discourse: The Nexus of Practice.* London: Routledge.

Scollon, R. and Scollon, S.W. (2004) *Nexus Analysis: Discourse and the Emerging Internet.* London: Routledge.

Shapson, S., Kaufman, D. and Durward, L. (1978) *BC French Study: An Evaluation of Elementary French Programs in British Columbia.* Burnaby: Faculty of Education, Simon Fraser University.

Sinclair, J. and Coulthard, M. (1975) *Towards an Analysis of Discourse.* Oxford: Oxford University Press.

Skerritt, D. (2003) Amount and function of English in Grade 3 French immersion teachers' discourse. Unpublished MA thesis, York University (Canada).

Skinner, D. (1985) Access to meaning: The anatomy of the language learning connection. *Journal of Multicultural Development* 6 (2), 369–389.

Strauss, A.L. (1987) *Qualitative Analysis for Social Scientists.* Cambridge University Press: New York.

Swain, M. (1985) Communicative competence: Some roles of comprehensible input and comprehensible output in its development. In S. Gass and C. Madden (eds) *Input and Second Language Acquisition* (pp. 235–254). Rowley, MA: Newbury House.

Swain, M. and Lapkin, S. (2000) Task-based second language learning: The uses of the first language. *Language Teaching Research* 4, 253–276.

Swain, M. and Lapkin, S. (2005) The evolving sociopolitical context of immersion education in Canada: Some implications for program development. *International Journal of Applied Linguistics* 15 (2), 169–186.

Sződy, E. (2001) *Practice Together.* Budapest: Szent István Társulat.

Thoms, J., Liao, J. and Szustak, A. (2005) The use of L1 in an L2 on-line chat activity. *The Canadian Modern Language Review* 62 (1), 161–182.

Tiemer, W. (2004) Code-switching repertoires in the language classroom: Contextualization and the enactment of shared perceptions in the talk of learners. Unpublished MA thesis, University of Alberta.

Tomlin, R.S. and Villa, V. (1994) Attention in cognitive science and SLA. *Studies in Second Language Acquisition* 16, 183–203.

Torres, L. (2002) Bilingual discourse markers in Puerto Rican Spanish. *Language in Society* 31, 65–83.

Torres, L. and Potowski, K. (2008) A comparative study of bilingual discourse markers in Chicago Mexican, Puerto Rican, and MexiRican Spanish. *International Journal of Bilingualism* 12 (4), 263–279.

Train, R. (2003) The (non)native standard language in foreign language education: A critical perspective. In C. Blyth (ed.) *The Sociolinguistics of Foreign-language Classrooms* (pp. 3–39). Boston: Heinle.

Turnbull, M. (1999) Multidimensional project-based second language teaching: Observations of four Grade 9 core French teachers. *Canadian Modern Language Review* 56, 3–35.

Turnbull, M. (2001) There is a role for the L1 in second and foreign language teaching, but ... *Canadian Modern Language Review* 57, 531–540.

Turnbull, M. (2005) Investigating and understanding Core French teachers' uses of English and French: Beliefs and practices. Final report submitted to Eastern and Western School Districts, P.E.I.

Turnbull, M. and Arnett, K. (2002) Teachers' use of the target and first languages in second and foreign language classrooms. *Annual Review of Applied Linguistics* 22, 204–208.

Turnbull, M. and McMillan, B. (2006) L'anglais en immersion tardive: Tabou? Défi complexe? Paper presented at the Canadian Association of Immersion Teachers Annual Conference, 22–29 October, Moncton, N.B.

Turnbull, M. and McMillan, B. (2007) Teachers' code-switching in French Immersion: Revisiting a core principle. Paper presented at the annual conference of American Association of Applied Linguistics, Costa Mesa, CA, April 2007.

Üstünel, E. and Seedhouse, P. (2005) Why that, in that language, right now? *International Journal of Applied Linguistics* 15 (3), 302–325.

Valdés, G. (1997) Dual-language immersion programs: A cautionary note concerning the education of language-minority students. *Harvard Educational Review* 67 (3), 391–429.

van Langenhove, L. and Harré, R. (1999) Introducing positioning theory. In R. Harré and L. van Langenhove (eds) *Positioning Theory: Moral Contexts of Intentional Action* (pp. 14–31). Oxford: Blackwell.

van Lier, L. (1996) *Interaction in the Language Curriculum: Awareness, Autonomy and Authenticity.* London: Longman.

van Lier, L. (2000) From input to affordance: Social-interactive learning from an ecological perspective. In J. Lantolf (ed.) *Sociocultural Theory and Second Language Learning* (pp. 245–259). New York: Oxford University Press.

van Lier, L. (2004) *The Ecology and Semiotics of Language Learning: A Sociocultural Perspective.* Dordrecht: Kluwer Academic Publishers.

Vesterbacka, S. (1991) Ritualized routines and L2 acquisition strategies in an immersion program. *Journal of Multilingual and Multicultural Development* 12, 35–43.

Vygotsky, L.S. (1978) *Mind in Society: The Development of Higher Psychological Processes.* In M. Cole, V. John-Steiner, S. Scribner and E. Souberman (eds). Cambridge, MA: Harvard University Press.

Walsh, A. and Yeoman, E. (1999) Making sense of the French in French immersion: Concept development in early FI. *Canadian Modern Language Review* 55 (3), 339–354.

Warner, C. (2004) 'It's just a game, right?' Types of Play in foreign language CMC. *Language Learning & Technology* 8 (2), 69–87.

Warschauer, M. (1999) *Electronic Literacies: Language, Culture, and Power in Online Education.* Mahwah, NJ: Lawrence Erlbaum Associates.

Watanabe, Y. (2008) Peer–peer interaction between L2 learners of different proficiency levels: Their interactions and reflections. *The Canadian Modern Language Review* 64 (4), 605–635.

Wieczorek, J. (1991) Spanish dialects and the foreign language textbook: A sound perspective. *Hispania* 74, 175–181.

Wieczorek, J. (1994) The concept of 'French' in foreign language texts. *Foreign Language Annals* 27, 487–497.

Wolf, R.M. (1977) *Achievement in America: National Report of the United States for the International Educational Achievement Project.* New York: Teachers College Press, Columbia University.

Wong-Fillmore, L. (1985a) When does teacher talk work as input? In S.M. Gass and C.G. Madden (eds) *Input in Second Language Acquisition* (pp. 17–50). Rowley, MA: Newbury.

Wong-Fillmore, L. (1985b) *Second Language Learning in Children: A Proposed Model.* Proceedings of a conference on issues in English language development, Arlington, VA: ERIC Document 273149.

Wood, D., Bruner, J.S. and Ross, G. (1976) The role of tutoring in problem-solving. *Journal of Child Psychology and Psychiatry* 17, 89–100.

Woods, D. (1996) An integrated view of teachers' beliefs, assumptions and knowledge. In D. Woods (ed.) *Teacher Cognition in Language Teaching: Beliefs, Decision-Making and Classroom Practice* (pp. 184–212). New York: Cambridge University.

Woods, D. (2003) The social construction of beliefs in the language classroom. In P. Kalaja and A. Barcelos (eds) *New Approaches to Research on Beliefs about SLA* (pp. 201–229). Amsterdam: Kluwer.

Young, R.F. and Miller, E.R. (2004) Learning as changing participation: Discourse roles in ESL writing conferences. *Modern Language Journal* 88 (iv), 519–535.

Zentella, A.C. (1997) *Growing Up Bilingual: Puerto Rican Children in New York.* Oxford: Blackwell.